# Destination Marketing

This book advances the current literature on destination marketing by using innovative up-to-date case studies from a wide geographical representation. The contributors examine new methods and marketing approaches used within the field through a combination of theoretical and practical approaches. With discussions of topics including image, branding, attractions and competitiveness, the chapters in this volume offer new insight into contemporary developments such as medical tourism, Islamic tourism and film-induced tourism. Presenting detailed findings and a range of methodologies, ranging from surveys to travel writings and ethnography, this book will be of interest to students, scholars and practitioners in the fields of tourism and marketing.

**Metin Kozak** is Professor of Tourism in the School of Tourism and Hospitality Management, Dokuz Eylul University, Turkey.

**Nazmi Kozak** is Professor of Tourism in the School of Tourism and Hospitality Management, Anadolu University, Turkey.

# Routledge Advances in Tourism
Edited by Stephen Page
*School for Tourism, Bournemouth University*

*For a complete list of titles in this series, please visit www.routledge.com.*

# Destination Marketing

An international perspective

**Edited by
Metin Kozak and Nazmi Kozak**

LONDON AND NEW YORK

First published 2016
by Routledge

2 Park Square, Milton Park, Abingdon, Oxfordshire OX14 4RN
711 Third Avenue, New York, NY 10017

*Routledge is an imprint of the Taylor & Francis Group, an informa business*

First issued in paperback 2018

*British Library Cataloguing in Publication Data*
A catalogue record for this book is available from the British Library

*Library of Congress Cataloging in Publication Data*
A catalog record for this book has been requested

ISBN: 978-1-138-85589-2 (hbk)
ISBN: 978-1-138-59225-4 (pbk)

Typeset in Times
by Book Now Ltd, London

# Contents

# Figures

# Tables

# Contributors

**Naeema Alhosani** obtained her Ph.D. and M.A. degrees in Geography with a specialization in Cartography from the University of Kansas, USA. Currently, she is Assistant Professor of Cartography at the UAE University, UAE. Her research interests are focused on cartography, cartographic design, GIS, and tourism. She is affiliated with many professional and international associations in the field of cartography.

**Justyna Bąkiewicz** is a Ph.D. candidate at Edinburgh Napier University, UK. Her main research interests are related to heritage tourism management, heritage interpretation and film-induced tourism. Justyna's Ph.D. research explores management challenges at film-induced tourism heritage attractions and focuses on the role of heritage interpretation as a valuable tool for effective heritage tourism management practices. Her research employs a qualitative methodology.

**Paul Barron** is Reader in Hospitality Management at Edinburgh Napier University. His research interests include the education experience of university students and an analysis of new and emerging markets in the tourism industry. Paul has authored over 50 articles in tourism and hospitality management and is currently Hospitality Editor for the *Journal of Hospitality, Leisure, Sport and Tourism Education*.

**Vivina Carreira** is Professor at the Higher School of Agriculture, Polytechnic Institute of Coimbra, Portugal. She earned a Ph.D. degree in Applied Linguistics from the University of Vigo, Spain and a postgraduate diploma in Cultural Tourism from the University of Barcelona, Spain. Her research focuses on the languages of tourism, multiculturalism and cultural tourism.

**Gürel Çetin** is Assistant Professor at the Faculty of Economics, Istanbul University, Turkey. He holds a Ph.D. degree in Business Administration, Istanbul University, Turkey. His research focuses primarily on tourism marketing, sustainable tourism, ICT in tourism and tourist experience.

**Joyce Hsiu-yu Chen** is Associate Professor in the Department of Food and Beverage Management at the National Kaohsiung University of Hospitality and Tourism, Taiwan. She received her Ph.D. in Management from National

Changhua University of Education, Taiwan. Her research focuses on hospitality human resource management training and development, hospitality and tourism service management, and tourist behavior.

**Yin Teng Chew** obtained her Ph.D. in Strategic HRM, Nagoya University, Japan. Currently, she is a senior lecturer in the School of Business, Monash University, Malaysia. Her research focuses on tourism management, medical tourism, consumer behavior and psychological contract. She often reviews manuscripts for well-ranked journals and works in collaboration with governments.

**Salvador Anton Clavé** is Full Professor of Regional Geographical Analysis at the Rovira i Virgili University in Catalonia, Spain, where he serves currently as the Director of the Science and Technology Park for Tourism and Leisure. His research concentrates on the analysis of the evolution of tourist destinations, the development and globalization of leisure facilities and issues concerning tourism and ICT.

**Antónia Correia** is Professor of Tourist Behaviour and Tourism Economics, University of Algarve, Portugal. Her main research interests focus on consumer behaviour, tourism economics and modelling. She has a number of papers published in tourism, leisure and economics journals. Antónia is also a member of the editorial board of several journals including *Journal of Travel Research, Journal of Business Research, Tourism Analysis,* and *Anatolia.*

**Füsun Istanbullu Dinçer** is Professor of Tourism in the Department of Tourism Management, Istanbul University, Turkey. She currently acts as a chair in the same department. She is the co-editor of *Journal of Tourismology.* Her research interests include epistemology of tourism, sustainable tourism, European Union, and destination management.

**Rita Gomes** works at the Bussaco Forest Foundation, Portugal. She holds a Bachelor degree in Tourism and a Master's degree in Ecotourism, both from the Polytechnic Institute of Coimbra, Portugal. She has taught on environmental and rural tourism professional courses. Her research interests are in the areas of ecotourism and rural tourism.

**Grace K. S. Ho** is pursuing the degree of Doctor of Hotel & Tourism Management, Hong Kong Polytechnic University, SAR China. She has a MSc degree in Hospitality and Tourism Management and a MBA degree concentrated in Marketing. She has more than 15 years in hospitality as a former general manager. She is now a consultant and part-time lecturer in hospitality management and marketing.

**Osama Ibrahim** is Associate Professor of Tourism Guidance in the Faculty of Tourism and Hotels at Fayoum University, Egypt and currently on exchange to Cardiff Metropolitan University, UK. He started his research career in egyptology, and then adopted an interdisciplinary approach to conduct research on ecotourism and sustainable development, cultural and natural heritage management, and heritage interpretation and presentation.

**Neven Ivandić** is a Senior Researcher at the Institute for Tourism in Zagreb, Croatia. He obtained his Ph.D. in Economics from the University of Split, Croatia. His research focuses on strategic management and on economic impacts of tourism.

**Nurliana Jafar** received her Master's degree in Tourism Management from the University of Technology MARA (UiTM), Malaysia. She has had more than four years experience in the tourism industry particularly in relation to destination and event planning. Her research focuses on destination marketing, tourism planning and place branding.

**Siti Aqilah Binte Jahari** graduated from Monash University, Malaysia with a degree in Bachelor of Business and Commerce with First Class Honors. She is currently a Ph.D. student at Monash University, Malaysia. She has published several papers in tourism journals. Her areas of research are travel risk, destination image and Islamic tourism.

**Salamiah A. Jamal** holds a Ph.D. degree in Hospitality and Tourism Management, Universiti Teknologi MARA (UiTM), Malaysia. Currently, she is the Head of Hotel Management Department at the Faculty of Hotel and Tourism Management, UiTM, Malaysia. Her research focuses on hospitality consumer behavior, community-based tourism and special interest tourism.

**Tang-Chung Kan** is Associate Professor of Department of Travel Management at the National Kaohsiung University of Hospitality and Tourism, Taiwan. He obtained his Ph.D. in Social Sciences from National Sun Yat-Sen University, Taiwan. His research focuses on tourist psychology and behavior, tourism marketing, and tourism development strategy.

**Sally Khalil** is Lecturer in the Department of Tourism Studies, Faculty of Tourism and Hotels at Fayoum University, Egypt and currently on exchange to Cardiff Metropolitan University, UK. Her research interests are ecotourism and sustainable development, service quality and customer satisfaction, and heritage management.

**Alan Darmasaputra Koeshendro** obtained a First Class Honours degree from Monash University, Malaysia. He has conducted a marketing and management study on the pull factors of Malaysia as a medical tourism destination for the Indonesian market. Currently, he is working in the corporate world to enhance his knowledge, skills and experiences.

**Metin Kozak** is Professor of Tourism in the School of Tourism and Hospitality Management, Dokuz Eylul University, Turkey. He holds both Master's and Ph.D. degrees in tourism management. His research focuses on consumer behaviour, benchmarking, destination management and marketing, and sustainability. He has attended various universities in the USA, Europe and Asia as a visiting scholar.

**Nazmi Kozak** is Professor of Tourism in the School of Tourism and Hospitality Management, Anadolu University, Turkey. He gained both his Master's and

Ph.D. degrees in tourism management. His research activities focus on tourism marketing, history of tourism, and bibliometrics. He is the Editor of *Anatolia: Turizm Araştırmaları Dergisi* and the co-editor of *Anatolia: An International Journal of Tourism and Hospitality Research* and has attended several universities in the USA as a visiting scholar.

**Anna Leask** is Professor of Tourism Management at Edinburgh Napier University, UK. Her teaching and research interests combine and lie principally in the areas of visitor attraction management and heritage tourism management. Recent research has focused on how visitor attractions can engage with Generation Y visitors and employees, with primary research being conducted in the UK, Hong Kong, Macau and Singapore.

**Estela Marine-Roig** is Visiting Professor at the AEGERN Department of the University of Lleida, Spain, and a post-doctoral researcher in the GRATET research group of the Rovira i Virgili University, Spain. She holds a European Ph.D. in Tourism and Leisure. Her research interests include the analysis of the image and identity of tourist destinations through tourism online sources.

**Giuseppe Marzano** is the Dean of the Graduate School at Universidad de Las Americas in Quito, Ecuador. Giuseppe earned his Ph.D. at the University of Queensland, Australia and his research focuses on multi-stakeholder decision making processes in the context of tourism.

**Rosana Mazaro** is Associate Professor of Tourism in the Program of Graduate and Postgraduate, Rio Grande do Norte Federal University, Brazil. She obtained her Ph.D. in Management from the Universidad de Barcelona, Spain. Her research focuses on competitiveness destinations, regional innovation, cost zones management and nautical tourism. She is PQ in CNPq and researcher group leader in Brazil.

**Bob McKercher** has wide ranging research interests. He received his Ph.D. from the University of Melbourne, Australia, a Masters degree from Carleton University, Canada and his Undergraduate degree from York University, Canada. Prior to entering academia, he worked in a variety of operational and advocacy positions in the Canadian tourism industry.

**Carlos Alberto Freire Medeiros** is Associate Professor of Marketing at the Federal University of Rio Grande do Notre, Brazil. He received his Ph.D. in Business Administration at the University of São Paulo, Brazil. His research focus is visitor attractions management, marketing and strategy. He was a subsecretary of tourism at the Rio Grande do Norte State, Brazil.

**Gonzalo Mendieta** holds a Ph.D. in Statistics from the University of Iowa, USA. He is currently the Academic Vice-Rector and Full Professor of Statistics at Universidad de las Americas, Quito, Ecuador. His research interest focuses in statistical models for market research.

**Sabrina Meneghello** is Senior Researcher at CISET- Ca' Foscari University Venice, Italy, where she is involved both in the education and research activities. Her research focuses mainly on destination image and brand, cultural tourism, exploitation of cultural and natural heritage, emerging tourist products, destination planning and management. She is lecturer on the same topics at CISET and institutions in Italy.

**Federica Montaguti** is Senior Researcher at CISET, and a member of the Board of Professors coordinating the Master's programme in the Economics and Management of Tourism offered at Ca' Foscari University Venice, Italy. Her research interests are mainly in the areas of destination image and branding, segmentation of tourist demand, tourist products, tourist attractiveness, mobility, and urban tourism.

**Carlos Larreategui Nardi** holds an MSc degree from the London School of Economics, UK, and Harvard University, USA. Currently, he is the Rector and Full Professor of Public Policies and Political Science at Universidad de las Americas, Ecuador.

**Nor'Ain Othman** is Associate Professor in the Faculty of Hotel and Tourism Management, Universiti Teknologi MARA, Malaysia. She received her Ph.D. in Tourism Management from University of Queensland, Australia. She has more than 10 years working experience as an Assistant Director with Tourism Malaysia. Her research interests focus on tourism management, tourism marketing, event management, heritage tourism and Islamic tourism.

**Tijana Rakić** is a Reader in Tourism and Marketing at the Department of Marketing, Events and Tourism at the University of Greenwich, UK. Her research interests and publications predominantly lie in visual research methods, visual culture, tourism and arts, narratives of travel and tourism, and the relationships between world heritage, tourism and national identity.

**Ana Isabel Rodrigues** is Assistant Professor of Tourism, Polytechnic Institute of Beja, Portugal. She holds a degree in Social and Cultural Communication from the Catholic University of Lisbon and a MSc in communication and destination image from ISCTE-Lisbon University Institute, Portugal. She is currently a Ph.D. student at the University of Algarve, Portugal. Her research focuses on destination marketing and image formation.

**Chelsea Su** obtained her Bachelors and Master's degrees from National Kaohsiung University of Hospitality and Tourism, Taiwan, and specializes in Hotel and Travel Management. She has had work experience in Mandarin Orchard Singapore as GSE for two years and in MGM Macau and Venetian for another two years.

**Neda Telišman-Košuta** is a Senior Researcher at the Institute for Tourism in Zagreb, Croatia. She obtained her Master's degree in Travel and Tourism Management from the George Washington University, USA. Her research interests and consulting work focus on destination development and strategic marketing.

**Yi-Wei Xiao** is a postgraduate student in the Faculty of Hospitality and Tourism Management at the Macao University of Science and Technology University, China. Recently, she studied ethnic residents' perception towards on tourism development from the perspective of destination marketing.

**Batıkan Yasankul** is a MSc student in the Department of Tourism Management, Istanbul University, Turkey. He is currently writing a thesis on tourist experiences in Middle East. His research interests include Middle East tourists and tourist experience.

**Yang Zhang** is Assistant Professor in the Faculty of Hospitality and Tourism Management at the Macao University of Science and Technology University, China. She obtained her Ph.D. in cultural heritage management from the Sichuan University, China. Her research focuses on cultural heritage tourism, tourism and lifestyle migration, serious leisure and identity, social media and tourist experience.

# Introduction

*Metin Kozak and Nazmi Kozak*

The subject of competitiveness has been central to the advancement of tourism research over the last two decades, as an increasingly large number of destinations and individual businesses have entered into the international tourism market. Many destinations have created their own icons, such as theme parks, tall buildings and food. These serve as background sources in the creation of destination-specific logos and slogans that offer a means of communicating with existing or potential visitors. There has also been a steady increase in international outbound tourism demand, and this has become more heterogeneous in terms of geographical distribution. This leads to competition between various destinations for certain tourist markets and certain product categories.

As a consequence, on the practical side, destinations have become central to the management and marketing of the international tourism and travel industry over the last few decades. Similarly, from an academic perspective, the tourism literature has increasingly directed its attention towards the inclusion of destinations. This has been achieved through a large number of empirical studies with the purpose of developing effective management and marketing tools similar or dissimilar to those of individual business establishments. Several books have appeared since the early millennium on the theme of marketing tourist destinations (such as Baker, 2012; Kotler, Haider & Rein, 2002; Kozak & Baloglu, 2010; Morrison, 2013; Pike, 2008, 2011). The topic is likely to receive increasing levels of attention in the future, for as long as tourism supply and demand continue to progress.

The present volume differs from the above-referenced books in that it is primarily intended to present the detailed findings of empirical studies and to substantiate and enrich the existing theoretical background, presenting first-hand case studies from an international perspective. The volume examines recent advances in the application of new methods, and will contribute to a better understanding of the marketing approaches used by destinations, as well as informing readers of recent practical developments in the field, providing a list of real case studies from a large range of countries across the world.

## Background

Over the years, we have become quite familiar with destination marketing, due to an increasing number of books, conference papers and journal articles on the topic. Moreover, new conference initiatives have been created with a clear focus on destination management or marketing. Many conference organizations have brought hot topics to the fore relating to destination marketing by making these their conference themes. The idea motivating the present volume originated during discussions prior to two conference series held in Istanbul, Turkey, on 4–9 June 2014, namely the *Interdisciplinary Tourism Research Conference* and the *World Conference for Graduate Research in Tourism, Hospitality and Leisure*. This series has attracted the participation of over 260 scholars from across the world, providing the opportunity for an interactive debate on key topics including destination marketing.

As in previous years, it was decided to publish selected conference papers in the form of a book series. The present volume is entitled *Destination Marketing: An International Perspective*. The reason for identifying this specific theme relates to the fact that in today's growing competitive environment, tourist destinations rather than individual attractions and businesses have become central to the management and marketing of national tourism sources. This highlights the importance of destination management and marketing.

By selecting some of the papers presented at these conferences for publication each year, it has become possible to enhance and deepen the existing body of tourism knowledge. The present volume includes 18 chapters by 40 invited contributors. The topics addressed include image, branding, supporting elements (attractions) and competitiveness. The book is composed of four main parts, moving from the specific to the general. Part I focuses on the specific, and is entitled 'Destination Image'. It includes five chapters, contributed by a total of 11 scholars. Part II has a similar focus, and is entitled 'Destination Branding'. It consists of a further four chapters contributed by eight scholars from across the world. Part III is entitled 'Supporting Elements of Destinations'. It covers a range of topics relating to the attractiveness of three destinations, and includes four studies written by 11 scholars. Part IV is devoted to a much broader subject, namely the empirical investigation of models of destination marketing and competitiveness. This last part, entitled 'Models of Destination Marketing and Competitiveness', includes five chapters contributed by ten scholars from across the world.

## Part I Destination image

The book begins by seeking to understand the importance of image as the basis of all substantial topics relating to destination marketing, such as branding and competitiveness. A perceived positive image will lead to success for destinations in accomplishing their marketing strategies. In contrast, a negative image, regardless of its occurrence as part of a stereotype or not, may lead to an imbalance in the perception of visitors, and/or force destination authorities to be more creative in eliminating negative consequences. The effective sources of image formation for destinations have become multi-dimensional and increasingly dynamic. Any information bombarded by formal or informal sources has substantial consequences (in the short or long term) that may or may not be easy to rectify.

Part I contains five chapters related to the image perception of destinations, which are explored using a range of different approaches, such as neural network content analysis, fictional literature, travel writings and travel blogs. Chapter 1, by Yin Teng Chew and Siti Aqilah Binte Jahari, shows how country image differs from destination image and confirms that these are different but inter-related constructs. Chapter 2, by Ana Isabel Rodrigues, Antónia Corrreia and Metin Kozak, tries to identify a list of the most frequently mentioned words that help in portraying visitors' image perceptions of a lake destination. Chapter 3, contributed by Yang Zhang and Yi-Wei Xiao, is an ethnographic study empha-sizing the importance of fictional literature in how tourists share their image of certain destinations. Chapter 4, by Sabrina Meneghello and Federica Montaguti, examines how texts have contributed to creating an image for specific destina-tions such as Venice, and how such destinations manage to sustain their image over a long period of time. Chapter 5, by Estela Marine-Roig and Salvador Anton Clavé, looks at how user-generated contents take place in the affective component of image creation, and how this can influence tourists' perceptions, satisfaction and behaviour.

## Part II Destination branding

Along with its role in image formation, branding has also become an important tool in allowing destinations to discover their primary or most attractive attrac-tions, in terms of conveying a message to their target markets. On the practical side, a wide number of logos and slogans have been developed in the early twenty-first century. Like individual businesses, destinations have also tended to benefit from the contents or possible meanings of their logos or slogans for potential visitors, as part of developing strategies to increase competitiveness. The brand development process has no unique route. Rather, it is an interactive process, involving the participation of different bodies on the supply and demand sides (stakeholders, tourists, residents, and so on).

Part II contains four chapters on the topic of destination branding that use a combination of qualitative and quantitative techniques. Chapter 6, by Carlos Larreategui Nardi, Giuseppe Marzano and Gonzalo Mendieta, undertakes an interview with a group of stakeholders and examines the role of 'collaborative thuggery' in destination branding, and how this emerges within a multi-stakeholder decision-making process. Chapter 7, by Sally Khalil and Osama Ibrahim, explores how stakeholders' perceptions may be of help in developing a brand, focusing on the specific case of Alexandria, Egypt. Chapter 8, by Nurliana Jafar, looks at how tourists' perceptions of destination components are likely to influence the development of destinations and their choices, and assesses the implications of this for destination rebranding and marketing. Chapter 9, by Neda Telišman-Košuta and Neven Ivandić, determines the reasons behind the disability of the development of proper and efficient branding strategies for destinations, and identifies the lack of 'destination thinking' and the inability of tourist boards to act as potential branding directors.

## Part III Supporting elements of destinations

In terms of their contribution to image formation and branding, attractions are of primary importance for destinations. There is no doubt that the existence of attractions is a vital way of giving the impression that a given destination is the right place to visit for a vacation. The contents of a vacation can also provide multiple reasons to visit for each tourist group. For instance, history and culture could be more attractive for culture-seeking tourists, while theme parks and leisure activities may be of greater appeal to family groups. The richness of attractions can also be helpful for destinations to promote themselves more easily promote to a target segment, or to develop their own identities as brands.

Part III contains four chapters, each focusing on a different attraction. Chapter 10, by Justyna Bąkiewicz, Anna Leask, Paul Barron and Tijana Rakić, tries to establish the link between film-tourism and heritage sources, and investigates how the former can influence visitors' expectations, and experiences and interpretations of the latter. Chapter 11, by Rita Gomes and Vivina Carreira, is set in the context of geology and geography, and demonstrates how to use stones as tourism sources in developing a route destination for visitors wishing to engage in urban and eco-tourism. Chapter 12, by Yin Teng Chew and Alan Darmasaputra Koeshendro, has a specific focus on medical tourism – another emerging type – as a major tourist attraction, and suggests some different ways of undertaking research to advance its contextual settings in knowledge development. Chapter 13, by Gürel Çetin, Batikan Yasankul and Füsun Istanbullu Dinçer, articulates Middle East tourists' experiential dimension in the destinations they visit, focusing on culture, nature, shopping, etc.

## Part IV Models of destination marketing and competitiveness

The tourism literature contains an increasing number of journal papers, conference papers, chapters, research projects and books addressing the importance of competitiveness for destinations and outlining how to succeed from a practical perspective (e.g. Kozak & Baloglu, 2010; Ritchie & Crouch, 2003). There are now a substantial number of empirical studies focusing on destination competitiveness. Some of these focus on taking into consideration the measurement of destination competitiveness through the evaluation of sources or attractions on the supply and demand sides (Bahar & Kozak, 2007; Kim & Agrusa, 2005; Kozak, Baloglu & Bahar, 2010). In addition, new thinking is emerging on ways of creating new models that will be more efficient in terms of destination marketing. Each creative model will benefit the destination both in terms of sustaining its continued success and in guaranteeing a quality experience for visitors.

Chapter 14, by Tang-Chung Kan, Joyce Hsiu-yu Chen and Chelsea Su, examines visitors' experience of gaming activity, and confirms a clear relationship between motivations, enduring involvement, and flow experience. Chapter 15, by Grace K.S. Ho and Bob McKercher, revisits the destination life cycle models refined by Plog and Butler, and suggests that a destination may appeal to various stages in its life cycle while catering for different types of tourists. Chapter 16, by Naeema Alhosani, presents a brief overview of the plans for Dubai Tourism Vision 2020 as a new tourism map, and examines Saudi tourists' preferences for Dubai, which offers them entertainment services not available in their home country. Chapter 17, by Nor'Ain Othman and Salamiah A. Jamal, presents a survey, conducted in three steps, and discusses the current and potential Islamic market in the international tourism industry. Chapter 18, by Rosana Mazaro and Carlos Alberto Freire Medeiros, compares various destination competitiveness models and analyses tourism policies and strategies in the context of the competitiveness of Brazilian destinations.

## Final words

To sum up, this volume contains chapters dealing with a wide range of topics related to destination marketing, including image, branding, attractions and competitiveness. The methodologies of the contributing authors include both qualitative and quantitative methods, and range from surveys (e.g. interviews, questionnaires) to additional advanced qualitative methods (e.g. travel writings, ethnography and neural network content analysis).

As part of a broad collaborative effort, a number of different perspectives on a wide diversity of topics on a particular aspect of destination marketing are presented by researchers from 25 different institutions and 11 countries. As such, the richness of the volume derives not only from the cultural diversity of its contributors, but also from the contents of the chapters, which explore the significance of understanding the multi-cultural characteristics of the tourism and hospitality industry in general, and of destination marketing in particular. In terms of Hofstede's cultural dimensions (Hofstede, 2001; Hofstede, Hofstede & Minkov, 2010), there remains much to think about with regard to possible marketing methods that would help to develop better communication between service providers and visitors (e.g. customer relationship marketing, experiential marketing), among service providers (e.g. self-governance, knowledge sharing) and among visitors (e.g. word of mouth recommendation), where each of these represents a piece of today's multi-cultural tourism and hospitality world.

As a result, the audience for this book may include students of tourism and hospitality programmes at both undergraduate and postgraduate levels, faculty members with teaching and research commitments, libraries in schools that run tourism, hospitality and business management programmes, and practitioners (e.g., destination managers, ministry of tourism staff and individual tourism establishments). This book would serve as an excellent supplement to existing textbooks that examine various aspects of tourism marketing, particularly in the context of world-wide case studies on destination marketing. The contributions accommodated in this volume will be a helpful reference resource, full of rich materials that refer to the applications of destination marketing practices via worldwide case studies.

We thank all the authors for their remarkable contributions and for their respectful commitment and continuous cooperation that has been of such help in bringing this proposal to fruition. We would also like to thank Routledge for giving us a unique opportunity to publish this volume in such a smooth and professional manner. Without your endless support, positivity and understanding, we would never have been able to make this happen.

Metin Kozak and Nazmi Kozak
*Volume editors*

## References

Bahar, O., & Kozak, M. (2007). Advancing destination competitiveness research: Comparison between tourists and service providers. *Journal of Tourism and Travel Marketing, 22*(2), 61–71.

Baker, B. (2012). *Destination branding for small cities.* 2nd ed., Portland, OR: Creative Leap Books.

Hofstede, G. (2001). *Culture's consequences: Comparing values, behaviors, institutions and organizations across nations.* 2nd ed., London: Sage.

Hofstede, G., Hofstede, G. J., & Minkov, M. (2010). *Cultures and organizations: Software of the mind.* 3rd ed., New York: McGraw-Hill.

Kim, S., & Agrusa, J. (2005). The positioning of overseas honeymoon destinations. *Annals of Tourism Research, 32*(4), 887–904.

Kotler, P., Haider, D., Rein, I. (2002). *Marketing places.* New York: The Free Press.

Kozak, M., & Baloglu, S. (2010). *Managing and marketing tourist destinations: Sustaining a competitive edge.* New York: Routledge.

Kozak, M., Baloglu, S., & Bahar, O. (2010). Measuring destination competitiveness: A comparison between three destinations. *Journal of Hospitality Management and Marketing. 19*(1), 56–71.

Morrison, A. (2013). *Marketing and managing tourism destinations.* Oxon: Routledge.

Pike, S. (2008). *Destination marketing.* Oxford: Butterworth-Heinemann.

Pike, S. (2011). *Destination marketing: An integrated marketing communication approach.* Oxford: Butterworth-Heinemann.

Ritchie, J.R.B., & Crouch, G.I. (2003). *The competitive destination: A sustainable tourism perspective.* Oxon: CABI.

# Part I
# Destination image

# 1　A study of the role of country image in destination image

*Yin Teng Chew and Siti Aqilah Binte Jahari*

## Introduction

Tourism is an industry that is highly driven by images that offer simplified and close representation of the actual destination (MacKay & Fesenmaier, 1997). Images are particularly crucial in determining the viability of the destination (Tasci & Gartner, 2007), tourist behaviours and their decision-making processes in choosing a travel destination (Baloglu & Brinberg, 1997; Chen & Hsu, 2000; Chen & Tsai, 2007). The formation of destination image (DI) is inextricably intertwined with several external factors (familiarity with a destination, previous visitation and socio-demographic factors) (Beerli & Martin, 2004a, 2004b; Baloglu, 1997; Chaudhary, 2000). A key aspect of the DI literature that still remains questionable and highly debated amongst scholars is its conceptualization.

Despite the existence of DI literature over a span of three decades, scholars have yet to arrive at a consensus on the conceptualization of DI constructs (Tasci, Gartner & Cavusgil, 2007). This lack of consensus is due to its multidimensionality characteristics that are defined as complex, multiple, relativistic and dynamic (Gallarza, Gil Saura & Calderon Garcia, 2002). Conventionally, past studies have conceptually and empirically demonstrated cognitive and affective images as a function of DI (Beerli & Martin, 2004a; Baloglu & McCleary, 1999a, 1999b; Tasci & Gartner, 2007) through which the combined interaction of these two constructs yields 'overall image' (Baloglu & McCleary, 1999a, 1999b; Beerli & Martin, 2004a, 2004b). Together with conative image (Gartner, 1994), these DI constructs capture the behavioural response of an individual.

Recent research has started to consider country image (CI) as conceptually part of DI. Some scholars attempt to draw parallels with DI (Gertner, 2010; Elliot, Papadopoulos & Kim, 2011; Martin & Eroglu, 1993; Mossberg & Kleppe, 2005; Nadeau, Heslop, O'Reily & Luk, 2008) although CI and DI have independently developed as two separate streams of research in international marketing and tourism. Martínez and Alvarez (2010) empirically revealed that DI and CI are two separate and distinct constructs. Conversely, several scholars concluded that greater integration between product-based CI and DI is required (Elliot *et al.*, 2011; Mossberg & Kleppe, 2005; Nadeau *et al.*, 2008).

Nadeau *et al.* (2008) and Kim *et al.* (2007) empirically revealed that perceived stereotypes and beliefs about the country and its people are significant in influencing visitation and recommendation intentions. These findings seem to suggest that there are considerable overlapping ideas between CI and DI. Nadeau *et al.* (2008) contended that the DI construct is thus far inconclusive as it has neglected several aspects such as the country and its people. He argues that similar perception may be extended to other product information and services (Hong & Wyer, 1989), including tourism. We concur with these scholars as our literature review indicates that DI constructs employed in past research (e.g., Beerli & Martin, 2004a) do not capture values, beliefs and national stereotypes that tourists might perceive about the country's people.

DI itself still lacks a conceptual framework as to the functions of its various constructs (cognitive, affective, conative, overall) when considered in an integrated model (Fakeye & Crompton, 1991; Mazanec & Schweiger, 1981) although cognitive and affective images are the dominant approach to measuring DI (Pike & Ryan, 2004). For instance, DI has been loosely defined (Fakeye & Crompton, 1991; Mazanec & Schweiger, 1981) as mirrored in several studies which had previously interpreted it as a city (Dadgostar & Isotalo, 1996; Oppermann, 1996), region (Ahmed, 1991; Fakeye & Crompton, 1991) or country (Chon, 1991; Sönmez & Sirakaya, 2002). Others have relied on individual attractions or resorts as the basis of DI (Alhemoud & Armstrong, 1996; Gibson, Qi & Zhang, 2008; Phelps, 1986).

Such a fragmented concept implies that past research seems to recognize non-travel-specific attributes as part of DI. This argument is consistent with Kotler's (1987) assertion that an association exists between a country's tourist image and its national image. In short, despite concerted effort by scholars, ascertaining the definition and conceptualization of DI still remains problematic owing to its multifaceted nature (Jenkins, 1999).

Given the inconsistent findings from previous research, this study attempts to empirically examine cognitive and affective images along with CI. By testing several models in a single study, our contributions to the literature are three-fold. First, adopting such a measure elucidates how cognitive and affective images may be studied in relation with CI. Second, while other research only considers a single model, this chapter will empirically examine and suggest the most suitable model for integrating country and destination image in understanding their respective effects on intention to visit. Third, the scale measuring CI will also include factors other than traditional DI that are commonly considered by tourists.

## Literature review

Advancement in DI literature in determining its definition over three decades has evolved to encapsulate various features of DI. Most definitions identify two facets of DI, namely cognitive and affective images. Despite concerted effort by scholars, ascertaining the definition and conceptualization of DI still remains problematic owing to its multifaceted nature (Jenkins, 1999). There are several aspects contributing to its multidimensional nature such as one's exposure to different types of information sources, past travel experience, familiarity, socio-demographics, constraints and motivations (Baloglu & McCleary, 1999a; Beerli

& Martin, 2004b, Kim & Chalip, 2004) and in a recent study, perceived destination risk (Chew & Jahari, 2014). Hence, more research is required to explore other factors or dimensions which have not been captured, but may potentially affect DI (Tasci & Gartner, 2007) or be a facet of DI.

A commonality amongst past definitions of DI is the identification of 'perception', 'impressions', 'ideas' and 'beliefs' as the accepted alternative expressions used to conceptualize tourist DI. Beyond the typical facets of cognitive and affective images, Echtner and Ritchie (1991) argue that certain aspects of the country that are non-observable prior to actual visitation should be considered as a construct of DI, since a clichéd impression of the destination regardless of accuracy of image could still be formed as a consequence of past knowledge acquired from various non-tourism and non-commercial sources of information such as education, news reports, magazines and books (Gunn, 1972).

To illustrate, various sources of information often feature the Japanese government as highly responsible towards its citizens' welfare. Japanese are often known for their discipline, kindness and courtesy. These positive images may be retained as a national image of Japan. Some tourists may believe that post-disaster intervention by the Japanese government on the radioactive leakage issue was effective and diligent. With such a perceived image of Japan resulting from images of its people and governance, tourists may feel less deterred by the threat of radioactive leakage in deciding whether to travel to Japan.

Further, while conceptualization of DI has given greater prominence to measuring the tourist destination's physical and functional attributes, less attention has been directed towards the holistic impression of a destination (Echtner & Ritchie, 1991). The functional construct measuring the tangible and measurable aspects of destinations has been successfully studied (Pike, 2002). However, the much neglected aspect of DI is the holistic impression that refers to the psychological, more abstract and unique features or perception accentuated by the country endowed with tourism destinations.

Existing cognitive image measurement uses some items that seem to feature cognitive image (quality of life, customs and ways of life, friendliness of local people). However, the majority of past studies have predominantly tested 'friendliness of local people' as the only psychological attribute. This weakness in capturing the psychological aspects has been lamented by various scholars (Baloglu & Martin, 2004a; Jenkins, 1996; San Martin & Rodríguez del Bosque, 2008). Yet, studies have been conservative in reflecting such inclusion in advancing research, since they have predominantly limited their studies to existing cognitive and affective images of a tourism destination. Hence, a revisit to the image constructs is warranted, as argued by Echtner and Ritchie (1991), to further examine if inclusion of CI enhances the conceptualization of DI to advance theory and practice.

## Methodology

The primary aim of this study was to determine the role of CI in relation to DI through analysis of data obtained from an online survey. The target population was Malaysian tourists, while the destination under examination was Japan following the Fukushima disaster. Malaysian tourists were chosen as they were ranked as one of the top 10 international tourists travelling to Japan (JNTO, 2011). Collaboration with organizations such as the Malaysian Travel and Tour Association (MATTA) and the Japan National Tourism Organization (JNTO) was sought for dissemination of the online survey questionnaire.

The survey instrument was adopted from previously established scales for DI (Baloglu & McCleary, 1999a) and intention to visit (Huang & Hsu, 2009). An exception was made for the CI instrument which was developed in congruence with the stereotype definition consisting of cognitive features that reflect country's people and beliefs. Considering the contextual influence of post-disaster Japan, the CI construct was developed to understand tourists' perceptions of values, traits and characteristics that Japanese people may adhere to in a homogeneous society.

Questions measuring CI were based on whether tourists believed that Japan, as a country, possesses the ability to maintain its holiday destinations and has good food quality control and civilized and polite people. In contrast, DI was measured using the traditional construct of cognitive and affective image. To measure cognitive image, respondents were asked whether they believed that Japan is able to offer good standards of hygiene and cleanliness, personal safety, beautiful scenery and attractions. Likewise, affective image was captured by measuring respondents' feelings towards Japan as a holiday destination.

A total of 298 responses were collected of which 286 were retained after data cleaning for current analysis. This study employed statistical software such as SPSS to output descriptive statistics and AMOS to run structural equation modelling. The KMO–Bartlett's test of sample adequacy value of 0.926 indicated that the sample size was sufficient. All constructs achieved satisfactory reliability, exceeding the minimum threshold level of 0.70 as recommended by Bagozzi and Yi (1988). The discriminant validity was also satisfied when the squared correlation of any pair of latent variables was less than the average variance extracted of the two paired variables (Anderson & Gerbing, 1988). Convergent validity was also achieved in this study when the average variance extracted for all latent variables exceeded 0.5 (Bagozzi & Yi, 1988).

## Findings

The variation in conceptualizing CI and DI inevitably produces mixed results and an inconclusive understanding of DI. To unlock the black box of DI conceptualization, future study should disentangle the concepts by testing out various models in a single study (see Figures 1.1–1.3) as such a study carries important theoretical and practical contributions. This study intended to examine CI as a moderator. However, since the reported ratings of the study sample had a small number of respondents with sharp differences in ratings, the moderation model could not be examined. The findings of this study suggest that CI plays a more prominent role as a predictor over mediator.

**Destination Image**

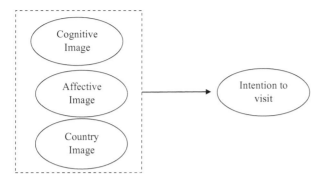

*Figure 1.1* Country image as an additional facet of destination image.

**Destination Image**

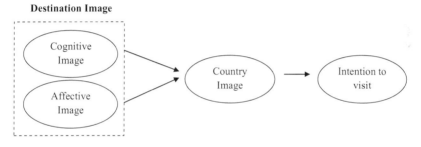

*Figure 1.2* Country image as a mediator.

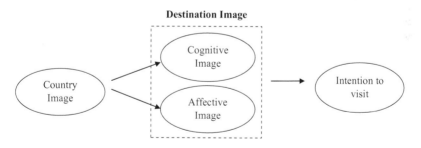

*Figure 1.3* Country image as a predictor of destination image.

In line with Echtner and Ritchie's (1993) suggestion on holistic representation of DI, the first model proposes CI as the third dimension of DI, in addition to the conventional cognitive and affective image (Figure 1.1). The model assumes that tourists may revert to cliché perceptions of CI which contribute to the overall

*Table 1.1* Comparison of goodness of fit indices between models

|  | Chi-square | Chi-square/df | CFI | TLI | RMSEA |
|---|---|---|---|---|---|
| CI as a facet of the DI construct | 178.990 | 1.884 | 0.969 | 0.961 | 0.056 |
| CI as a mediator | 289.127 | 1.701 | 0.971 | 0.964 | 0.050 |
| CI as a predictor of DI | 271.855 | 1.668 | 0.974 | 0.966 | 0.048 |

Source: Authors.

evaluation of destination, thus expressing their intention to visit. Based on empirical testing, this model highlights the nature of CI as being indeed a part of DI given the model fit. However, fit indices, albeit being significant and meeting the cut-off criteria for a best-fit model, are acceptable and thus seem to suggest that further investigation is required to explore other roles of CI in relation to DI.

Consistent with Martin and Alvarez's (2010) suggestion, the second (Figure 1.2) and third (Figure 1.3) models consider CI as a separate construct. The second model suggests that not only can the image of a country as a tourist destination be affected by the cognitive and affective images but more importantly, CI plays a mediating role between DI and visit intention, thereby influencing tourist decision-making and travel intention. The empirical results in Table 1.1 show the model fit for the mediation model. CI mediates the relationship between affective image and visit intention. While CI is influenced by cognitive image, it was not a mediator for the relationship between cognitive image and visit intention. Partial mediation indices fit better. Therefore, CI partially mediates the relationship between DI and visit intention.

The third model (Figure 1.3) assumes that CI is a predictor of the conventional components of DI (cognitive and affective images). This model asserts that CI plays a significant role in influencing DI. The empirical finding shows that across the three tested models, this model has the best fit. CI predicts both cognitive and affective images. However, due to the insignificant path from cognitive image to visit intention, the CI–cognitive image–visit intention path was insignificant.

## Conclusion

This study advances theoretical knowledge by comparing three different models that examine the relationship between CI and DI. Based on the comparison of the three model fit indices, CI is best studied as a predictor of DI. First, this finding supports Martin and Alvarez's (2010) study that CI and DI exist as two separate, yet interrelated constructs. Tourists' beliefs that Japanese possess qualities such as environmental awareness in ensuring strict control on food quality and maintenance of holiday destinations directly influenced their intention to visit. Such perception can help restore the tarnished image of Japan as a holiday destination. Second, respondents showed strong positive feelings towards post-disaster Japan which mediate the relationship between CI and intention to visit. Tourists may ascribe to similar values and traits of Japanese that instil confidence in tourists which consequently encourage travel to post-disaster Japan.

In terms of practical implications, destination marketing organization (DMO) may capitalize on advertising campaigns that depict Japanese manners or values to restore the image of post-disaster Japan as a departure from traditional marketing strategy that places greater emphasis on destination attributes. By concentrating on CI attributes, DMO can divert prospective tourists' attention from negative DI to positive CI. Such a softer approach may arouse tourists' positive feelings towards post-disaster Japan and instil confidence in tourists regarding Japan's capabilities to recover from natural disaster.

Countries subjected to hazards resulting from natural disasters may consider shifting their promotion strategy to identifying attributes unique to the country. In the case of Japan, the homogeneity of the value system along with the strong influence of non-governmental organizations on environmental protection represent attributes unique to Japan that can easily be related to or admired by prospective tourists. Therefore, non-travel-related features may also play an influential role in shaping one's intention to visit. Future studies examining DI should consider studying DI together with CI as two separate constructs, by identifying positive facets unique to the country that can further enhance its overall image as a holiday destination.

## References

Ahmed, Z. U. (1991). The influence of the components of a state's tourist image on product positioning strategy. *Tourism Management, 12*(4), 331–340.

Alhemoud, A. M., & Armstrong, E. G. (1996). Image of tourism attractions in Kuwait. *Journal of Travel Research, 34*(4), 76–80.

Anderson, J. C., & Gerbing, D. W. (1988). Structural equation modeling in practice: A review and recommended two-step approach. *Psychological bulletin, 103*(3), 411–423.

Bagozzi, R. P., & Yi, Y. (1988). On the evaluation of structure equations models. *Journal of the Academy of Marketing Science, 16*(1), 76–94.

Baloglu, S. (1997). The relationship between destination images and socio-demographic and trip characteristics of international travellers. *Journal of Vacation Marketing, 3*(3), 221–233.

Baloglu, S., & Brinberg, D. (1997). Affective images of tourism destinations. *Journal of Travel Research, 35*(4), 11–15.

Baloglu, S., & McCleary, K. W. (1999a). A model of destination image formation. *Annals of Tourism Research, 26*(4), 868–897.

Baloglu, S., & McCleary, K. W. (1999b). US international pleasure travelers' images of four Mediterranean destinations: A comparison of visitors and non-visitors. *Journal of Travel Research, 38*(2), 144–152.

Beerli, A., & Martin, J. D. (2004a). Factors influencing destination image. *Annals of Tourism Research, 31*(3), 657–681.

Beerli, A., & Martín, J. D. (2004b). Tourists' characteristics and the perceived image of tourist destinations: A quantitative analysis – a case study of Lanzarote, Spain. *Tourism Management, 25*(5), 623–636.

Chaudhary, M. (2000). India's image as a tourist destination – a perspective of foreign tourists. *Tourism Management*, *21*(3), 293–297.

Chen, C. F., & Tsai, D. (2007). How destination image and evaluative factors affect behavioral intentions? *Tourism Management*, *28*(4), 1115–1122.

Chen, J. S., & Hsu, C. H. (2000). Measurement of Korean tourists' perceived images of overseas destinations. *Journal of Travel Research*, *38*(4), 411–416.

Chew, E. Y. T., & Jahari, S. A. (2014). Destination image as a mediator between perceived risks and revisit intention: A case of post-disaster Japan. *Tourism Management*, *40*, 382–393.

Chon, K. S. (1991). Tourism destination image modification process: Marketing implications. *Tourism Management*, *12*(1), 68–72.

Dadgostar, B., & Isotalo, R. M. (1996). Content of city destination image for near-home tourists. *Journal of Hospitality & Leisure Marketing*, *3*(2), 25–34.

Echtner, C. M., & Ritchie, J. B. (1993). The measurement of destination image: An empirical assessment. *Journal of Travel Research*, *31*(4), 3–13.

Elliot, S., Papadopoulos, N., & Kim, S. S. (2011). An integrative model of place image exploring relationships between destination, product, and country images. *Journal of Travel Research*, *50*(5), 520–534.

Fakeye, P. C., & Crompton, J. L. (1991). Image differences between prospective, first-time, and repeat visitors to the Lower Rio Grande Valley. *Journal of Travel Research*, *30*(2), 10–16.

Gallarza, M. G., Saura, I. G., & García, H. C. (2002). Destination image: Towards a conceptual framework. *Annals of Tourism Research*, *29*(1), 56–78.

Gartner, W. C. (1994). Image formation process. *Journal of Travel & Tourism Marketing*, *2*(3), 191–216.

Gertner, R. K. (2010). Similarities and differences of the effect of country images on tourist and study destinations. *Journal of Travel & Tourism Marketing*, *27*(4), 383–395.

Gibson, H. J., Qi, C. X., & Zhang, J. J. (2008). Destination image and intent to visit China and the 2008 Beijing Olympic Games. *Journal of Sport Management*, *22*(4), 427–450.

Gunn, C. A. V. (1972). *Designing tourist regions.* New York: Von Nostrand Reinhold.

Hong, S. T., & Wyer, R. S. (1989). Effects of country-of-origin and product-attribute information on product evaluation: An information processing perspective. *Journal of Consumer Research, 16*, 175–187.

Huang, S. S., & Hsu, C. H. (2009). Effects of travel motivation, past experience, perceived constraint, and attitude on revisit intention. *Journal of Travel Research, 48*(1), 29–44.

Japan National Tourism Organization [JNTO]. (2011). Foreign visitors & Japanese departures. Retrieved January 24, 2012 from http://www.jnto.go.jp/eng/ttp/sta/PDF/E2011.pdf.

Jenkins, O. H. (1999). Understanding and measuring tourist destination images. *International Journal of Tourism Research*, *1*(1), 1–15.

Kim, N. S., & Chalip, L. (2004). Why travel to the FIFA World Cup? Effects of motives, background, interest, and constraints. *Tourism Management*, *25*(6), 695–707.

Kim, S. S., Agrusa, J., Lee, H., & Chon, K. (2007). Effects of Korean television dramas on the flow of Japanese tourists. *Tourism Management*, *28*(5), 1340–1353.

Kotler, P. (1987). Semiotics of person and nation marketing. In J. Umiker-Seboek (ed.), *Marketing and semiotics* (pp. 3–12). Berlin: Mouton de Gruyter.

MacKay, K. J., & Fesenmaier, D. R. (1997). Pictorial element of destination in image formation. *Annals of Tourism Research*, *24*(3), 537–565.

Martin, I. M., & Eroglu, S. (1993). Measuring a multi-dimensional construct: Country image. *Journal of Business Research*, *28*(3), 191–210.

Martínez, S. C., & Alvarez, M. D. (2010). Country versus destination image in a developing country. *Journal of Travel & Tourism Marketing, 27*(7), 748–764.

Mazanec, J., &. Schweiger, G. (1981). Improved marketing efficiency through multiproduct brand names? An empirical investigation of image transfer. *European Research, 9,* 32–44.

Mossberg, L., & Kleppe, I. A. (2005). Country and destination image – different or similar image concepts? *The Service Industries Journal, 25*(4), 493–503.

Nadeau, J., Heslop, L., O'Reilly, N., & Luk, P. (2008). Destination in a country image context. *Annals of Tourism Research, 35*(1), 84–106.

Oppermann, M. (1996). Convention destination images: Analysis of association meeting planners' perceptions. *Tourism Management, 17*(3), 175–182.

Phelps, A. (1986). Holiday destination image – the problem of assessment: An example developed in Menorca. *Tourism Management, 7*(3), 168–180.

Pike, S. (2002). Destination image analysis – a review of 142 papers from 1973 to 2000. *Tourism Management, 23*(5), 541–549.

Pike, S., & Ryan, C. (2004). Destination positioning analysis through a comparison of cognitive, affective, and conative perceptions. *Journal of Travel Research, 42*(4), 333–342.

San Martin, H., & Rodríguez del Bosque, I. A. (2008). Exploring the cognitive–affective nature of destination image and the role of psychological factors in its formation. *Tourism Management, 29*(2), 263–277.

Sönmez, S., & Sirakaya, E. (2002). A distorted destination image? The case of Turkey. *Journal of Travel Research, 41*(2), 185–196.

Tasci, A. D., & Gartner, W. C. (2007). Destination image and its functional relationships. *Journal of Travel Research, 45*(4), 413–425.

Tasci, A. D., Gartner, W. C., & Cavusgil, S. T. (2007). Conceptualization and operationalization of destination image. *Journal of Hospitality & Tourism Research, 31*(2), 194–223.

# 2 Lake-destination image attributes

## A neural network content analysis

*Ana Isabel Rodrigues, Antónia Correia
and Metin Kozak*

## Introduction

Forty years of research have clearly demonstrated that destination image (DI) is nowadays an important field of tourism studies, more specifically destination marketing inquiry. However, an apparent absence of homogeneity related to DI theory and empirical work have led to a lack of theoretical framework, continuously pointed out by several researchers in the field (Baloglu & McCleary, 1999; Echtner & Ritchie, 1993; Fakeye & Crompton, 1991). This is mainly due to the fact that DI can be classified as an 'umbrella construct' which requires an evolutionary approach when investigating this field of research (Rodrigues, Correia & Kozak, 2011, 2012).

Embraced by a cyclical process, different theories, perspectives, methods and techniques have been emerging in recent decades and new trends in the DI field are arising (Stepchenkova & Mills, 2010). For example, new methodologies for DI measurement based on Jenkins' (1999) model which incorporates two phases of research (both qualitative and quantitative), started to emerge. As stated by Walle (1997, p. 535), 'the field of tourism needs to embrace a general recognition of the legitimacy of a variety of research tools'. In the last decade, multi-method studies have been increasing in this field of research (e.g. Martin & Bosque, 2008; Rolo-Vela, 2009), where computer-aided text analysis, specifically the use of CATPAC software has been highlighted (Ryan & Cave, 2005; Govers & Go, 2005; Govers, Go & Kumar, 2007; Ryan, 1998).

In addition, as a result of an intensive competitive environment non-traditional entities have started to be the focus of recent DI studies, such as regions (Kastenholz, Davis & Gordon, 1999; Silvestre & Correia, 2005), resorts (Alcaniz, Garcia & Blas, 2009) or types of tourism (Silva, Kastenholz & Abrantes, 2013). Particularly related to lake tourism, very little is known about destination marketing and image applied to the lake tourism context (Tuohino, 2006). This is a relatively unexplored research theme of tourism studies, specifically in the DI field.

In this context, this chapter aims to advance knowledge of lake tourism as a recent research area in tourism studies and to extract image attributes more related to lake-destination areas (LDAs). For this purpose, the study's goal is to explore and analyse the findings obtained through content analysis and validate their interpretation. In order to assure the reliability of these outputs, a different method of analysis was adopted through the use of a computer-aided text analysis named CATPAC (v. III, Woelfel, forthcomimg), which 'is able to identify the most important words in a text and determine the patterns of similarity based on the way they are used in the text' (Woelfel, 1998, p.11). CATPAC is as a self-organizing artificial neural network software package that has been optimized for reading text.

## Literature review

The literature review of DI research over the last forty years clearly demonstrated that: (1) destinations under study were mainly large-scale entities; (2) only three DI scales were considered to be reliable and valid (Rolo-Vela, 2009); (3) there is no consensus about which attributes should be selected and included in a DI scale; and finally, (4) DI scales should progressively include attributes that really match the object under study (Rodrigues *et al.*, 2012).

Additionally, recent studies (Stepchenkova & Mills, 2010) argue that the scope of DI measurement has become wider including non-traditional entities, such as national parks, resorts, rural areas and sport events. In this line of thought there is also Beerli and Martin's (2004, p. 659) rationale, for whom

> the selection of the attributes used in designing a scale will depend largely on the attractions of each destination, on its positioning, and on the objectives of the assessment of perceived image, which will also determine whether specific or more general attributes are chosen.

Also, Correia, Santos and Barros (2010) posit that the probability of choice by tourists is strongly affected by different attributes related to destination characteristics, among other variables.

Given this, and considering the fact that due to the multifaceted nature of tourism new typologies have come into existence over the last decade, DI scales should consider the attribute differences not only based on geographical scope, but also on the type of entity/object, such as types of tourism and destinations. In this context and particularly related to water as a tourism resource, a new type of tourism has emerged – lake tourism – as a relatively unexplored research theme of tourism studies with an emerging body of literature (Cooper, 2006; Tuohino, 2006). Lakes are open bonds of water (natural or man-made) which can either be considered as a tourism resource, which adds value to the whole destination experience or arise as the core of the destination's attractiveness. In fact, tourism development not only on the lake itself but in the surrounding area might constitute a valuable resource for some countries if properly developed.

Based on this, due to the emergence of LDAs all over the world, it is assumed that DI might represent a relevant basis for the development and management of this new type of destination. According to Pike and Ryan (2004), DI is considered a key construct in destination positioning, and destinations should be oriented to target positioning in their own competitiveness set (Bahar & Kozak, 2007; Kozak, 2002; Kozak & Rimmington, 1999). For this reason, the objective of this chapter is to explore what attributes might be involved in the image formation of LDAs, as a possible basis for developing a future image measurement scale applied to this particular type of destination.

Grounded on the premise that various methods should be used to explore DI attributes, both qualitative and quantitative (e.g. Martin & Bosque, 2008; Rolo-Vela, 2009), this study assumes that unstructured and semi-structured techniques should be employed to obtain more knowledge concerning image attributes (Prebensen, 2007; Ryan & Cave, 2005). Similarly to Cave, Ryan and Panakera (2003), this study also advocates that there are advantages in employing qualitative techniques, particularly in the early stages of DI research, since it apprehends more aspects of image.

## Methodology

The qualitative phase began with an analysis of the image measurement variables found in the literature for other types of tourist destinations. A meta-analysis paper concerning DI as a field of research since the emergence of the construct in the 1970s was examined. Having as a base line the list of the most common DI attributes proposed by Gallarza, Saura and Garcia (2002), an extension of the period was considered (2000 to 2012) and twenty-four research studies were analysed (Rodrigues, Correia, Kozak & Tuohino, 2015). With this in mind, and since the scales analysed did not correspond well to the object of the study (LDAs in this case), the goal of the study is to explore the cognitive image of LDAs, analysing both its functional and psychological attributes, and also to investigate the nature of the lake tourism concept.

This chapter focuses on validating the results obtained through the content-analysis method in a previous research stage (Rodrigues *et al.*, 2015). As suggested by Ryan (1998), other steps of analysis might be implemented for the refinement of the final results and one way of attempting to assess the qualitative data is by trying to establish relationships between phrases and words. Therefore, by matching the results from content analysis with the establishment of associations between words (attributes) through perceptual maps, it becomes possible to assess whether the data are mutually supportive. With this in mind, this chapter focuses on the use of a neural content analysis with CATPAC software.

As a reminder, the general objective of this chapter is to explore the cognitive image of LDAs, analysing both its functional and psychological attributes, and also investigate the nature of the lake tourism concept. This general objective is reflected in the following research question:

- What attributes might be involved in the image formation of LDAs, as a possible basis for developing a future image measurement scale applied to this particular type of destination?

The extracting process was carried out based on a content analysis of text and pictures in the database of an online directory for lake enthusiasts (cf. Lakelubbers.com). A total of 40 lake descriptions (units of analysis) constitute the sample of this study (for a more detailed explanation see Rodrigues *et al.*, 2015). As a first step a 'deductive procedure' was conducted since the goal here was to conceptually validate a theoretical framework of DI dimensions (e.g. 'natural resources', 'tourism infrastructures') by using Beerli and Martin's (2004) scale, but particularly applied to the lake-destination context.

As analysis proceeded, additional codes were developed more related to lake-destinations, and the initial coding scheme was revised. Subcategories were then defined through 'inductive procedure' as a method of coding (e.g. A.1. 'Physical features of the lake'; A.2. 'Richness of nature'; A.3. 'Weather' under category A. 'Natural resources'). Through a deductive-inductive approach it was possible to generate a set of over 100 potential attributes related to LDAs, grouped into 23 subcategories, classified in nine predetermined categories or domains (see Table 2.1). These items might be included in an image measurement scale for this type of destinations in the future.

After this and in order to respond the second research question, a holistic method of coding was applied and five dimensions of lake tourism concept were extracted (resource, supply, logistical, organizational and representational). Based on these results of the conventional content analysis mentioned above, and aiming to enrich the interpretation of those results, a different method of analysis was used. CATPAC is a self-organizing artificial neural network software package, which 'is able to identify the most important words in a text and determine the patterns of similarity based on the way they are used in the text' (Woelfel, 1998, p. 11).

Simply, CATPAC is based on a neural modelling technique that generates a frequency table and proximity for the most common words. As Govers and Go (2005) explain, proximities between words consists of artificial neurons or nodes which are connected by communications channels of varying strength within a sliding text window chosen by the researcher (standard size is seven words, i.e., CATPAC moves a window of seven words over the text and calculates proximities based on the number of times words are found together within these frames). For a good overview, refer to Woelfel (1998), Doerfel and Barnett (1999).

Conjointly, other researchers have supported the use of CATPAC as a helpful tool for content analysis in tourism studies (Cave & Ryan, 2005; Choi, Lehto & Morrison, 2007; Govers & Go 2005; Govers, Go & Kumar, 2007; Ryan, 1998). Summarizing, the resulting neural network output was used to identify the words that were most frequently mentioned to portray image attributes related to LDAs.

Similar to Choi *et al.*'s procedure (2007), some technical operations were needed to achieve interpretable results. The program: (1) eliminates 'stop words' (Doerfel & Barnett, 1999), which include a list of articles, prepositions, conjunctions and intransitive verbs that do not contribute to the meaning of the text (e.g. *if, and, to, is*); (2) combines two and more words into one so that they are not counted separately (e.g. *NationalPark, RealEstate*); and (3) replaces plurals with singulars (e.g. *lake, mountain, island, city, village* all in singular) and past tense with present tense.

Table 2.1 Defining dimensions and attributes of lake-destination areas from content analysis

| Categories | Subcategories | Attributes/properties (examples) |
| --- | --- | --- |
| A. Natural resources | A.1. Physical features of the lake | A.1. Origin, type, surface, depth, elevation, length, topography (…) |
| | A.2. Richness of nature | A.2. Protected areas, flora and fauna (birds, fish); sky, beaches, islands (…) |
| | A.3. Weather | A.3. Temperature, snow, frozen or unfrozen lake (…) |
| B. General infrastructure | B.1. Development and quality of roads | B.1. Access roads to the lake, circular drives |
| | B.2. Transport facilities | B.2. Existence of nearby airport, between villages around the lake, between lakes, between islands on the lake |
| | B.3. Nautical facilities and other infrastructures | B.3. Marinas, ports, public ramps, boat slips, public piers, berths, swimming areas, boardwalks (…) |
| C. Tourist infrastructure | C.1. Accommodation and catering facilities | C.1. Caravan parks, cottages, real estate, camping, hotels, chalets, vacation rentals (…) |
| | C.2. Available packages | C.2. Sightseeing tours, excursions, cruises (half-day, whole-day, evening, lunch), fishing trips (…) |
| | C.3. Signed trails and paths | C.3. Bicycle trails, climbing trails, hiking trails, nature/scenic trails, walking trails (…) |
| | C.4. Tourist services and information | C.4. Maps, tourist offices, visitor/information centres, nature centres, picnic areas, rental services), charter services (…) |
| D. Tourist leisure and recreation | D.1. Water activities, sports and recreation | D.1. Boating, boardwalk, canoeing, fishing, houseboating, lake sightseeing, kayaking, kite surfing, sailing, swimming |
| | D.2. Land-based activities, sports and recreation | D.2. Biking, birdwatching, climbing, hiking, paragliding, picnicking, sightseeing, rock climbing trekking, walking |
| | D.3. Winter activities, sports and recreation | D.3. Alpine and Nordic skiing, dog sledding, ice fishing, ice skating, ice climbing, snowboard, snowshoeing, toboggan |
| | D.4. Entertainment and events | D.4. Sport competitions (regattas, tournaments, parades), themed events (wine festivals, evening parties), local attractions (swimming pools, casinos), nightlife |

| Category | Sub-category | Description |
|---|---|---|
| E. Culture, history and art | E.1. History of the lake and surrounding region | E.1. Historic ruins, archaeological ruins and artefacts, local architecture, legends/stories, caves, UNESCO |
| | E.2. Museums and historic buildings | E.2. Museums, castles, fortresses, fortifications, churches, monasteries, abbeys, chapels, cathedrals, monasteries (…) |
| | E.3. Cultural attractions and events | E.3. Music festivals and demonstrations, concerts, recitals, exhibitions, theatre, dance performances |
| | E.4. Gastronomy | E.4. Local dishes, wine (…) |
| F. Political and economic factors | F.1. Geographical location and territorial division | F.1. Location, countries and region boundaries, geo-political significance of the lake |
| | F.2. Lake purposes (past and present) | F.2. Salt extraction, fishery, energy production, supply of drinking water, agriculture, transportation |
| G. Natural environment | G.1. Attractiveness of the communities | G.1. Historic villages, mountain villages, cities, hamlets, lakeside towns, small towns (…) |
| | G.2. Beauty of the landscape/scenery | G.2. Rural, natural, alpine, mountain, vineyards, orchards, vegetable farms, deep valleys, foothills, alpine |
| H. Social environment | H.1. Host community | H.1. Presence of local people, way of life, hospitality and friendliness |
| I. Atmosphere | No sub-category | Active, amazing scenery, breathtaking views, challenging, dramatic scenery, friendly and family-oriented lake, inspired, simplicity, tranquillity, beauty, memorable, outdoor destination, picturesque, quiet, rejuvenation, relaxing, unspoiled, romantic |

Source: Own elaboration.

Multiple runs of the CATPAC were then conducted to further exclude other words that do not contribute to a meaningful interpretation of the results. According to Doerfel & Barnett (1999, p. 592), CATPAC

> then counts the occurrences of the remaining words yielding the most fre-
> quently occurring words equal to the value set by the user. CATPAC creates
> a words-by-words matrix which cell containing the likelihood that the occur-
> rence of one word will indicate the occurrence of another.

This matrix is then entered into a variety of multivariate analytic procedures through the use of two familiar techniques: cluster analysis and multidimensional scaling ('perceptual mapping'). A 'dendogram' as a graphic representation of the clusters in the text is produced indicating the degree of clustering (for a more in-depth explanation see Doerfel & Barnett, 1999; Woelfel, 1993). In order to enrich the analytic procedure, a visual plot of the symbols by multidimensional scaling is produced by CATPAC.

Based on the results of the content analysis as previously presented, the text data analysed by CATPAC was classified under themes or domains. The process of defining these themes was derived from the intersection of the first and second research question results. Therefore, five themes were extracted and the text data disposed, namely: *theme 0* based on a total combined lake description (40 texts of all units of analysis); *theme 1* corresponding to lake natural resources (about the lake itself); *theme 2* with a destination description (natural and social environment, atmosphere); *theme 3* comprising text data about destination heritage; (e) *theme 4* with the activities and facilities (general and tourist infrastructures and activities on and around the lake).

## Findings

As previously explained, the initial set of image attributes extracted from the literature review reveals that they are too generic (e.g. landscape, sport facilities, culture attractions, accommodation). The list was considered inadequate and did not incorporate all salient attributes for LDAs. Through a content analysis deductive approach, nine image categories were determined based on Beerli and Martin's (2004) classification and 21 subcategories identified through a more inductive approach. Each subcategory includes several image attributes more related to LDAs. The outcomes of the conventional content analysis were the nine categories and 23 subcategories. A set of over 100 potential variables were extracted from textual analysis.

Using CATPAC content-analysis software, the totality of qualitative responses for each theme or subcategory was processed (Choi *et al.*, 2007; Gretzel & Fesenmaier, 2003; Ryan, 1998). Table 2.2 displays and compares the top 30 most frequent words for each theme and shows the combined total frequencies for all themes extracted from CATPAC outputs. This procedure was undertaken since the purpose behind the study was to obtain key descriptors that could be incorporated into a subsequent questionnaire.

*Table 2.2* Most frequent words related to LDA in rank order

| Rank | Theme 0 | Theme 1 | Theme 2 | Theme 3 | Theme 4 |
|------|---------|---------|---------|---------|---------|
| 1 | Lake | Lake | Lake | Lake | Lake |
| 2 | Water | Water | Visitor | Castle | Boating |
| 3 | Area | Feet | Area | Northern | Fishing |
| 4 | Visitors | Acres | Beautiful | History | Water |
| 5 | Along | Largest | Shoreline | Historical | Visitor |
| 6 | Fishing | River | Northern | Century | Area |
| 7 | Shoreline | Depth | City | Shore | Along |
| 8 | Around | Miles | Water | Area | Shoreline |
| 9 | Miles | Area | Town | Early | Holiday |
| 10 | City | Known | Village | Dates | Offer |
| 11 | Island | Over | Museum | Time | Rentals |
| 12 | Enjoy | Northern | Forest | Abbey | Around |
| 13 | Holiday | Island | Nature | Island | Enjoy |
| 14 | popular | Sea | Around | Ruins | Available |
| 15 | Large | Fishing | Mountain | Years | Popular |
| 16 | Over | Fish | Over | Western | Town |
| 17 | Offer | Located | Miles | Visitors | Skiing |
| 18 | Mountain | Shoreline | Largest | Place | Several |
| 19 | Village | Surface | Enjoy | First | Vacation |
| 20 | Year | Part | NationalPark | NationalPark | Trails |
| 21 | North | Reservoir | Lough | Built | Island |
| 22 | Known | Smaller | Find | Lies | Mountain |
| 23 | Home | Includes | Home | Thousands | Cruise |
| 24 | Town | Trout | Along | City | Including |
| 25 | Provide | Natural | Located | Stone | Village |
| 26 | River | Years | Feet | Ohrid | Local |
| 27 | Feet | Canal | Irland | Goods | Find |
| 28 | Vacation | Species | Popular | Sweden | Hiking |
| 29 | Several | Salmon | Destination | Ancient | Provide |
| 30 | Located | Provide | Castle | UNESCO | Home |

Source: Own elaboration. Generated by CATPAC.

Theme 0: total combined lake description; theme 1: lake natural resources; theme 2: destination description; theme 3: destination heritage; theme 4: activities and facilities.

Not surprisingly, 'lake' was the most frequently used word in all themes, followed by 'water' in *theme 0* and *theme 1*. This reinforces the idea that 'lake' and 'water' are the two main attributes related to LDAs, indicating that lake itself is the core resource of lake tourism as a type of tourism. 'Visitor', 'castle' and 'boating' were the second most ranked words in *theme 2, theme 3* and *theme 4*, correspondingly. This is an evident outcome since *theme 2* includes the visit to the surrounding region where the lake is located, therefore the tourist truly becomes a 'visitor'; *theme 3* specifies heritage as an important element of the destination, where 'castle' was ranked higher than the other themes; and *theme 4* shows that 'boating' is undoubtedly the utmost important activity in LDAs.

Another interesting analysis might set out a more focused observation on each theme. In *theme 1*, which characterizes the lake itself, emphasizing its natural resources, the ranks of words such as 'feet', 'largest', 'depth', 'surface', 'island' might indicate that natural features (e.g. depth, surface or topography) seem to be important attributes when promoting lakes for tourism. Seemingly, natural resources such as icthyofauna through the words 'fishing', 'fish', 'trout', 'species' or 'salmon' also reveal the relevance of this type of attributes related to LDAs. Another interesting observation is 'shoreline', which is used across all themes (except *theme 3*), and was the eighteenth most frequent word in *theme 1*. This reinforces the notion that LDAs are being described or projected based on a strong association between lakes and their shorelines.

In *theme 2* examples of the most frequently mentioned terms are 'city', 'town' or 'village', which are intertwined. These words constitute an important group, emphasizing the description of the region where the lake is located. It can be inferred that the cities or villages around the lake are relevant attributes when promoting lake tourism. In addition, natural and cultural attributes located in the surrounding region also add value to the lake itself (e.g. 'forest', 'nature', 'mountain', 'National Park'). Similarly the words 'museums' and 'castle' also indicate the relevance of cultural attributes. Not surprisingly, in this theme the word 'water' emerges only as the eighth most frequent word, since the core here is not the lake, but the surrounding region.

In *theme 3*, in which the text data is related to destination heritage, the tendency appears to be the promotion of the destination history and its historical elements. That is evident through the words 'history' and 'historical' ranked in fourth and fifth position, correspondingly. Words such as 'century', 'ruins' and 'ancient' corroborate this assumption. Another interesting observation refers to the word 'UNESCO' revealing that the classification as World Heritage Sites by UNESCO, namely cultural sites, is a relevant attribute for LDAs. The tendency appears to be that UNESCO cultural sites might add a significant value to the lake, suggesting its importance when promoting LDAs.

*Theme 4* refers to the activities and facilities located on and around the lake. The top 30 most frequent words highlight the occurrence of activities on water (e.g. 'boating', fishing', 'cruise') and at the surrounding region (e.g. 'skiing', 'hiking' and 'mountain') as a key attribute for lake tourism and, consequently LDAs. Following this line of thought, words such as 'available', 'offer' and 'provide' clearly demonstrate that for LDAs it not only is the existence of lakes important as a resource, but also a supply of nautical and touristic infrastructures and activities. Interestingly, and corroborating this inference is the word 'trails' ranked in twentieth position, which provides evidence once more of the need to support the existence of natural and cultural resources with signed trails and paths.

A final remark on *theme 0* shows the combined total frequencies for all themes (40 texts of all units of analysis). This means that 'lake' and 'water' not surprisingly are the most frequent words when characterizing LDAs. These attributes refer to the nuclear resource of lake tourism, the lakes themselves. The words 'city', 'village' and 'town' also appear in this top 30, demonstrating once more that these places are of utmost importance when promoting lakes. This means that not only is the lake itself relevant, but also the territory where the lake is located. In a similar way this is also expressed through the word 'enjoy' ranked in twelfth

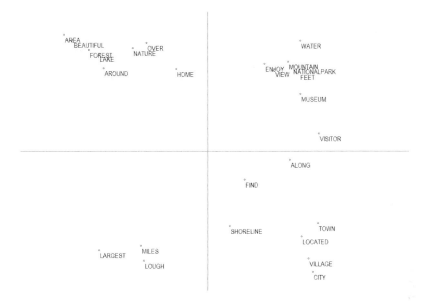

*Figure 2.1* Two-dimensional perceptual map of theme 2 (destination). (Source: Generated by CATPAC.)

position. The idea is to have a pleasurable time near the lake and to appreciate a sum of attributes that define the destination where the lake is located.

The next step was to return to the text and develop a perceptual map with CATPAC. Figure 2.1 presents a two-dimensional perceptual map of *theme 2* as an example. The analysis contains the results from *theme 2*, which shows attributes more related to the surrounding region where the lake is located. The analysis was restricted to 30 keywords. As in textual analysis, the top left-hand cell of the diagram exhibits a clustering of words ('nature', 'around', 'forest') associated with nature and the landscape which surrounds the lakes. The top right cell also corroborates this revealing a cluster with the words like 'mountain' and 'national park' and 'view'. The bottom right cell shows 'town', 'village' and 'city' related closely to each other. This word association brings into the discussion the value that the communities located around the lakes have in terms of tourism development.

## Conclusion

The findings of this study, based on CATPAC analysis, suggest that certain themes or domains exist in lake tourism conceptualization (e.g. 'lake natural resources', 'destination description', 'activities and facilities'), corroborating the need to understand better lake tourism as a particular type of tourism. The text data analysed by CATPAC classified under five themes confirms the conclusions of Rodrigues *et al.* (2015) that the lake tourism concept should be analysed according two main spatial levels of development: (i) the lake itself and lakeshore, and (ii) the destination/surrounding region. This is also in line with the five dimensions of the lake tourism concept obtained through a content-analysis process. It is thus believed that conceptualizing lake tourism facilitates a move forward in developing an image measurement scale more adapted to LDAs.

This chapter examined image attributes which are more related to this type of tourism for a more accurate picture of lake tourism. The first stage of a qualitative study confirms that several dimensions and attributes exist specifically related to LDAs, through an analysis of information contents provided by a lake-lovers' online directory (Lakelubbers.com). As a result of the initial data collecting-phase and content analysis, a set of more than 100 variables that potentially influence the image formation of LDAs was obtained.

These results were then validated by the use of CATPAC, as a self-organizing artificial neural network software package, in order to assure the reliability of the outputs. Certain words or attributes which represent the image projected by LDAs, following specific patterns of associations was obtained. The rank words by themes extracted by CATPAC related to LDAs corroborate the set of variables obtained by content analysis. The projected image of LDAs related to 'lake natural resources' is represented by words such as 'feet', 'largest ', 'depth', 'miles' or 'area', which means that lake features as 'surface area', 'depth' or 'length' might be important attributes when promoting LDAs. Additionally, words such as 'city', 'town' or 'village' also came up, showing how relevant they are for LDA image, adding value to the lake itself. In the theme 'destination heritage', words such as 'castle', 'century', 'abbey' or 'ruins' demonstrated the importance of highlighting these attributes when promoting LDAs. The theme 'activities and facilities' also revealed that 'boating', 'fishing' or 'cruising' are some examples of nautical activities intertwined with LDAs.

Based on these results, future research will focus on this issue and also aim to validate the results here obtained through stakeholder interviews, based on the case of the Alqueva Lake as a recent LDA. Located in the south of Portugal, in the Alentejo region, this is the biggest man-made lake in western Europe. Future lines of research should be directed towards reliable and valid scales for this type of tourism.

The development of this scale could provide relevant and useful information for tourism decision makers in order to design a marketing management strategy for this type of destinations. This is in line with several researchers who argue that image is an important component for a more competitive destination (Ritchie & Crouch, 2003) and directly influences the choice of a destination, valued attributes and purchase process (Morgan & Pritchard, 1998). All the decisions to create or improve an LDA's image, its positioning in the market and enhance competitive advantage of such locations are based on the implementation of elements related to the set of image attributes extracted from the content analysis and validated by CATPAC.

## Acknowledgements

The authors would like to thank Joseph K. Woelfel, the author of CATPAC, for all his support and insightful comments.

# References

Alcaniz, E.B., Garcia, I.S., & Blas, S.S. (2009). The functional-psychological continuum in the cognitive image of a destination: A confirmatory analysis. *Tourism Management*, 30, 715–723.

Bahar, O., & Kozak, M. (2007) Advancing destination competitiveness research. *Journal of Travel & Tourism Marketing*, 22 (2), 61–71.

Baloglu, S., & McCleary, K.W. (1999). A model of destination image formation. *Annals of Tourism Research*, 26, 268–897.

Beerli, A., & Martin, J.D. (2004). Factors influencing destination image. *Annals of Tourism Research,* 31 (3), 657–681.

Cave, J., Ryan, C., & Panakera, C. (2003). Residents' perceptions, migrant groups and culture as an attraction–The case of a proposed Pacific Island cultural centre in New Zealand. *Tourism Management*, 24, 371–385.

Choi, S., Lehto, X.Y., & Morrison, A.M. (2007). Destination image representation on the web: Content analysis of Macau travel related websites. *Tourism Management*, 28, 118–129.

Cooper, C. (2006). Lakes as tourism destination resources. In M. Hall & T. Härkönen (eds.), *Lake Tourism. An integrated approach to lacustrine tourism systems* (pp. 27–42). Clevedon: Channel View Publications.

Correia, A., Santos, C.M., & Barros, C.P. (2010). Tourism in Latin America: A choice analysis. *Annals of Tourism Research*, 34 (3), 610–624.

Doerfel, M. L., & Barnett, G.A. (1999). A semantic network analysis of the international communication association. *Human Communication Research*, 25 (4), 589–603.

Echtner, C., & Ritchie, B. (1991). The meaning and measurement of destination image. *Journal of Tourism Studies,* 2 (2), 2–12.

Echtner, C., & Ritchie, B. (1993). The measurement of destination image: An empirical assessment. *Journal of Travel Research,* 31 (3), 3–13.

Fakeye, P. C., & Crompton, J. L. (1991). Image differences between prospective, first-time, and repeated visitors to the Lower Rio Grande Valley. *Journal of Travel Research,* 30 (10), 10–16.

Gallarza, G., Saura, G., & Garcia, H. (2002*).* Destination image: Towards a conceptual framework. *Annals of Tourism Research,* 29 (1), 56–78.

Govers, R., & Go, F.M. (2005). Projected destination image online: Website content analysis of pictures and text. *Information Technology & Tourism*, 7, 73–89.

Govers, R., Go, F. M., & Kumar, K. (2007). Promoting tourism destination image. *Journal of Travel Research,* 46, 15–23.

Gretzel, U., & Fesenmaier, D.R. (2003). Experienced-based internet making: An exploratory study of sensory experiences associated with pleasure travel to the Midwest United States. In A. Frew, M. Hitz, & P. O'Connor (eds.), *Proceedings of the International Conference on Information and Communication Technologies in Tourism* (pp.49–57). Wien-New York: Springer Verlag.

Jenkins, O. H. (1999). Understanding and measuring tourist destination images. *International Journal of Tourism Research*, 1, 1–15.

Kastenholz, E., Davis, D., & Gordon, P. (1999). Segmenting tourism in rural areas: The case of North and Central Portugal. *Journal of Travel Research*, 37, 353–363.

Kozak, M. (2002). Destination benchmarking. *Annals of Tourism Research*, 29 (2), 497–519.

Kozak, M., & Rimmington, M. (1999). Measuring tourist destination competitiveness: Conceptual considerations and empirical findings. *International Journal of Hospitality Management*, 18, 273–283.

Lakelubbers.com. Lakes for vacation and recreation. Retrieved from http://www. lakelubbers.com/

Martin, H.S., & Rodriguez del Bosque, I.A. (2008). Exploring the cognitive–affective nature of destination image and the role of psychological factors in its formation. *Tourism Management*, 29, 263–277.

Morgan, N. & Pritchard, A. (1998). *Tourism promotion and power: Creating images, creating identities.* New York: John Wiley.

Pike, S., & Ryan, C. (2004). Destination positioning analysis through a comparison of cognitive, affective, and conative perceptions. *Journal of Travel Research*, 42 (May), 333–342.

Prebensen, N.K. (2007). Exploring tourists' images of a distant destination. *Tourism Management*, 28, 747–756.

Ritchie, J.R.B., & Crouch, G.I. (2003). *The competitive destination: A sustainable tourism perspective,* London: CABI.

Rodrigues, A.I., Correia, A., & Kozak, M. (2011). A multidisciplinary approach on destination image construct. *Tourisms: An International Multidisciplinary Journal of Tourism* 6 (3), 93–110.

Rodrigues, A.I., Correia, A., & Kozak, M. (2012). Exploring the life-cycle model applied to `Umbrella Constructs´: Destination image as an example. *Tourism Recreation Research*, 37(2), 133–143.

Rodrigues, A.I., Correia, A., Kozak, M., & Tuohino, A. (2015). Lake-destination image attributes: Content analysis of text and pictures. In A. Correia, J. Gnoth, M. Kozak, & A. Fyall (eds.), *Advances in marketing places and spaces*, Bingley: Emerald (forthcoming).

Rolo-Vela, M. (2009). Rural-cultural conceptualization: A local tourism marketing management model based on tourism destination image measurement. *Tourism Management*, 30, 419–428.

Ryan, C. (1998). Saltwater crocodiles as tourist attractions. *Journal of Sustainable Tourism*, 6(4), 314–327.

Ryan, C., & Cave, J. (2005). Structuring destination image: A qualitative approach. *Journal of Travel Research*, 44; 143–150.

Silva, C., Kastenholz, E., & Abrantes, J.L. (2013). Place-attachment, destination image and impacts of tourism in mountain destinations. *Anatolia: An International Journal of Tourism and Hospitality Research,* 24(1), 17–29.

Silvestre, A., & Correia, A. (2005). A second-order factor analysis model for measuring tourists' overall image of Algarve/Portugal. *Tourism Economics*, 11, 539–554.

Stepchenkova, S., & Mills, J.E. (2010). Destination image: A meta-analysis of 2000–2007 research. *Journal of Hospitality Marketing & Management*, 19, 575–609.

Tuohino, A. (2006). Lakes as an opportunity for tourism marketing: In search of the spirit of the lake. In M. Hall & T. Härkönen (eds.), *Lake Tourism. An integrated approach to lacustrine tourism systems* (pp. 101–118). Clevedon: Channel View Publications.

Walle, A. H. (1997). Quantitative versus qualitative tourism research. *Annals of Tourism Research*, 24(3), 524–536.

Woelfel, J. (1993). Artificial neural network in police research: A current assessment. *Journal of Communication*, 63(1), 63–80.

Woelfel, J. (1998). *CATPAC II: User's Guide.* Amherst, NY: Rah Press.

Woelfel, J. (forthcoming 2016). *CATPAC III.* Amherst, NY: Rah Press.

# 3 Literature creation of the tourist imaginary

*Yang Zhang and Yi-Wei Xiao*

## Introduction

Discourse on literature–tourism relations has positioned literature as a reservoir of cultural expressions and revealed perspectives on the relationships between people and places at various space scales (Crang, Dwyer & Jackson, 2003; Drabble, 1979). In the main the focal point for studies has been the tripartite relationship between the author, his or her writings and the concepts of place/landscape (Herbert, 1995, 2001; Seaton, 1998; Watkins & Herbert, 2003). Desforges (1999) points out that tourism is certainly no exception in that it is disclosed by words as the building blocks of image creation and projection, and the conveyers of people's expectations and experiences. Literature is a fundamental reservoir of words that can inform, describe, stimulate, motivate and inspire. Moreover, it is a potent and pervasive force that runs deep within and across societies, shaping the way we see the world and each other.

The tourism industry, in pursuit of image creation/re-creation and ultimately economic gain, is largely responsible for the designation of notional bounded areas associated with writers and their works. New tourism destinations have been marked out according to fictive and factual reference points which not only reflect the self-contained nature of fictional settings but also refer to the spatial and temporal geographies of the writer. Literary motifs thus are promoted by tourism authorities as redefining and reinventing certain places (Duffy, 1997). But these 'created spaces' (Robinson, 2001) are not recent 'top-down' impositions but are more organic, with various stakeholders such as local communities, local and regional authorities, literary societies and figures of academic authority proud and astute enough to be associated with their factual and fictional progenies as part of identity building (Earl, 2008; Light, 2007; Robinson, 2001).

Previous works that have explicitly explored the many relations between literature and tourism have mostly focused on literary works and tourism activities associated with Western countries. Some researchers have stated that future studies in this field and its associated destination image should be investigated and contextualized with more consideration of cultural perspectives derived not only from Western culture, but also with more of an Asian voice (Salazar, 2012). This chapter focuses on a Chinese literature destination with an oriental cultural background, and so differs from the current mainstream of literature tourism research, thereby introducing a Chinese cultural perspective.

The literary work, *Peach Blossom Fan*, is a musical play and historical drama in 44 scenes that was completed in 1699 by the early Qing dynasty (1644–1911) playwright Kong Shangren after more than 10 years of effort. The play depicts the drama that resulted in the collapse of the Ming Dynasty in 1644 and recounts the death of the Ming Dynasty through the love story of its two main characters, young scholar Hou Fangyu and courtesan Li Xiangjun, the Fragrant Princess. The key theme of this drama is the emotions arising from separation and union, to depict feelings about rise and fall (Kung, 1976). As a traditional literary work, it has been performed thousands of times since it was published. Because of the high reputation of this drama, it was translated into English in 1976 by Chen, Shih-hsiang and Harold Acton.

The story takes place mainly in Nanjing, located in Jiangsu province, China. Many scenic spots in Nanjing such as Qin Huai River, Swallow Rock, Imperial Palace, and the Mausoleum of the Ming Emperor feature in the storyline. In particular, the house in which Li Xiangjun lived according to the drama has been reconstructed and promoted by local tourism authorities as a thematic literary attraction. This chapter therefore attempts to connect the tourists' imaginaries and the construction of destination through an interpretation of a literary work in a Chinese context. The key objective of this chapter is to bridge tourism and literature, connecting tourists' imaginaries and fictional literature. Through constructions of economic and architectural imaginaries, tourist's imaginaries are shaped.

## Literature review

Literature, along with any number of other cultural forms, is particularly well suited to satisfying mental cravings for a fictional reality and a dream-come-true world (Bendix, 1999) through various guises in the contemporary touristic realm such as well-visited theme parks and packaged trails of fictionally derived experiences to the preserved and revered places of writers' creativity, and subtle and less subtle denotations of literary association (Robinson, 2001). Travellers have a need for narratives and imaginaries with which to individually enliven and animate landscapes and thus experience them afresh. The tourism industry attends to this need with an ever increasing number of initiatives of cultural tourism. The motion towards an experience of a literary or narrative themed landscape requires and provokes not only narration but also material reminiscences.

Sheller and Urry (2004) argue that tourism spaces are changeable systems. Diverse actors – both the travellers and the visited – continually create and redefine them with their performances. It is not just the hospitality industry and the services offered to cultural tourists that render the link between narrative or literary imagination, landscape and tourism into a profitable economic resource. The narrated landscape is also, an identity resource for both literary sites and tourists as idealized and nostalgic memories of youth, family life and countryside as well (Fussell, 1980; Squire, 1994, 1996). Thus, the potentially chaotic takes on a cultural shape and thus becomes manageable and aesthetically pleasing (Bendix, 2002, 2009; Greenwood, 1989). A tourist, by contrast, juggles his or her actual experience against the promised experiences that have been purchased, and depending on his or her disposition, can end up with a memory pragmatically (Bendix, 2002).

The tourist group that visits literary destinations, overall, is a group which signals their membership of a cultivated class, preferring the words of a 'knowledgeable expert' to those of a guidebook (Bourdieu & Darbel, 1991, p. 52). Earl (2008) found out that tourists who visited literary destinations prefer to spend a relatively long time on such a visit which marked the group out as belonging to a higher social stratum than the day-trippers and had an unusually high level of cultural capital. Meanwhile, almost all of the visitors had 'literary' backgrounds, having either worked in academia or teaching, or as librarians (Rojek, 2005). Therefore, consumption of literature is in itself a marker of class (Baudrillard, 1997) whose disposition was towards a cultivated taste. Travel is seen as 'pursuing the ageless aristocratic principle of broadening the mind' (Rojek, 1993, p. 175).

Words are the building blocks of image creation and projection, and the conveyers of tourists' expectations and experiences. Creative writings do not seek deliberately to tell anything about tourism processes or tourist destinations but inhabit the world of organic information sources (Anderson, 1983; Gunn, 1972) as an alliance of imagination. In order to respond to consumer preferences for activity, interaction, adventure, high visibility, education and sensory experience, literary works are represented in purpose-built attractions, theme parks and heritage sites by a tourism industry that has sought to condense elements of imaginative writing – characters, story and setting – within a created, controlled and possibly artificial environment (Macdonald & Alsford, 1995; Swarbrooke, 2000) to create 'countries' or improve negative image (Duffy, 1997).

## Methodology

Knowledge of the location was gained by repeated visits to Nanjing, each of which took several days, up to a week, based on several readings of the play's text along with critiques of it. Overlapping these procedures were conversations held on an informal basis with the local tourism officers about the tourism attractions of *Peach Blossom Fan* in Nanjing. Once familiarity with both drama and physical landscapes had been established, a more formal sequence took place by interviewing in a semi-structured way, tourists found in the house of Li Xiangjun over a two-day period as described below, while continuing conversations with tourism officers when tourists were absent. According to the feedback of local tourism authorities, the house of Li Xiangjun, which is located in the historical street of Qinghuai River, is the most popular attraction for tourists. Therefore, the field work of this study was conducted there.

Open-ended questions were asked. The tourist sample was chosen on a convenience basis. In addition, formal interviews were undertaken within the house, with the interpreters, salesman of the souvenir shop, the administrators in charge of entrance ticket sales and other staff members. In total there were 12 such interviews. The questionnaire used with tourists asked first a filter question as to whether the respondents were familiar with the play *Peach Blossom Fan*, or alternatively had read or heard of it. They were then asked what their key impressions were in the house of Li Xiangjun, and these questions were supplemented with further ones requiring, where appropriate, comparisons with the scenes in the play. Thus imaginaries were constructed. The final part of the questionnaire related to the collection of socio-demographic data. The purpose of the questionnaire, as just noted, was to elicit and analyse imaginaries. The final number of interviewers was 100. The text was analysed by using thematic analysis in accordance with principles established by Patton (1980) and Saldaña (2009).

## Findings

The background period to the creation of *Peach Blossom Fan* is the early Qing dynasty (1644–1911); the rise and fall of the Ming dynasty (1368–1644) touched many poets and playwrights, especially intellectuals, which pushed them into thinking of the historical lessons taught by the downfall of the Ming. Kong Shangren, with other scholars expressed hatred and regret at its collapse through their works and a sense of historical responsibility. The story is set in the late Ming dynasty. The reformist Donglin movement reinstituted the 'Restoration Society' in Nanjing to fight corrupt officials. Hou Fangyu, one of the Society's members, falls in love with courtesan Li Xiangjun beside the Qinhuai River. He sends Li Xiangjun a fan as a gift and becomes engaged to her. An official called Ruan Dacheng delivers a trousseau through celebrity Yang Longyou for Hou in order not to be isolated from the royal court. Hou is persuaded into accepting it, but Li Xiangjun rejects the gift firmly, which wins Hou Fangyu's respect.

After Hou and Li's marriage, the Nanjing officials ask Hou to write a letter to discourage a commander, who terrifies the court, from moving his army to Nanjing, but he is slandered by Ruan for betraying the country, forcing him to flee to Yangzhou to find shelter. Li Xiangjun and Hou Fangyu are separated. At that time, the political situation runs out of control. Li Zicheng captures the capital Beijing, and the Chongzhen Emperor hangs himself. Ruan and other governors crown the Prince of Fu as the new Emperor in Nanjing and indulge the Emperor with lust. One of the local governors covets Li's beauty and wants to take her as concubine. At the marriage ceremony, Li resists and tries to kill herself by striking her head against a pillar, leaving blood spots on the fan which was given by Hou Fangyu. After that, Yang draws a branch of peach blossoms with Li's blood on the fan, and it is sent to Hou to show Li Xiangjun's determination and integrity.

The Qing's army continues to go south, threatening the Nanjing court. However, the internal conflicts among generals who are in charge of strategic posts in north of the Yangtze River and the new Emperor never cares about politics, only losing himself in song and dance. Li is sent into the court as a gift to cater to the Emperor. Li Xiangjun scolds the evil officials to their faces and is beaten cruelly. Hou Fangyu flees to Nanjing during the chaotic war but is caught and sent to prison by Ruan. The new Emperor is captured by the Qing army. The end of the play features a Taoist ceremony mourning the loss of the Ming Dynasty in Nanjing. Hou Fangyu and Li Xiangjun accidentally meet during that ceremony. When they declare their affection, Zhang Yaoxing, a Taoist master, criticizes them for the affair, asking 'when there are such tremendous changes, you still indulge in love?' This gives them both a realization. Li Xiangjun thus becomes a nun, while Hou Fangyu follows her example to become a Taoist priest.

The house of Li Xiangjun by Qinghuai River is the place where the love story between Li and Hou happened and which appears many times in this play. As the background of many important scenes, the house of Li Xiangjun extends the narrative space from a single building to the general scenery of the Qinghuai River district in the late Ming dynasty, and enriches the storyline. Frequent appearances of the house of Li Xiangjun make it a symbol of the whole play. It was the place that the beautiful Li used to live in, the symbol of a journey from romantic love to separation and thence to the tragic end. At present, the house of Li Xiangjun includes two floors and 14 rooms with a garden which were built exactly to the description in the play. Meanwhile, there is also a small exhibition in that house about the research of *Peach Blossom Fan* in various disciplines.

In fact, the current house of Li Xiangjun is a reconstructive attraction. But it is deemed to be a landmark in the play due to its frequent appearance at important points in the plot. In order to promote the Qinghuai River district to attract tourists, the local tourism bureau and government rebuilt this house in the 1990s according to its description in the play. It appears from nearly half of the respondents that readers of the play tended to be impressed by the setting, so the tourists visiting this building were likely to search for the narration of the house and Li Xiangjun herself in the play. The house of Li Xiangjun becomes an element of tourists' imaginaries, and its image is enhanced by reappearance in the play.

At the same time, the presence of the house will enable tourists to recall memories of the plot, thus replicating a dramatic atmosphere in this location to become part of their tourist reality. Therefore, the tourism authorities has built the house and made itself more like the images of Li's house (and hence tourists) have from the drama to set up a landmark for the real street, in order to suit the imaginaries from tourists.

The peach blossom fan owned by Li Xiangjun in the play is obviously a very important item. At the beginning of the play, the fan is given by Hou Fangyu as an engagement gift to Li. Even it is just a simple fan, the perfect romantic couple and their happy life in Li's house create a view of harmony and joy in the play. With the subsequent tragic separation suffered by Li Xiangjun and Hou Fangyu, Li's blood on the fan indicates that the symbol of happiness and well-being is gone. However, the peach painting by scholar Yang based the bloody fan becomes the witness of Li's integrity to her love of Hou Fanyu. At the end of the play, Li and Hou accidentally find the peach blossom fan after the collapse of Ming dynasty. It is impossible for them to reunite as the happy couple when faced with such huge change in the whole country. The peach blossom fan thus turns out to be just an old memory.

As the item created by the drama, it now has been created as a significant local tourism souvenir. It is the rationale for the story line and the relationship between Li and Hou. Therefore, it is not only in the reader's perception, and in the tourists' imaginaries about this drama. When the local tourism authorities realize it is the most popular flavour souvenir to tourists, there are many stores in and around the Li's house sell the 'copy' peach blossom fan which is just exact as the drama described. For those tourists, this souvenir is given symbolic meanings that it represents not only a thematic tourism experience but also the emotional attachment in the drama. It carries the meanings from the drama, like 'happiness' and 'integrity of love', into reality. Tourists encounter the destination by engaging all the senses: touch, smell, sight, hearing and taste (Andrews, 2009; 2011), the tourism souvenir of the peach blossom fan makes the 'touch' experience available for tourists, who have an expectation in mind.

## Conclusion

The literary work *Peach Blossom Fan* by Kong Shangren has scored a remarkable success since it was published. Not only was it a landmark drama, but also it created an affective, impressive imaginary between the lines that reinforced the storyline, and has contributed significantly to its ongoing popularity. In the first case of the house of Li Xiangjun, an image already exists in tourists' minds and the narration of that drama reminds readers that they would like to visit this place; in the latter case of the peach blossom fan, which is not a mainstream tourism product, indeed not even on the tourists' 'must buy' list, the story of this drama supplies the readers with brand new imaginaries of it. The imaginaries thus are constructed with detail and symbolic meanings by dramatic fiction. It has the reconstructive power to transform itself from virtual to real, if physical settings, places and social situations are purposefully structured to comply with the ambience of a 'constructed authenticity' (Buchmann, Moore & Fisher, 2010; Wang, 1999).

In Salazar's (2012, p. 865) words, 'lived spaces are shaped by and are shaping tourism practices and fantasies'. Actually, the border between the imaginaries and the physical space is barely distinguishable (Ingold, 2010). Relationships between literature and tourism may be based on cultural identity, and the relationship between space and tourism is material, metaphorical or imagined (Crouch, 2000). Tourism and literature both appeal to the public as source materials for aesthetic appreciation, providing distraction or challenge, evading or embracing social reality and comprehending the needs of others. Although a work of classical literature like *Peach Blossom Fan* seems too far away from current Chinese life, and moreover, the readership (visitors) is limited, while having relative high education and literature reading background, the imaginary it created through the fiction successfully transformed tourists' fantasy from words to real attractions.

This chapter has concentrated on spatial relationships of literature and destination, but one means of extending the study reported in this chapter is to further examine the temporal dimension of the relationship between fictional literature and the reconstruction of destination. Any further study can also involve the soundtrack and linguistic components as well.

## References

Anderson, B. (1983). *Imagined communities: The origins and spread of nationalism.* London: Verso.

Andrews, H. (2009). Tits out for the boys and no back chat: Gendered space on holiday. *Space & Culture, 12*(2), 166–182.

Andrews, H. (2011). *The British on holiday: Charter tourism, identity and consumption.* Tonawanda, NY: Channel View.

Baudrillard, J. (1997). *Art and artefact.* Brisbane: Institute of Modern Art.

Bendix, R. (1999). On the road to fiction. *Ethnologia Europaea, 29*, 29–40.

Bendix, R. (2002). Capitalizing on memories past, present, and future: Observations on the intertwining of tourism and narration. *Anthropological Theory, 2*(4),469–487.

Bendix, R. (2009). *In search of authenticity: The formation of folklore studies.* University of Wisconsin Press.

Bourdieu, P., & Darbel, A. (1991). *The love of art.* Cambridge: Polity.

Buchmann, A., Moore, K., & Fisher, D. (2010). Experiencing film tourism: Authenticity & fellowship. *Annals of Tourism Research, 37*(1), 229–248.

Crang, P., Dwyer, C., & Jackson, P. (2003). Transnationalism and the spaces of commodity culture. *Progress in Human Geography, 27*(4), 438–456.

Crouch, D. (2000). Places around us: Embodied lay geographies in leisure and tourism. *Leisure studies, 19*(2), 63–76.

Desforges, L. (1999). Touring cultures: Transformations of travel and theory. (Book review.) *Journal of Rural Studies, 15*(2), 226–227.

Drabble, M. (1979). *A writer's Britain – landscapes in literature.* London: Thames and Hudson.

Duffy, P. J. (1997). Writing Ireland: Literature and art in the representation of Irish place. In G. Brian (ed.), *In search of Ireland – a cultural geography* (pp. 64–83). London: Routledge.

Earl, B. (2008). Literary tourism constructions of value, celebrity and distinction. *International Journal of cultural studies, 11*(4), 401–417.

Fussell, P. (1980). *Abroad: British literary traveling between the wars.* Oxford University Press.

Greenwood, D. (1989). Culture by the pound: An anthropological perspective on tourism as cultural commoditization. In V. Smith (ed.), *Hosts and guests* (pp.171–185). 2nd ed., Philadelphia: University of Pennsylvania Press.

Gunn, C. (1972). *Vacationscape: Designing tourist regions.* Austin: Bureau of Business Research, University of Texas.

Herbert, D. (1995). *Heritage, tourism and society.* London: Mansell Publishing.

Herbert, D. (2001). Literary places, tourism and the heritage experience. *Annals of Tourism Research, 28*(2), 312–333.

Ingold, T. (2010). Ways of mind-walking: Reading writing painting. *Visual Studies, 25*(1), 15–23.

Kung, S. J. (1976). *The peach blossom fan: Tao-hua-shan.* Berkeley: University of California Press.

Light, D. (2007). Dracula tourism in Romania cultural identity and the state. *Annals of Tourism Research, 34*(3), 746–765.

Macdonald, G. F., & Alsford, S. (1995). Museums and theme parks: Worlds in collision? *Museum Management and Curatorship*, *14*(2), 129–147.

Patton, M. Q. (1980). Qualitative evaluation methods. Beverly Hills, CA: Sage.

Robinson, M. (2001). Tourism encounters: Inter- and intra- cultural conflicts and the world's largest industry. In N. AlSayyad (ed.), *Consuming tradition, manufacturing heritage* (pp. 34–68). London: Routledge.

Rojek, C. (1993). *Ways of escape: Modern transformations in leisure and travel.* Basingstoke: Macmillan.

Rojek, C. (2005). P2P leisure exchange: Net banditry and the policing of intellectual property. *Leisure Studies*, *24*(4), 357–369.

Salazar, N. B. (2012). Tourism imaginaries: A conceptual approach. *Annals of Tourism Research*, *39*(2), 863–882.

Saldaña, J. (2009). The coding manual for qualitative researchers. Los Angeles, CA: Sage.

Seaton, A. V. (1998). The history of tourism in Scotland: Approaches, sources and issues. In M. Rory & R. Smith (eds.), *Tourism in Scotland* (pp. 1–41). London: International Thomson Business Press.

Sheller, M., & Urry, J. (2004). *Tourism mobilities: Places to play, places in play.* London: Routledge.

Squire, S. (1994). The cultural values of literary tourism. *Annals of Tourism Research* 21, 103–120.

Squire, S. (1996). Literary tourism and sustainable tourism: Promoting 'Anne of Green Gables' in Prince Edward Island. *Journal of Sustainable Tourism, 4*(3), 119–134.

Swarbrooke, J. (2000). Museums: Theme parks of the third millennium?, In M. Robinson (ed.), *Tourism and heritage relationships: Global, national and local perspectives* (pp. 417–432). Sunderland: Business Education Publishers.

Wang, N. (1999). Rethinking authenticity in tourism experience. *Annals of Tourism Research, 26*(2), 349–370.

Watkins, H., & Herbert, D. (2003). Cultural policy and place promotion: Swansea and Dylan Thomas. *Geoforum*, *34*(2), 249–266.

# 4 Travel writings and destination image

*Sabrina Meneghello and Federica Montaguti*

## Introduction

Images, words and films contribute to defining 'what' a tourist destination is, and the kind of experience that should be had there (Sheller & Urry, 2004). Destinations are described, illustrated and 'mobilised' both by promotional and organic sources. As demonstrated in literature (Gunn, 1972; Mansfeld, 1992), the narrative structures built by this mix of sources synchronically and diachronically animate the discourse about places defining, and being influenced by, the tourist gazes and behaviours (MacCannell, 1989; Sheller & Urry, 2004; Urry, 1990). Travel writings play an essential role in these narratives, not only by defining the history of tourism at a destination but also by 'tagging' the main features of a destination image. The tourists' own production of images and stories entangles with this narrative, reproducing (Crang & Travlou, 2009) and posting it on social media boards.

The study presented here explores how travel writings can affect the image of a destination, and discusses if some travel writings play a different role than others in influencing this image. It is a part of the results of a wider research analysing the perception of Venice by US tourists. The general objective of the study, conducted by CISET in cooperation with Ca'Foscari Department of Linguistics and Comparative Cultural Studies, was to understand if a well-conducted semiotic analysis on a selected corpus of organic 'texts' (films, travel books and blogs, novels, etc.) and promotional ones, could provide the main features of the image and the positioning of a destination in a specific market.

This chapter shows how, using an appropriate criterion to select relevant texts within a wide corpus, and applying a semiotic analysis to the selected texts, it is possible to understand how these texts affect the tourists' perception of a destination, but also to highlight that, even for a world-famous destination like Venice, only a few texts provided the main features of the destination image. Through a quantitative and qualitative research, it also shows how this specific image still affects the tourists' perception today.

## Literature review

The concept of destination image was introduced in tourism studies in the late 1970s (Gunn, 1972; Hunt, 1975; Mayo, 1973). Analyses on this issue have become more widespread over the last few years, also through the exploration of the impact that different media, including social media, have on the image of places. Many underlined the importance of creating appropriate destination brands (Morgan, Pritchard & Pride, 2002). Echtner and Ritchie (1993) point out that a destination image has multiple dimensions.

The definition of the destination image is strictly correlated with the process of choosing an ideal destination from a number of different options, and with the final evaluation of the experience once back home. Starting from Crompton (1979) and later with Yoon and Uysal (2005), two factors have been identified to explain the process of choosing a destination. This process is important because the same factors need to be considered to explain the role the image of the destination has in the process:

- *Whether to travel:* push factors that describe the desire to travel and considerations about the set of possible destinations. They include sociological and psychological motivations (desire for entertainment or interest in cultural aspects, self- realisation, etc.) and the capability of the selected destinations, i.e. of their perceived images, to meet each specific motivation.
- *Where to travel:* pull factors that describe the destination selection and that, again, are influenced by the image (elements of perceived atmosphere, attractions, typologies of possible fruition, weather, landscape, lifestyle, social environment, etc.).

At what point do specific sources of image in the selection process influence the potential client? The destination marketing strategist's job is to answer this question. The above-mentioned authors suggest that effective promotion strategies should address 'organic' image, i.e. informative and persuasive sources before the journey, as well as 'induced' image, i.e. images of tourists enjoying travel experiences after the journey. In fact, some images are more effective as a tool in client attraction strategies while in contrast, some images are essential as a tool in customer loyalty management.

The definition of an overall destination image is important to define how many categorisations and stereotypes weigh on the final destination perception (Crang, 2003). Moreover, monitoring specific globalised marketing projects that lead consumers' choices and tendencies (Deighton & Grayson, 1995; Kozinets, 2002) – and so identifying 'hegemonic' cultural producers (Arnould & Thompson, 2005) strongly impacting the destination's image – helps in understanding how and why different segments of tourism demand create or redefine their itineraries within the destination.

Many authors seem to prefer qualitative methodologies to investigate 'cultural texts' defining the destination image in its entirety, and semiotic approaches answer this need well (Gartner, 1993; Pike, 2002; Prebensen, 2007; Ryan & Cave, 2005). In particular, a semiotic approach applied to 'induced' texts such as guidebooks and tourism catalogues has been adopted by several scholars (Bhattacharyya, 1997; Dioguardi, Giannitrapani & Parroco, 2009; Lew, 1991; Quinlan, 2005; Smyth, 2008; Travlou, 2002). The same approach has been used to 'organic', i.e. non-promotional, texts, by Dann (2004), and Robinson and Andersen (2004). These approaches have been criticised as lacking strict statistical analyses and leading to data interpretation heavily influenced by the researcher's personal view, but, due to the advantages they bring in interpreting the image feature and positioning, they have often been used in marketing studies (Floch & Pinson, 2001).

The methodological approach adopted in this study is based on this recent literature, and tries to demonstrate how organic and induced sources affect the tourists' perception of a destination, comparing the semiotic analysis results with the ones obtained through a more traditional marketing survey.

## Methodology

As mentioned, the results presented in this chapter are part of a wider study on how cultural productions influence a destination image in a specific market. The research aimed at understanding how strong the cultural productions' impact is when they interrelate with tourist practice, and with tourist promotional materials. The specific case analysed was that of Venice as perceived by the North American market.

Having to deal with very different materials and art forms, and needing to understand how the interaction between a series of productions creates and changes a discourse on a specific place in a specific cultural context, a semiotic approach was used to analyse all the different texts.

The first step was to identify a corpus of promotional (guidebooks, tour operator brochures) and organic (novels, films, etc.) sources about Venice, ranging from the 1820s to the 2010s. The total corpus included about 200 films, 230 books and 50 guidebooks. However, it was evident that not all of these sources could have an impact on current perception of Venice as a tourist destination.

Therefore, the second step was to select significant 'texts'. Two criteria were adopted. For the most recent productions, the criterion adopted was popularity, measured, according to the kind of 'text', on the basis of:

- for novels, guidebooks, etc. the position on the amazon.com bestselling list – with 244 million active customer accounts globally (amazon.com) it dominates the publishing market in the United States – and, when available, the number of copies sold on the US market;
- American box office results (films) reported at imdb.com.

For those nineteenth century books for which we do not have similar data available, the criterion chosen was the number of times a specific author was referred to by the other sources examined.

On each of the 70 selected texts, a semiotic analysis was applied, in order to identity, first, denotative aspects, and then, recurring connotative meanings associated to Venice. The connotative meaning led to understanding the discourse about Venice in the US cultural context, and how it interacts with specific cultural dimensions, and their evolution over time. The use of text analytics – applied in tourism research on destination reputation (Vulic *et al.*, 2012) – was considered as not being particularly helpful in this case, because of the nature of the corpus of selected texts, as well as the study goals. First of all, web semantics or text analytics could not be used for the films, or for a number of sources which were not available in electronic format. Furthermore, the results provided by this kind of semi-automatic system still present different limits, linked to disambiguation difficulties (Gabrilovich & Markovitch, 2009; Piskorski & Yangarber, 2013), but also to the impossibility to provide a diachronic semantic analysis, and to interpret the text when the usual order of words is changed (Friedman, Rindflesch & Corn, 2013). These two features are however essential when dealing with a corpus including poetry texts and a literary production over the course of two centuries.

Once the semiotic analysis was conducted, a more 'conventional' marketing approach was used to survey the perceptions and imageries of a sample of US tourists who had visited Venice at least once. A qualitative (two focus groups) and quantitative (200 questionnaires collected online) survey was conducted, in order to compare the results of the semiotic analysis to the perception of Venice as expressed directly by tourists.

## Findings

One of the first results of the analysis was that tourists' practice and 'mobilites' (Sheller & Urry, 2004) and the organic sources were so strictly linked that all the texts analysed could de facto be considered as travel writings (Antelmi & Santulli, 2012; Crang & Travlou, 2009; Francescato, 2013). As suggested by von Martels (1994), therefore, every cultural product somehow related to a travel experience can be defined as 'travel writing'.

Focussing on books, the analysis showed that only a few had a strong influence, and not all were by American authors. Among the contemporaries, Rick Steves' accounts are undoubtedly influential – in the bestselling books about Venice (travel category) amazon.com lists five titles by Steves in the first 15. In his case, the boundary between guidebook and travel book is almost non-existent.

Another strong influence is the one retained by Shakespeare – still six titles in the first 24 bestsellers, and a vast amount of quotes in the more popular guidebooks. Other very popular authors are Thomas Mann, Donna Leon, J. Berendt and M. De Blasi. They all recurred one or more times in the first 40 bestsellers on Venice at the time the research was conducted. When US tourists were asked which novels they read and remembered about Venice, they named mainly these titles (Figure 4.1). Among the guidebooks used by the surveyed tourists those by Steves were the most popular after the Lonely Planet (Figure 4.2).

What kind of image of the city is projected by these texts? Leon, de Blasi, Berendt, and also other very popular writers like Sklepowich and Dan Brown in his *Inferno* (2013) present a decadent, mysterious, gloomy, and 'southern' Venice. They insist on an idea of Venice as a place of death (Ghose, 1999; Urry, 2004), which is easy to trace back to T. Mann – in itself the most read book about Venice (Figure 4.1).

The discourse on Venice in these sources is polarised between 'death' and the idea of the mask and the maze (the topographic correspondence to the mask), of a city always shifting and changing. D. Leon, in her choices of 'perspective' and description of the city emphasises this theme (Mahler, 1999). The idea of a

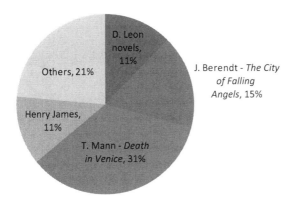

*Figure 4.1* US tourists in Venice – the most-read novels about Venice. (Source: CISET data, 2012.)

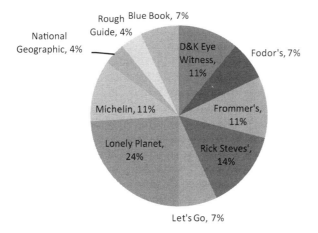

*Figure 4.2* US tourists – guidebooks used during their stay in Venice. (Source: CISET data, 2012.)

constant 'displacement' and re-discussion of the identity is obviously working only if the author and the reader share a tourist perspective. In fact, no Italian author identifies Venice so univocally with the binomial death-deception (Perosa, 1999). This identification possibly explains why, at amazon.com, the majority of the literature and fiction that has 'Venice' as a key word is crime fiction.

The idea of a shape-shifting Venice, as of a city of death, can be easily traced back to its origin – Lord Byron's *Childe Harold's Pilgrimage*. Descriptions of the city echoing Byron's words – 'fairy city', 'out of the waves her structure rises as from the stroke of the enchanter's wand' – and similar, can be found in the writings of Leon, 'moral decline behind respectable façades' (Sepeda, 2011), Brown (2013, p. 305), 'had somehow risen out of the sea', but also Jong (1987, p. 8), 'Venice, that chimera, that city of illusions where reality becomes fantasy and fantasy becomes reality' and Steves (1999, p.126), 'After Venice, with its mysterious and feminine charms'.

Thus, as all fiction is de facto travel writing, the *topoi* of literature are used as tourist *topoi*. And Lord Byron is one of the *topoi* these authors, but also guide-books, refer to often, by quoting him, focusing on his adventures in the city, or using descriptions which recall his own: 'improbable cityscape of stone palaces that seems to float on water' (*Frommers' Northern Italy,* 2010, p. 91); 'improbably waterlogged and persistently picturesque' (*Time Out Venice,* 2001).

Byron's travel writings still heavily influence the US perception of Venice, which is a nineteenth century landscape (Francescato, 2013).

### The image according to the tourists

Given what has been discussed in the previous section, it is hardly surprising that, when surveyed, the US tourists found that the statements about Venice they most agreed upon were: the city is mysterious and gloomy, a maze, out of time, opposite to America (Figure 4.3).

It is interesting, though, that this kind of view is lingering longer in the American cultural context than in its original English one – UK publishers' guidebooks (e.g. *The Rough Guide*) do not quote Byron so much and do not dwell so much on gothic images. This could be related to the fact that, while Byron presented Venice as a metaphor for every nation's decay (von Koppenfels, 1994) – and for the British Empire in the first place – American mainstream culture does not seem to perceive that this metaphor could be applied to the United States ('Venice represents the contrary of where they live').

On the other hand, Venice represents a sort of southern 'otherness', where every-thing is possible and allowed, haunted and chaotic, and so associated with American port cities such as Savannah, New Orleans. The Gulf of Mexico, in fact, is often considered a second Mediterranean, and New Orleans is identified as a 'Latin' city

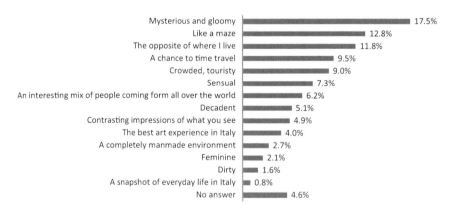

*Figure 4.3* US tourists – statements about the city of Venice they most agree with. (Source: CISET data, 2012.)

(Gore, 1992; Gruesz, 2006; Horden & Purcell, 2000). This could explain why this metaphor is still meaningful in that culture, while the European view, although still influenced by this, has evolved to a slightly different kind of relationship with Venice.

## Conclusion

The study presented shows, first, that a semiotic analysis on a selected corpus of popular 'texts' provides reliable results on how tourists from a specific market perceive a place, representing a good alternative to the more traditional surveys. Second, it highlights how interaction between various kinds of travel writing – and in particular between promotional and organic sources – shapes the image of a destination, and how – thanks to this interaction – few writers have a massive long-term effect on this image. Third, it shows how a semiotic approach has the advantage to explore not only the features of a destination image, but also how they have been created, providing the destination with more refined tools to manage this image, promote new marketing strategies and reduce bias and distortions.

It also underlines the importance of the organic sources in the process of construction of a destination image, but also how strongly these sources are inter-related with 'tourist' practice and discourse.

Finally, the specific focus on Anglo-American cultural production stresses how certain powerful cultural producers hold hegemony in perpetuating, and even twisting, some 'texts', defining the perception of the destination not only for American 'readers', but also for 'readers' belonging to cultures influenced by American preferences and behaviours.

From a destination management point of view, the results of this study might have different implications. They underline how cultural productions are effective in positioning and repositioning a place in a way no promotional source can achieve. Some destination management organisations such as VisitBritain have been working on this aspect for some years now, but generally the role of creative productions in shaping or even creating a destination is not acknowledged nearly enough, also because it is not so easy to assess their actual impact. This results in lost opportunities to promote or reposition the destination, or even to create business out of a novel's success (e.g. often the territory is taken by surprise by the sudden presence of novel or film-induced tourism).

To underestimate the 'power' of these productions can also be risky from a more general perspective, as it means that the destination does not monitor its image, and does not take part in the discourse about itself. In this situation, the representations produced and re-produced by the tourists' culture – and often masked as reified, commoditised authenticities – might end up corresponding to the image the local community uses to describe itself.

In this context, the results of this study show how guidebooks are still able to heavily influence the way tourists see a place, and what they see. As guidebook authors become bloggers, and the publishing houses use the guidebooks' content on websites, apps, their influence is destined to grow stronger. For a destination manager, to know and maintain a dialogue with the authors of guidebooks and their publishers, might prove more effective to control the destination image than more expensive advertising campaigns.

The information deriving from a semiotic analysis might also be useful to approach a new market, as it can highlight the features of the destination the new market will more easily be attracted by, the position the destination might hold in that cultural context, and the marketing opportunities.

Finally, this kind of analysis is useful to better understand the origins and reasons of the web reputation and the 'sentiment' about a place. It underlines how sentiment might be 'culture specific', and influenced by a series of sources that 'filter' the experience the tourist has during his/her stay. The next step planned for this research is to conduct a 'sentiment' analysis to verify how much US tourists re-project on social networks the image of Venice as shaped and defined by popular cultural productions and the guidebooks analysed in this chapter.

## References

Antelmi, D., & Santulli, F. (2012). Travellers' memories: The image of places from literature to blog chatter. *Pasos,* 10(4), 13–24.

Arnould, E. J., & Thompson, C. J. (2005). Consumer culture theory (CCT): Twenty years of research. *The Journal of Consumer Research*, 31(4), 868–882.

Bhattacharyya, D. P. (1997). Mediating India: An analysis of a guide book. *Annals of Tourism Research,* 24(2), 371–389.

Brown, D. (2013). *Inferno*. Bantam Press.

Byron, G. G. *The works of Lord Byron. Vol. 2*. E. Coleridge (ed.). Project Gutenberg, 2008 [EBook #25340].

Crang, M. (2003). Placing Jane Austen, displacing England: Touring between book, history and nation. In S.R. Pucci & J. Thompson (eds.), *Jane Austen and Co.: Remaking the past in contemporary culture* (pp. 111–132). Albany: SUNY Press.

Crang, M., & Travlou P. (2009). The island that was not there: Producing Corelli's island, staging Kefalonia. In P. Obrador, M. Crang, & P. Travlou (eds.), *Cultures of mass tourism. Taking the Mediterranean tourists seriously* (pp. 75–90). Farnham: Ashgate.

Crompton J. L. (1979). Motivations for pleasure vacation. *Annals of Tourism Research*, 6(4), 408–424.

Dann, G. M. S. (2004), La Serenissima: Dreams, love and death in Venice. In M. Robinson & H. C. Andersen (eds.), *Literature and tourism* (pp. 240–278). London: Thomson.

Deighton, J., & Grayson, K. (1995). Marketing and seduction: Building exchange Relationships by managing social consensus. *Journal of Consumer Research,* 21(4), 660–676.

Dioguardi, V., Giannitrapani, A., & Parroco, A.M. (2009). Destination image and tourism intermediation. A possible interdisciplinary approach. Paper presented at 8th International Congress Marketing Trends, Paris, 6–17 January.

Echtner, C. M., & Ritchie, J. R. B. (1993). The measurement of destination image: An empirical assessment. *Journal of Travel Research*, 31(4), 3–13.

Floch, J. M., & Pinson, C. (2001). *Semiotics, marketing, and communication: Beneath the signs, the strategies*. Basingstoke: Palgrave.

Francescato, S. (2013). I risultati dell'analisi delle fonti sul Veneto e Venezia. In S. Menghello & S. Francescato. *L'immagine del Veneto e di Venezia e il turismo nordamericano: un approccio interdisciplinare*. CISET-Ca' Foscari Internal research report.

Friedman C., Rindflesch T., & Corn, M. (2013). Natural language processing: State of the art and prospects for progress. *Journal of Biomedical Informatics,* 46(5), 765–773.

*Frommers' Northern Italy. With Venice, Milan, and the lakes* (2010). Hoboken: John Wiley.

Gabrilovich, E., & Markovitch, S. (2009). Wikipedia-based semantic interpretation for natural language processing. *Journal of Artificial Intelligence Research,* 34, 443–498.

Gartner, W. C. (1993). Image formation process. *Journal of Travel and Tourism Marketing,* 2, 191–216.

Ghose, I. (1999). Confidential Venice. In M. Pfister & B. Schaff (eds.), *Venetian views, Venetian blinds: English fantasies of Venice* (pp. 213–224). Amsterdam-Atlanta: Rodopi B.V.

Gore, R. H. (1992). *The Gulf of Mexico.* Sarasota, FL: Pineapple.

Gruesz, K. S. (2006). The Gulf of Mexico system and the 'Latinness' of New Orleans. *American Literary History,* 18(3), 468–495.

Gunn, C. (1972). *Tourism planning.* New York: Taylor and Francis.

Horden, P., & Purcell, N. (2000). *The corrupting sea.* Oxford: Blackwell.

Hunt, J. D. (1975). Image as a factor in tourism development. *Journal of Travel Research,* 13(3), 1–17.

Jong, E. (1987). *Shylock's daughter: A novel of love in Venice.* WW Norton & Company, 2003.

Kozinets, L. V. (2002). Can consumers escape the market? Emancipatory illuminations from 'Burning Man'. *Journal of Consumer Research,* 29 (June), 20–38.

Lew, A. A. (1991). Place representation in tourist guidebooks: An example from Singapore. *Singapore Journal of Tropical Geography,* 12(2), 124–137.

MacCannell, D. (1989). *The tourist.* London: Macmillan.

Mahler, A. (1999). Writing Venice: Paradoxical signification as connotational feature. In M. Pfister, & B. Schaff (eds.), *Venetian views, Venetian blinds: English fantasies of Venice* (pp.29–37). Amsterdam-Atlanta: Rodopi B.V.

Mansfeld, Y. (1992). From motivation to actual travel. *Annals of Tourism Research,* 19(3), 399–419.

Mayo, E.J. (1973). Regional images and regional travel behavior. *Proceedings of the Travel Research Association Conference,* 211–218.

Morgan, N., Pritchard, A., & Pride, R. (2002). *Destination branding: Creating the unique destination proposition.* Oxford: Elsevier Butterworth-Heinemann.

Perosa, S. (1999). Literary deaths in Venice. In M. Pfister & B. Schaff (eds.), *Venetian views, Venetian blinds: English fantasies of Venice* (pp. 115–128). Amsterdam-Atlanta: Rodopi B.V.

Pike, S. (2002). Destination image analysis – a review of 142 papers from 1973 to 2000. *Tourism management,* 23(5), 541–549.

Piskorski, J. E., & Yangarber, R. (2013), Information extraction: Past, present and future. In T. Poibeau, H. Saggion, J. Piskorski, & R. Yangarber (eds.), *Multi-source, multilingual information extraction and summarization.* Berlin: Springer Science & Business Media.

Prebensen, N. K. (2007). Exploring tourists' images of a distant destination. *Tourism Management,* 28(3), 747–756.

Quinlan, S. (2005). *Never short of smile: A content analysis of travel guidebooks.* Dissertation, University of Waterloo.

Ryan, C., & Cave, J. (2005). Structuring destination image: a qualitative approach. *Journal of Travel Research,* 44 (2), 143–150.

Sepeda, T. (2011). *Brunetti's Venice. Walks through the novels.* Random House Ebooks.

Sheller M., & Urry, J. (2004) Places in play, places to play. In M. Sheller & J. Urry (eds.), *Tourism mobilities. Places to play, places in play* (pp. 1–10). London: Routledge.

Smyth, F.T. (2008). *Constructing place, directing practice?: Using travel guidebooks.* Edinburgh Working Papers in Sociology No. 28. Sociology Subject Group of Social & Political Studies, University of Edinburgh.

Steves, R. (1999). *Rick Steves' Postcards from Europe.* Berkeley, CA: Avalon Travel Pub.

*Time Out Venice* (2001). London: Penguin books.

Travlou, P. (2002). Go Athens: A journey to the centre of the city. In S. Coleman & M. Crang (eds.), *Tourism: Between place and performance* (pp. 108–127). New York: Berghahn Books.

Urry, J. (1990). *The tourist gaze: Leisure and travel in contemporary societies, theory, culture & society.* London: Sage.

Urry, J. (2004). Death in Venice. In M.Sheller & J. Urry (eds.), *Tourism mobilities: Places to play, places in play* (pp. 205–233). London: Routledge.

von Koppenfels, W. (1994). Sunset City – City of the Dead. Venice and the 19th century apocalyptic imaginary. In M. Pfister, & B. Schaff (eds.), *Venetian views, Venetian blinds: English fantasies of Venice* (pp. 99–114). Amsterdam-Atlanta: Rodopi B.V.

von Martels, Z. R. W. M. (Ed.). (1994). *Travel fact and travel fiction: Studies on fiction, literary tradition, scholarly discovery, and observation in travel writing* (Vol. 55). Leiden, The Netherlands: Brill.

Vulic I., De Smet, Tang, J., & Moens M. (2012). Probabilistic topic modelling in multilingual settings: A short overview of its methodology with applications. *Proceedings of the NIPS Workshop on Cross-Lingual Technologies* (xLiTe), pp. 1–11.

Yoon, Y., & Uysal, M. (2005). An examination of the effects of motivation and satisfaction on destination loyalty: A structural model. *Tourism Management*, 26(1), 45–56.

# 5 Affective component of the destination image

## A computerised analysis

*Estela Marine-Roig and Salvador Anton Clavé*

## Introduction

The social media have revolutionized communication (Agarwal, Mondal & Nath, 2011) in the travel and tourism industry (Xiang & Gretzel, 2010) especially due to the experiential nature of the tourism product. User-generated content (UGC), with no economic interest behind opinions and accounts, is highly credible and trustworthy for users (Leung, Law, van Hoof & Buhalis, 2013; Litvin, Goldsmith & Pan, 2008) and highly influential for tourist decision-making (Schmallegger & Carson, 2010; Yoo & Gretzel, 2010). As a consequence, knowing what is said by user-tourists on the web 2.0 becomes of major importance for destinations.

UGC has proved to be a good source for the study of destination reputation, branding and image, as well as for the study of tourist experiences and behaviour (Költringer & Dickinger, 2015; Lu & Stepchenkova, 2015; Pan, MacLaurin & Crotts, 2007). However, there is room to maximize the usefulness of travel blogs and reviews as sources of information for businesses, destination marketing organizations (DMOs) and academics (Pan *et al.*, 2007) doing research concerning the affective image of a destination as expressed by tourists online through data analysis systematization and computerization of the online UGC (Marine-Roig & Anton Clavé, 2015). This allows overcoming the disadvantage of collecting data manually, which is still done in most analyses of UGC in spite of their enormous growth (Banyai & Glover, 2012; Lu & Stepchenkova, 2015) and gives new opportunities for understanding the role of affective components of the image of a tourism destination within the whole image construct (Marine-Roig, 2015).

## Feelings and emotions within tourist image

As defined by some scholars, destination image is the expression of knowledge, impressions, prejudice, imaginations, expectations, ideas, feelings and emotional thoughts people hold about a place over time (Bandyopadhyay & Morais, 2005; Kim & Richardson, 2003). Indeed, images and representations contain various elements of identity that are the different values, elements, ideas and feelings that build up the tourist image (Almeida & Buzinde, 2007; Marine-Roig, 2011).

The destination image is created or formed by different components (Andsager & Drzewiecka, 2002; Baloglu & McCleary, 1999; Gartner, 1994; Kim & Richardson, 2003; Krizman & Belullo, 2007). The cognitive and the affective components are the most mentioned in the tourism-related research literature as being central to the formation of the overall destination image. In fact, for many authors, the tourist image construct consists of these two interrelated components 'woven into overall impressions' (Baloglu & McCleary, 1999; Krizman & Belullo, 2007).

The cognitive component has been the most widely studied, by focusing on the evaluation of physical attributes of places (Kim & Richardson, 2003), while the affective component, representing the evaluation of the destination at an emotional level, has been far less analysed despite its huge implications for tourist satisfaction, decision-making and behaviour. In this vein, Russell and Pratt (1980) created a spatial model of eight adjectives that describe the affective image component, dividing them into positive ones (exciting, arousing, pleasant and relaxing) and negative ones (sleepy, distressing, unpleasant and gloomy). The aspect of positivity or negativity of the affective image, which is related to feelings, has been studied by authors such as Govers, Go and Kumar (2007) who detected some negative image components in a destination's image and stressed their importance for tourist authorities at the destination.

The affective component of image is meaningful as the cognitive process that gives meaning to the emotion has already occurred. In this respect, the affective image appears later than the cognitive one (Russell & Pratt, 1980). Therefore, 'in tourism contexts, evaluation of affective qualities of places might become even more important than objective, perceptible properties of places' (Kim & Richardson, 2003). Furthermore, for Andsager and Drzewiecka (2002) the affective component is strongly related to the notion of difference, which addresses value-based responses to images that fit or do not fit pre-established images of destinations. This emotional interpretation of a place is greatly related with the conative component of image, and thus will influence tourist behaviour and decision-making, destination choice, as well as the degree of satisfaction with the tourist experience (Bandyopahyay & Morais, 2005; Gartner, 1994; Kim & Richardson, 2003).

UGC is of great interest in the study of the affective component of image or the feelings attached to the destination. It is seen as a representative source of the 'real' thoughts and feelings of tourists (Carson, 2008) and can greatly influence people reading it (Chen, Shang & Li, 2014; Filieri & McLeay, 2013) as it communicates experiences, and 'experience involves personal or intersubjective feelings activated by the liminal process of tourist activities' (Wang, 1999).

Travel blogs and online travel reviews (OTRs) are of great relevance due to their trip-diary nature of recounting travel experiences (Bosangit, McCabe & Hibbert, 2009; Chen *et al.*, 2014; Filieri & McLeay, 2014; Pan *et al.*, 2007). They are written freely by tourists (with no constraints) (Jones & Alony, 2008; Marine-Roig & Anton Clavé, 2015) usually after the trip has taken place. Post-visit image is perhaps the most elaborate and processed. It can be understood as an unreal image as it is an idealization of the trip (Anton Clavé, Fernández & González, 2008).

The most popular research methods for the analysis of travel diaries have been content analysis, both qualitative and quantitative, narrative analysis (Banyai & Glover, 2012) and, more recently, sentiment analysis techniques (Schmunk, Höpken, Fuchs & Lexhagen, 2014). This chapter explores a new methodology enabling massive data analysis of the affective component of the destination image as expressed in these online sources through data systematization and computerization.

The analysis is applied to the case of Catalonia, a Mediterranean destination with a millenary history, its own culture and language and a wealthy historical and natural heritage that according to the official statistics of the Catalan Government (http://empresaiocupacio.gencat.cat/en), welcomed about 16.8 million foreign tourists in 2014. The capital of Catalonia, Barcelona, is its principal destination.

## Methodology

The methodological framework proposed in this chapter is based on web content mining. It aims to discover and extract useful data or information from webpage contents, especially by automating the harvesting and analysis of contents (Liu, 2011). Web content mining has been used to analyse destination branding and image from online sources (Költringer & Dickinger, 2015). Abburu and Babu (2013), for instance, propose a framework for web data extraction and analysis based on three main steps: finding URLs of webpages; extracting information from webpages; and data analysis. In this research, although we use a similar process, we download all useful HTML pages, and then eliminate all the noise in order to leave only what the user has written and posted, preserving the original HTML format, to conduct data analysis.

The first major step to deal with large quantities of information in a computerized manner has been to create a consistent and suitable dataset. Several authors manifest difficulties in locating travel blogs in relation to a given case study (Carson, 2008). Here we have targeted blogs and reviews in specialized websites due to their clear advantages for blog mining, data-download and analysis as they concentrate thousands of travel blogs and reviews about a destination in a single space. After the exploration of specialized websites, a selection criterion has been applied: the presence of blogs or reviews concerning the case study should be significant (more than 100 entries) and allow obtaining date and destination. A total of 11 websites were found that fulfil this criterion. They were ranked by applying a weighted formula 'TBRH = 1*B(V) + 1*B(P) + 2*B(S)' (Marine-Roig, 2014), where 'B' corresponds to Borda's ordering method, 'V' to the visibility of the website (quantity and quality of inbound links), 'P', its popularity (received visits and traffic in general) and 'S', the size (number of entries related to the case study). The first four in the ranking were selected: TravelBlog.org (TB), TripAdvisor.com (TA), TravelPod.com (TP), and VirtualTourist.com (VT).

Most studies gather very small samples of blogs and reviews, usually not exceeding a few hundred entries, and they do so manually (Lu & Stepchenkova, 2015). The best way to gather and process large numbers of entries is to download all relevant travel blogs and reviews onto the computer via a web copier. In this chapter, manual exploration of websites hosting blogs and reviews was undertaken to view their structure and locate the HTML files relative to the case study (Marine-Roig & Anton Clavé, 2015). In the case of Catalonia more than 250,000 files were retrieved (all existing entries, excluding lodgings and restaurants, until January 2015). However, 139,122 files were empty (with no contents) and were eliminated. Finally 133,477 entries remained for content analysis.

Data mining was conducted in order to extract useful information from the HTML structure of tags such as the destination, date of writing or update, travellers' country of origin, theme or webpage title. We arranged the data following the format below through a batch programme to enable multiple classifications:

*root\host\brand\destination\entrydate_lang_[isfrom]_pagename_[theme].htm*

Online sources, often full of 'noise' (Carson, 2008), were cleaned prior to analysis removing from the downloaded webpages all information not generated by the user without losing the HTML format.

Language detection was done after the cleaning stage (Marine-Roig & Anton Clavé, 2015). The language of blog and review entries was detected through an ad hoc Java programme, based on the Language Detection Library (LDL) of N. Shuyo. This library, based on the Naive Bayes classifier, detects each language with a probability higher than 99 per cent. For this case study the only files that remained were those with a probability of more than 85 per cent of being written in English.

The next step was the analysis of text within travel blogs and reviews through quantitative content analysis. This approach is objective, systematic, relies on scientific methods (Neuendorf, 2002) and usually deals with the number of appearances of a subject, how it is distributed, and its relation to other subjects. Categorization was crucial and, to be useful, categories should be very well defined, structured and mutually exclusive (Stemler, 2001).

We used a thematic approach following an a priori (deductive) (Stemler, 2001) model of categories, according to certain theoretical backgrounds or established frameworks (Banyai & Glover, 2012). Concerning the affective component of image, Carson (2008) and Pan *et al.* (2007), among others, show the value of assessing whether the feelings tourists have about a place, activity, or event are positive or negative. Besides, other authors state that the affective component of image can also be targeted through the analysis of several opposite concepts or dichotomies (Andreu, Bigne & Cooper, 2000; Baloglu & Mangaloglu, 2001; Baloglu & McCleary, 1999; Russell & Pratt, 1980).

In this analysis the categories to classify travel blog and review content in order to unveil the affective image component were divided into: (1) opposite feelings, represented by good (positive) vs. bad (negative) feelings extracted from standard lists in American and British English; and (2) opposite concepts/dichotomies, formed by related keywords (see Table 5.1). The lists of keywords within each opposite concept were mainly built using the *Oxford Dictionary of Synonyms and*

*Antonyms* (2007). Concerning negative forms, we tried as much as possible to use attributes that are usually only used positively or negatively (amazing vs. disgusting, for example) and do not lead to doubt. Some negative forms (e.g. 'not nice') have been transformed into composite words to avoid possible problems.

In this chapter, the smaller analysis units are keywords within categories. The most basic counting system is word frequency counts that are then accumulated by categories. 'The assumption made is that the words that are mentioned most often are the words that reflect the greatest concerns' (Stemler, 2001).

Site content analyser (SCA) software was selected to conduct keyword counts. This software generates a CSV file for each blog entry, conveying all the words appearing in that entry-file, their total count (total number of appearances), density (percentage of appearance relative to total words) and weight (prominence or visibility of the word according to HTML structure, e.g. a word in the title has a much higher weight than a word appearing in a smaller font within the text). The HTML tags in weight order are: first, 'title' (required in all HTML documents to define the title of the document), then the headings ('h1', 'h2' and 'h3'), followed by 'a' (defines a hyperlink, which is used to link from one page to another), 'img alt' (alternative text for an image), then, with the same weight, come h4, 'b': bold font, 'i': italic font, 'u': underline font, 'strong' (defines important text), 'em' (renders as emphasized text) and 'h5', etc.

SCA was chosen because it provides the advantages of computer-assisted text-analysis (CATA) software for text analysis but is especially designed for web analysis, enabling the processing of HTML information (no need to 'copy–paste') maintaining HTML hierarchy. It can process thousands of files at the same time. This software enables working with composite words and providing a black list with stop words.

## Findings

The application of the methodology to the study of feelings and dichotomies in travel blogs and reviews about Catalonia shows the different types of results summarized in Table 5.1.

Concerning the categories of good feelings and bad feelings, quite remarkably, good feelings are far more mentioned and more dense in tourists' accounts than bad feelings, over 10 times more. This may indicate that tourists had an overall positive experience at the destination, that positive elements are much more representative of their perception than negative ones (probably showing satisfaction with the experience as stated by Bandhyopahyay and Morais (2005) and also that the destination has a positive reputation (Lu & Stepchenkova, 2015).

The weight of good feelings is about double that of bad feelings, meaning that when good feelings are mentioned they are in more visible or prominent positions on average in website HTML texts (in the title, in bold fonts, in bigger fonts, etc.). This is very interesting as it could correspond to the fact that a posteriori image, as a construction, is not a real image, but an idealization of the trip that is shared and transmitted to others (Anton Clavé *et al.*, 2008). Post-visit perceived image

Table 5.1 References to good and bad feelings and to dichotomies

| Good feelings | Count | Density (%) | Weight | Bad feelings | Count | Density (%) | Weight |
|---|---|---|---|---|---|---|---|
| Total | 473,909 | 6.67 | 20.25 | Total | 45,664 | 0.64 | 10.75 |
| Love | 25,403 | 0.36 | 12.30 | Hate | 1,145 | 0.02 | 5.46 |
| Beautiful | 88,762 | 1.25 | 21.45 | Ugly | 514 | 0.01 | 9.14 |
| Pleasant | 8,014 | 0.11 | 10.79 | Unpleasant | 657 | 0.01 | 10.84 |
| Friendly | 7,037 | 0.10 | 8.04 | Unfriendly | 138 | 0.00 | 17.39 |
| Fun/interesting | 65,456 | 0.92 | 17.31 | Boring | 3,059 | 0.04 | 8.96 |
| Lively | 4,694 | 0.07 | 12.16 | Gloomy | 1,073 | 0.02 | 4.46 |
| Noisy | 9,204 | 0.13 | 12.18 | Quiet | 5,950 | 0.08 | 12.41 |
| Full | 17,067 | 0.24 | 11.17 | Empty | 1,248 | 0.02 | 4.88 |
| Orderly | 3,258 | 0.05 | 5.62 | Chaotic | 1,741 | 0.02 | 12.12 |
| Clean | 4,212 | 0.06 | 11.49 | Dirty | 3,061 | 0.04 | 7.78 |
| Relax | 9,684 | 0.14 | 9.62 | Distress | 548 | 0.01 | 3.50 |
| Authentic | 19,518 | 0.27 | 14.37 | Inauthentic | 1,572 | 0.02 | 9.97 |
| New/fashionable | 15,251 | 0.21 | 25.81 | Old/old-fashioned | 19,574 | 0.28 | 14.30 |
| Cheap | 6,129 | 0.09 | 5.37 | Expensive | 11,721 | 0.17 | 17.24 |
| Modest/poor | 4,288 | 0.06 | 11.42 | Luxurious/wealthy | 1,769 | 0.02 | 11.41 |
| Safe | 2,377 | 0.03 | 4.87 | Unsafe | 3,694 | 0.05 | 8.96 |

Dataset: 133,477 entries in English (7,102,487 words).

Source: Authors.

will omit some elements and preserve others that tourists will purposefully select. Probably, although negative experiences may have occurred, as can be seen by the presence of some negative feelings, tourists will not be willing to express these negative experiences as the most prominent features of their 'idealized' trips, for others to read. Moreover, this generally positive image in blogs and reviews is then more likely to reach other tourists who read them, given their high degree of visibility on the webpage and their greater likelihood of being disseminated (Marine-Roig, 2014) since search engines will give more prominence and weight to the highest-level words in HTML structures (the most prominent ones) when looking for and delivering contents related to user searches.

Concerning the dichotomies of analysis, in general categories of attributes related to positive feelings are more frequently mentioned that their negative counterparts. Indeed, the three most mentioned attributes for the destination are 'beautiful', 'fun/interesting', 'love', while their negative counterparts are mentioned far less. Then come the attributes 'old/old-fashioned' and 'authentic', which are related rather to the type of true experience and traditional values of the destination tourists were looking for, and that may have been confirmed by the experience. However, some of the most prominent attributes have negative connotations and appear more strongly than their more positive counterparts. These are 'full', 'expensive' and 'noisy', which may be related to the type of tourism coming to the destination and the influence of high-season congestion which is reflected in tourists' comments. In other cases, such as 'friendly' vs. 'unfriendly', the negative counterpart, although much less frequent, has a much higher weight or visibility, indicating that when tourists feel unfriendliness they express it more strongly. In this sense, quite remarkable is the case of the 'safe' vs. 'unsafe' dichotomy. The negative sentiment (unsafe) is expressed much more strongly than 'safe'. This may be explained by the fact that tourists expect certain safety standards, and only feel the need to mention the issue of safety when they feel unsafe or some event such as pickpocketing has occurred. This also indicates that, although in general positive attributes and feelings are more prominent, in some specific issues such as feeling unsafe, both the total mentions and the weight and visibility of these words are higher.

Finally, a very relevant issue here is that of all words written by tourists in online travel blogs and reviews (7,102,487), a large proportion (about 10 per cent) are feelings and affective items (6.67 per cent are positive feelings, 0.64 per cent negative feelings, and many others). This indicates the great importance of the affective image component for the construction of the overall tourist image and its great potential for online dissemination to other people during the post-trip phase. It also reinforces the idea of the utility and relevance of the study of the affective component of image by DMOs to assess tourists' satisfaction with the experience, tourist behaviours and perceptions in general (Bandyopahyay & Morais, 2005; Gartner, 1994; Kim & Richardson, 2003) and that UGC such as travel blogs and reviews is a rich and meaningful source of information to do so (Schmunk *et al.*, 2014). At the same time, it disputes other studies such as Carson's (2008), which claims that blog content is relatively shallow and provides little detail about tourists' satisfaction or expectations.

## Conclusion

The study of the affective component of image is highly relevant for DMOs in order to get an insight into tourists' perceptions, satisfaction and behaviour. UGC in the form of travel blogs and OTRs has proven a very rich and useful source to study this. Our results have shown the huge importance of feelings and affective attributes when tourists express their perceived images, indicating their importance as elaborations of the experience during the post-trip phase and as an integral part of the overall image construct and its formation, and of what image will be transmitted to other users. In this case, positive feelings and attributes were dominant and more prominent and visible online, although in some specific cases negative attributes were also remarkably dense and weighty.

The implementation of this methodology allows dealing with massive datasets of travel blogs and reviews about a destination and giving insights into the affective component of image, while also preparing data for analysis and systematizing procedures so that the data can become useful for destinations. SCA software was especially useful to study not just the total word counts within categories, but also their density across files and their weight, which is especially relevant to ascertain the visibility and potential dissemination of certain contents.

Future research should continue to analyse the affective component of image in UGC, and its role and prominence in the overall image construct. Additional studies should assess the prominence and visibility of positive feelings and attributes in online trip diaries, and the differential affective images of various destinations at different geographical levels.

## Acknowledgements

This work was supported by the Spanish Ministry of Economy and Competitiveness (Grant id.: MOVETUR CSO2014-51785-R).

## References

Abburu, S., & Babu, G. S. (2013). A frame work for web information extraction and analysis. *International Journal of Computers & Technology, 7*(2), 574–579.
Agarwal, S., Mondal, A., & Nath, A. (2011). Social media – the new corporate playground. *International Journal of Research and Reviews in Computer Science, 2*(3), 696–700.
Almeida, C., & Buzinde, C. (2007). Politics of identity and space: representational dynamics. *Journal of Travel Research, 45*(3), 322–332.
Andreu, L., Bigne, J. E., & Cooper, C. (2000). Projected and perceived image of Spain as a tourist destination for British travellers. *Journal of Travel & Tourism Marketing, 9*(4), 47–67.
Andsager, J. L., & Drzewiecka, J. A. (2002). Desirability of differences in destinations. *Annals of Tourism Research, 29*(2), 401–421.
Anton Clavé, S., Fernández, A., & González, F. (2008). Los lugares turísticos [tourist places]. In S. Anton Clavé & F. González (eds.), *A propósito del turismo. La construcción social del espacio turístico* [About tourism: The social construction of the tourism space] (pp. 101–204). Barcelona, Catalonia, Spain: Editorial UOC.

Baloglu, S., & Mangaloglu, M. (2001). Tourism destination images of Turkey, Egypt, Greece, and Italy as perceived by US-based tour operators and travel agents. *Tourism Management*, 22(1), 1–9.

Baloglu, S., & McCleary, K. W. (1999). A model of destination image formation. *Annals of Tourism Research, 26*(4), 868–897.

Bandyopadhyay, R., & Morais, D. (2005) Representative dissonance: India's self and Western image. *Annals of Tourism Research*, 32(4), 1006–1021.

Banyai, M., & Glover, T. D. (2012). Evaluating research methods on travel blogs. *Journal of Travel Research, 51*(3), 267–277.

Bosangit, C., McCabe, S., & Hibbert, S. (2009). What is told in travel blogs? Exploring travel blogs for consumer narrative analysis. In W. Hopken, U. Gretzel, & R. Law (eds.), *Information and Communication Technologies in Tourism 2009* (pp. 61–71). The Netherlands: Springer-Verlag.

Carson, D. (2008). The 'blogosphere' as a market research tool for tourism destinations: A case study of Australia's Northern Territory. *Journal of Vacation Marketing, 14*(2), 111–119.

Chen Y. C., Shang, R. A., & Li, M. J. (2014). The effects of perceived relevance of travel blogs' content on the behavioral intention to visit a tourist destination. *Computers in Human Behavior, 30*(2014), 787–799.

Filieri, R., & McLeay (2014). E-WOM and accommodation: An analysis of the factors that influence travelers' adoption of information from online reviews. *Journal of Travel Research, 53*(1), 44–57.

Gartner, W. C. (1994). Image formation process. *Journal of Travel and Tourism Marketing, 2*(2–3), 191–216.

Govers, R., Go, F. M., & Kumar, K. (2007). Virtual destination image: A new measurement approach. *Annals of Tourism Research, 34*(4), 977–997.

Jones, M., & Alony, I. (2008). Blogs – the new source of data analysis. *Journal of Issues in Informing Science and Information Technology, 5*, 433–446.

Kim, H., & Richardson, S. L. (2003). Motion picture impacts on destination images. *Annals of Tourism Research, 30*(1), 216–237.

Költringer, C., & Dickinger, A. (2015). Analyzing destination branding and image from online sources: A web content mining approach. *Journal of Business Research*, (available online 13 February 2015).

Krizman, D., & Belullo, A., (2007). Internet – an agent of tourism destination image formation: Content and correspondence analysis of Istria travel related websites. *4th International Conference: Global Challenges for Competitiveness: Business and Government Perspective* (pp. 541–556). Pula: Juraj Dobrila University of Pula, Department of Economics and Tourism.

Leung, D., Law, R, van Hoof, H., & Buhalis, D. (2013). Social media in tourism and hospitality: A literature review. *Journal of Travel & Tourism Marketing, 30*(1–2), 3–22.

Litvin, S. W., Goldsmith, R. E., & Pan, B. (2008). Electronic word-of-mouth in hospitality and tourism management. *Tourism Management, 29*(3), 458–468.

Liu, B. (2011) *Web data mining: Exploring hyperlinks, contents, and usage data*. Berlin, DE: Springer.

Lu, W., & Stepchenkova, S. (2015). User-generated content as a research mode in tourism and hospitality applications: Topics, methods, and software. *Journal of Hospitality Marketing & Management, 24*(2), 119–154.

Marine-Roig, E. (2011). The image and identity of the Catalan coast as a tourist destination in twentieth-century tourist guidebooks. *Journal of Tourism and Cultural Change, 9*(2), 118–139.

Marine-Roig, E. (2014). A webometric analysis of travel blogs and reviews hosting: the case of Catalonia. *Journal of Travel & Tourism Marketing, 31*(3), 381–396.

Marine-Roig, E. (2015). Identity and authenticity in destination image construction. *Anatolia – An International Journal of Tourism and Hospitality Research* (in press), 1–14.

Marine-Roig, E., & Anton Clavé, S. (2015). A method for analysing large-scale UGC data for tourism: Application to the case of Catalonia. In Tussyadiah, I. and Inversini, A. (eds.), *Information and Communication Technologies in Tourism 2015* (pp. 3–17). Cham, Switzerland: Springer.

Neuendorf, K. A. (2002). *The content analysis guidebook*. Thousand Oaks, CA: Sage.

Pan, B., MacLaurin, T., & Crotts, J., C. (2007). Travel blogs and the implications for destination marketing. *Journal of Travel Research, 46*(1), 35–45.

Russell, J. A., & Pratt, G. (1980). A description of the affective quality attributed to environments. *Journal of Personality and Social Psychology, 38*(2), 311–322.

Schmallegger, D., & Carson, D. (2010). Destination image projection on consumer generated content websites (CGC): A case study of the Flinders Ranges. *Journal of Information Technology & Tourism, 11*(2), 111–127.

Schmunk, S., Höpken, W., Fuchs, M., & Lexhagen, M. (2014). Sentiment analysis: Extracting decision-relevant knowledge from UGC. In Xiang, Z. & I. Tussyadiah (eds.), *Information and Communication Technologies in Tourism 2014* (pp. 253–265). Cham, Switzerland: Springer.

Stemler, S. (2001). An overview of content analysis. *Practical Assessment, Research & Evaluation, 7*(17). Retrieved from http://PAREonline.net/getvn.asp?v=7&n=17

Wang, N. (1999). Rethinking authenticity in tourism experience. *Annals of Tourism Research, 26*(2), 349–370.

Xiang, Z., & Gretzel, U. (2010). Role of social media in online travel information search. *Tourism Management, 31*(2), 179–188.

Yoo, K. H., & Gretzel, U. (2010). Antecedents and impacts of trust in travel-related consumer-generated media. *Information Technologies & Tourism, 12*(2), 139–152.

# Part II
# Destination branding

# 6 Shaping collaboration in tourism

## Thuggery in a destination branding process

*Carlos Larreategui Nardi, Giuseppe Marzano and Gonzalo Mendieta*

## Introduction

This study examines how collaborative thuggery emerges within a multi-stake-holder decision-making process, such as the Gold Coast VeryGC destination branding process. Although collaboration has been widely (Bramwell & Sharman, 1999; Erkuş-Öztürk & Eraydın, 2010), yet arguably (Marzano & Scott, 2009), described as a necessary condition for destination competitiveness (Baggio, 2010), the tourism literature did not thoroughly examine how multi-stakeholder decision-making processes could be shaped to match the needs and interests of a few stakeholders. By examining the Gold Coast (Australia) VeryGC destination branding process, this study shows evidence of the existence of collaborative thuggery, defined as the behaviour of stakeholders who invest time and effort in shaping the agenda to fit their interests, and who play politics (Huxham, 2003). However, the question of whether thuggery is pathology, a necessity or just an unforeseen occurrence within a multi-stakeholder decision-making process in the context of tourism is outside the scope of this study.

## Literature review

According to Wood and Gray (1991), 'collaboration occurs when a group of autonomous stakeholders of a problem domain engages in an interactive process, using shared rules, norms and structures, to act or decide on issues related to that domain' (p. 146). Fyall and Garrod (2005) consider collaboration in tourism as a teleological process, which is expected to occur amongst stakeholders in the context of a fragmented industry that involves multiple players, such as the tourism industry (Reid, Mair & George, 2004). From the same perspective, Jamal and Getz (1995) link the success of community tourism planning processes to the inclusion of a broad base of legitimate stakeholders within the process and to the capacity of the convener to facilitate the reconciliation of the different perspectives and diverse goals that the parties carry into the process. However, in accordance with general planning theory (Healey, 1997), collaborative processes, and the multi-stakeholder decision-making processes in tourism among them, are not value free.

Stakeholders not only have different interests (Ramírez, 2001), an expression of the different ways they define their role within a certain community (von Friedrichs Grangsjo, 2001), but it has also been observed within a tourism destination that stakeholders' 'interests cannot be summarily restricted to consideration of a single variable' (Sautter & Leisen, 1999, pp. 316-317). As a consequence, the ability of a stakeholder, or a coalition of them, to advance a will or impose an interest (West, 1994), that is, the ability of stakeholders to exert power, is a critical element in understanding how collaboration works. In fact, as Reed (1997) points out, both theory (Rees, 1990) and empirical evidence (Timothy, 1998) confirm that all parties involved in a collaborative process, including public sector organisations, carry individual interests and pursue specific agendas (Hardy & Phillips, 1998).

Furthermore, human input is a necessary condition for sustaining a collaborative group (Mattessich & Monsey, 1992). Accordingly, Healey (2003) noted that the presence of a skilled convener gives legitimacy to a collaborative process and facilitates a successful outcome. As Wood and Gray (1991) explain in discussing facilitation, 'the convener has no formal authority to establish the collaboration and to enforce the rules, or ensure outcomes and must depend on the trust of participants to be effective' (p. 152). Stakeholders who convene by mandate 'elect to exercise the formal power they possess with the domain to assemble other stakeholders' (Gray, 1996, p. 65). Conveners who use participation need to be able to present arguments and convince stakeholders to become involved in the collaborative process because they do not have any formal clout to induce participation.

Jamal and Getz discuss the role of the convener as a facilitator of the collaborative process in the context of tourism and propose that:

> A convener is required to initiate and facilitate community-based tourism collaboration. The convener should have the following characteristics: legitimacy, expertise, resources; plus authority, and may be derived from a government agency, an industry firm, or group such as the local Chamber of Commerce, or the local tourist organization.
>
> (Jamal & Getz, 1995, p. 198)

The success of the convener in facilitating a collaborative process in tourism is also linked to their ability to use the leadership role to encourage 'collective decision-making and consensus building' (Bramwell & Sharman, 1999, p. 399). However, according to Björk and Virtanen (2003), the ability of the convener to play a useful role in bringing tourism stakeholders together and to make a collaborative project work is limited by the support they receive from the stakeholders of the project.

Reflecting on how conveners exert leadership, Huxham (2003) observes that in some cases, conveners can be engaged in activities that shape and interfere with collaboration. As one of the interviewees in Huxham's (2003) study observes, 'the convener is a thug: if people are not pulling their weight, he pushes them out' (p. 417). Huxham (2003) calls this behaviour collaborative thuggery, which she defines as the behaviour of the stakeholders who invest time and effort in shaping the agenda to fit their interests and play politics. Beech and Huxham (2003) also consider that being the convener of a collaborative process involves both 'facilitative activities that are in the "spirit of collaboration" and the manipulative activities that we label "collaborative thuggery"' (p. 49). As Vangen and Huxham (2003) suggest, thuggery could be considered a way to achieve a pragmatic leadership role by manipulating a collaborative agenda and playing politics.

## Methodology

This study examines thuggery in a destination branding process such as the creation of the Gold Coast (Australia) VeryGC brand. Semi-structured interviews were used to collect data from the stakeholders in the branding process (including both those involved and excluded). Purposive sampling and snowball sampling were used in combination to select interviewees who were familiar with the branding process for participation in the study. Through snowballing, 42 interviewees were identified and 32 individuals participated in this study. The interviewees ranged from the CEO of Tourism Queensland (TQ), to the CEO of the Gold Coast Tourism (GCT) Bureau to the top managers of the major hotels and theme parks at the Gold Coast. For privacy reasons, all names that were mentioned during the interviews were changed to fictitious ones and all interviewees were identified by codes.

## Findings

The determination of the agenda for the VeryGC destination branding process appeared to be a privilege Simon Doyle (CEO of the GCT Bureau) assigned to himself. As Respondent VGC3 clearly stated, 'the agenda for the brand was set by Simon Doyle'.

The same view was shared by Respondent VGC9, who suggested that Simon Doyle had sole responsibility for determining the direction of the VeryGC destination branding process: 'From an agenda-setting perspective, [it] was with Simon Doyle, on behalf of Gold Coast Tourism'.

Although Mr Doyle was part of an organisation, he was able to use his experience and personality to acquire the responsibility of providing direction to the destination branding process, without sharing the agenda-setting process with the Board of Directors of GCT.

Respondent VGC8 remembered their experience within the GCT Board of Directors, and related the behaviour of Simon Doyle to that of a general who would fight a war without waiting for consent or looking at the consequences of his initiative:

> I think from where I've been sitting with the Board not having a very strong position and he came in as the very strong personality. He said this is the direction we're going in. So the role was slightly reversed. As in the CEO

was basically saying, this is what we're going to do, rather than the Board. And he basically went off and started doing it, exercising it, and said, you know, everybody follow me, you know. This is what I'm doing. This is where I'm going. So how did he exercise it? I think he just did. He just went off and did it, you know. I suppose it's a bit like in the army, you know. Generals just say, we're going to war and we're going that way. And he just went off and did it. And what are the consequences? I won't ask anybody. I'll just go ahead and do it, I suspect. Also within Tourism Queensland it was clear that Simon Doyle was the sole person responsible for deciding which direction the VeryGC destination branding process was going to take.

(Respondent VGC8)

As Respondent VGC5 explained, 'the previous CEO [Simon Doyle] decided that the Gold Coast was at a three-star level and he wanted to take it to a five-star level'.

As long as Simon Doyle occupied the position of CEO of GCT, the stakeholders felt alienated from the branding process. But, as Respondent VGC5 stated, as soon as Simon Doyle left GCT, setting the agenda for the brand became a concern shared among the stakeholders:

Immediately the person [Simon Doyle] departed, who was the, let's say, the founder or the person who's driving it, immediately they left, it was very much a situation of no one wants to own it, because people were criticising it. So it was much easier for the people there to agree to the critics rather than to defend it; because they probably haven't been that involved in its conception in the first place. So I think it's a classic example. If you don't involve people in the concept and the inception, then you can expect to get a lot of criticism rather than the support that you probably would prefer.

(Respondent VGC5)

The departure of Simon Doyle reopened the door for Tourism Queensland to provide direction in shaping the agenda of the VeryGC destination branding process.

## Conclusion

The VeryGC destination branding process case offers an example of what Huxham (2003) refers to as collaborative thuggery: Simon Doyle exerted his role of convener not to embrace, empower, involve and mobilise members towards the creation of a negotiated order (Gray 1989), but as a vehicle to push forward his personal agenda. These findings contribute to tourism theory by adding new dimensions to Jamal and Getz's (1995) conceptualisation of the role of the convener's multi-stakeholder decision-making processes in tourism, such as a destination branding process. The results of this study are relevant not only for tourism, but they may also inform collaboration theory. In particular, when discussing collaborative thuggery, Huxham (2003) does not discuss the circumstances in which a convener may transform themselves from a facilitator into a thug, and Gray (1989) discusses the power of the convener only in terms of their ability to induce stakeholders to participate within a collaborative process. The study of the VeryGC destination branding process revealed that a convener is not necessarily a facilitator. The resources and power they provide to the convener of a multi-stakeholder decision-making process, such as the VeryGC destination branding process, may help to explain some of the circumstances in which a convener can 'reincarnate' into a thug. Collaboration theory may therefore benefit from an understanding of the behaviour of the convener within a multi-stakeholder decision-making process.

## References

Baggio, R. (2010). Collaboration and cooperation in a tourism destination: A network science approach. *Current Issues in Tourism, 14* (2), 183–189.

Beech, N., & Huxham, C. (2003). Cycles of identity formation in interorganizational collaborations. *International Studies of Management and Organization, 33* (3), 28–52.

Björk, P., & Virtanen, H. (2003, August). *Tourism project management and cooperation facilitators.* Paper presented at the 17th Nordic Conference on Business Studies, Reykjavik, Finland.

Bramwell, B., & Sharman, A. (1999). Collaboration in local tourism policymaking. *Annals of Tourism Research, 26* (2), 392–415.

Erkuş-Öztürk, H., & Eraydın, A. (2010). Environmental governance for sustainable tourism development: Collaborative networks and organisation building in the Antalya tourism region. *Tourism Management, 31* (1), 113–124.

Fyall, A., & Garrod, B. (2005). *Tourism marketing: A collaborative approach.* Clevedon: Channel View Publications.

Gray, B. (1989) Collaborating: Finding common ground for multiparty problems. San Francisco: Jossey Bass.

Gray, B. (1996). Cross-sectoral partners: Collaborative alliances among business government and communities. In C. Huxham (Ed.), *Creating collaborative advantage* (pp. 57–79). London: Sage.

Hardy, C., & Phillips, N. (1998). Strategies of engagement: Lessons from the critical examination of collaboration and conflict in an interorganizational domain. *Organization Science, 9* (2), 217–230.

Healey, P. (1997). *Collaborative planning: shaping places in fragmented societies.* London: Macmillan.

Healey, P. (2003). Collaborative planning in perspective. *Planning Theory, 2* (2), 101–123.

Huxham, C. (2003). Theorizing collaboration practice. *Public Management Review, 5* (3), 401–423.

Jamal, T. B., & Getz, D. (1995). Collaboration theory and community tourism planning. *Annals of Tourism Research, 22* (1), 186–204.

Marzano, G., & Scott, N. (2009). Power in destination branding. *Annals of Tourism Research, 36* (2), 247–267.

Mattessich, P. W., & Monsey, B. R. (1992). *Collaboration-what makes it work: A review of research literature on factors influencing successful collaboration.* St. Paul, MN: Amherst H. Wilder Foundation.

Ramírez, R. (2001). Understanding the approaches for accommodating multiple stakeholders' interests. *International Journal in Agricultural Resources, Governance and Ecology, 1* (3/4), 264–285.

Reed, M. G. (1997). Power relations and community-based tourism planning. *Annals of Tourism Research, 24* (3), 566–591.

Rees, J. A. (1990). *Natural resources: allocation, economics, and policy* (2nd ed.). London: Routledge.

Reid, D. G., Mair, H., & George, W. (2004). Community tourism planning: A self-assessment instrument. *Annals of Tourism Research, 31* (3), 623–639.

Sautter, E. T., & Leisen, B. (1999). Managing stakeholders. A tourism planning model. *Annals of Tourism Research, 26* (2), 312–328.

Timothy, D. J. (1998). Cooperative tourism planning in a developing destination. *Journal of Sustainable Tourism, 6* (1), 52–68.

Vangen, S., & Huxham, C. (2003). Enacting leadership for collaborative advantage: dilemmas of ideology and pragmatism in the activities of partnership managers. *British Journal of Management, 14* (1), S61–S76.

von Friedrichs Grangsjo, Y. (2001, August). *Destination networking: Co-opetition in a ski resort.* Paper presented at the Nordiska Företagsekonomiska Ämneskonferensen, Uppsala.

West, P. C. (1994). Natural resources and the persistence of rural poverty in America: A Weberian perspective on the role of power, domination, and natural resource bureaucracy. *Society and Natural Resources, 7* (5), 415–427.

Wood, D. J., & Gray, B. (1991). Toward a comprehensive theory of collaboration. *The Journal of Applied Behavioral Science, 27* (2), 139–162.

# 7 Revealing internal stakeholders' perceptions of developing 'Brand Alexandria'

*Sally Khalil and Osama Ibrahim*

In today's extremely competitive global tourism market environment, it is crucial to differentiate tourism destinations to encourage and inform potential visitors. In terms of Alexandria's competitive position, this chapter aims to investigate Alexandria's branding initiatives and reveal official internal stakeholders' (OIS's) perceptions. The study applies collage technique to explore stakeholder perceptions and develop 'Brand Alexandria' accordingly. The findings show that different OIS's perceptions reveal different identities in relation to 'Brand Alexandria'. The chapter presents the perception of OISs in Alexandria as posters which are integrated into a single composite poster.

## Introduction

Alexandria was not only the ancient mysterious capital of Egypt from Ptolemy I until the end of the Roman period, but is also the present-day Egyptian cultural capital to which the intelligentsia flock, nationally and internationally. In addition to its great heritage, it offers fabulous beaches and good weather all through the year. Many cities with tourism destinations have identified their unique selling proposition based on their comparative advantage and develop a brand to enhance their competitive advantage. Although Alexandria has a variety of heritage resources, its brand has never been fully developed in a systematic and scientific manner to enhance its competitive position. Therefore, the purpose of this chapter is to investigate branding initiatives and to reveal internal stakeholders' (OIS's) perceptions in relation to 'Brand Alexandria'.

The chapter investigates branding initiatives undertaken by Alexandria's destination managers. It is limited to OISs and does not investigate the perspectives of tourists or local communities which will be studied in other papers. Further research will be undertaken to support the findings of this research and to develop the final brand of Alexandria. The study applies the collage technique which analyses picture and word associations of different tourism types of Alexandria. The empirical study identifies the most important tourism types in Alexandria that could be integrated into 'Brand Alexandria' and who the OISs of Alexandria are. It also displays the selection of photos, symbols, logos, words or graphics that identify and differentiate Alexandria as a tourist destination. They were collected via the internet and photos taken by researchers during their fieldwork.

## Literature review

The marketing literature has primarily focused on destination image (Blain, Levy & Ritchie, 2005; Boo, Busser & Baloglu, 2009; Chen & Phou, 2013; Kotler & Gertner, 2004). Branding, as a concept, has developed within the tourism industry during the last few decades and actually became a topic of investigation in the late 1990s (Anholt, 2003; Barnes, Mattsson & Sørensen, 2014; Morgan, Pritchard & Piggott, 2003; Pike, 2002, 2012; Tasci & Kozak, 2006). The differences and similarities between the 'brand' and the 'image' concepts in the tourist destination context have been critically discussed in the literature (Blain, Levy & Ritchie, 2005; Haugland, Grønseth & Aarstad, 2011; Hosany, Ekinici & Uysal, 2006; Qu, Kim & Im, 2011; Tasci & Kozak, 2006).

The marketing literature reveals different ways to define a destination brand (Hankinson, 2004). Among several definitions of the term, Kerr (2006, p. 277) has defined destination branding as:

> name, symbol, logo, word or other graphic that both identifies and differentiates the destination; furthermore it conveys the promise of a memorable travel experience that is uniquely associated with the destination; it also serves to consolidate and reinforce the recollection of pleasurable memories of destination experience.

Thus, branding is considered the good name of a product/service, an organization or a destination; a guarantee of quality experiences; a short-cut to an informed decision and, most importantly, a promise of value (Blain, Levy & Ritchie, 2005; García, Gómez & Molina, 2012; Vallaster & de Chernatony, 2006).

Hence, in terms of tourism destination marketing, branding is a very important step. In today's competitive marketplace, only those destinations that have a unique selling proposition, a clear market position and appealing attractions will be competitive and remain at the top of tourists' minds when they book their holidays (Anholt, 2003; Hankinson, 2004; Pike, 2005).

Destination branding also helps identify target markets, describes the planned offer and experience, communicates the offer to consumers, and guides the future development of the offer. Therefore, Morgan and Pritchard (2004, p. 60) assert that 'Branding is perhaps the most powerful marketing weapon available to contemporary destination marketers'. This is true because many destinations have amazing natural and cultural heritage attractions, brilliant five-star hotels, superb customer services, friendly people and more. It becomes very complicated to differentiate a unique brand identity for a destination from other competitors.

## Stakeholders and destination brand development

Destinations are a complex of components, including: hotels; restaurants; tourist attractions; art types; entertainment places; cultural sites; natural sites (Buhalis, 2000; Ritche & Crouch, 2000). However, the tourism industry in a destination is managed by a number of stakeholders, who are considered as destination managers (Bornhorst, Ritchie & Sheehan, 2010; Sheehan, Ritchie & Hudson, 2007). A destination brand is considered the conclusion of the collaboration of an extremely complex multi-stakeholder managerial process in which the various stakeholders may carry different interests and define their role in different ways (Marzano & Scott, 2009).

Destination stakeholders can be classified into a group of primary and a group of secondary stakeholders (García, Gómez & Molina, 2012; Jones, 2005; Sheehan & Ritchie, 2005). Primary stakeholders show a regular high level of interactivity and are crucial to the survival of a destination (Boo, Busser & Baloglu, 2009; Konecnik & Gartner, 2007) and its brand equity with its five dimensions, i.e. awareness, image, quality, loyalty and cultural brand assets (Kladou & Kehagias, 2014). Secondary stakeholders are not directly involved in the development of a destination but have to be involved as they are important hidden assets of a destination (García, Gómez & Molina, 2012; Hosany, Ekinici & Uysal, 2006; Merrilees *et al.*, 2005). Secondary destination stakeholders include: hotel owners; tour operators; landowners; banks; permanent residents (Flagestad, 2002).

While the literature on brand development is focused on consumer products until lately, a different stream of research directly associated with the Service Dominant Logic (Vargo & Lusch, 2004), in which the brand plays a broader role (Brodie, Whittome & Brush, 2009). García, Gómez and Molina (2012) emphasize that little research developing an empirical application has been conducted as most studies are elementary and only involve some stakeholders and more importantly, many studies do not include members of local communities as stakeholders. In this context, Freire (2009) and Marzano and Scott (2009) discussed the risks of neglecting local communities when developing the destination-brand identity. Yet, most of the literature has been directed towards external stakeholders or customers (Park & Petrick, 2006).

Morgan and Pritchard (2004, p. 70) addressed six features that destination managers should consider to be successful in creating an emotional attachment when developing a brand. Hence, a destination brand should be: 'credible; deliverable; differentiating; conveying powerful ideas; enthusing for stakeholders and partners; resonating with the consumer'. Moreover as far as destination brand development is concerned, Hudson (2014) highlighted the importance of a multi-stage approach for successful brand development identifying four stages: (I) evaluating the current situation via market analysis; (II) developing brand identity; (III) communicating the brand by engaging with clients; and (IV) evaluating brand effectiveness.

When it comes to brand development, perhaps the most difficult task facing any marketer is the question of identification and differentiation (Jin & Weber, 2013). Wales, for instance, has developed a challenging brand as a golfing destination, 'Wales, Golf as it should be', and it was successful in revitalizing the number of visitors because it differentiates Wales from its competitor destinations (De Chernatony & Segal-Horn, 2003; Pride, 2004). Moreover, the success of countries such as Spain shows that destinations can develop brands that are both contemporary and timeless, and so can remain in the mature phase of their product life cycle over a prolonged period (Blain, Levy & Ritchie, 2005; Morgan, Pritchard & Piggott, 2003).

Successful destination brands have a social and emotional identity to enhance their desirability to tourists to visit the destination through creating an emotional relationship. For this reason, Morgan and Pritchard (2004, p. 61) assert that 'the battle for consumers in tomorrow's destination market place will be fought not over price but over hearts and minds'. Hence, the development of an emotional relationship with tourists can hold the key to destination differentiation (Barnes, Mattsson & Sørensen, 2014). More importantly, if destination managers focus only on logos and slogans in their branding initiatives but ignore emotions, they might be more accurately termed as 'sloganeering' (Morgan & Pritchard, 2004).

The value of a successful brand development lies in its potential to meet tourists' interests and enhance visit intentions (Ferns & Walls, 2012; Morgan, Pritchard & Pride, 2004). In a word, tourist branding encapsulates the competitive advantage of a destination by creating a memorable and highly differentiated image in the minds and emotions of tourists (Murphy, Moscardo & Benckendorff, 2007).

## Methodology

Prebensen (2007) asserted that there is a paucity of qualitative research in the field of branding. The collage technique is an unstructured qualitative method that comprises exploratory techniques to identify stakeholders' perceptions of a place's identity. Apparently, the advantage of using qualitative techniques in branding studies is to develop a richer picture of stakeholders' images of a destination. Therefore, a respondent can choose between several real images and discuss only those pictures which are relevant in his/her mind. Thus, it can be argued that the collage technique helps to recognize important dimensions of places through picture and the word association (Wagner & Peters, 2009).

After introducing a general framework for brand development in destination branding, this empirical study involves three phases; the first one specified the most important tourism types in Alexandria which could be marketed to potential visitors to enhance Alexandria's competitive position. The second phase displayed the selection of photos, symbols, logos, words, or graphics that identify and differentiate Alexandria as a tourist destination. The third phase identified the OISs of Alexandria assigned to developing 'Brand Alexandria'. An unstructured interview protocol was prepared in this phase and interviews with OISs were conducted. Data collected from the interviews were then transcribed and translated.

### *Phase one: Major tourism types in Alexandria*

In this phase, the most important tourism types in Alexandria were surveyed via literature, especially the proceedings of Alexandria conference 'Alexandria the city of civilizations and culture' in 2003. Each of these major types was also subdivided into a number of activities. The chart in Figure 7.1 is the conclusion from this analysis.

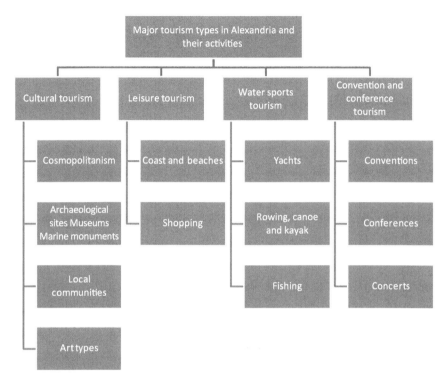

*Figure 7.1* Major tourism types in Alexandria.

## Phase two: The selection of textual and pictorial tools

The selected tools (photos, symbols, logos, words and graphics) bear a strong association that identifies and differentiates Alexandria from its competitors. They represent the surveyed major tourism types in Alexandria: 37 pictures and 4 slogans represent cultural tourism; 16 pictures and 2 slogans represent leisure tourism; 5 pictures and 2 slogans represent water sports tourism; and 3 pictures and 1 slogan represent convention/conference tourism. Seven common slogans had no association with the previous tourism types; however, they are famous sayings about Alexandria and should not be neglected. Their classification as 'common' indicates that they have the least emotional association that links visitors' hearts to Alexandria.

## Phase three: Interviewing OISs of Alexandria

Interviewees were asked about who are the OISs in charge of tourism develop-ment and marketing in Alexandria and, in turn, developing 'Brand Alexandria'. The targeted interviewees were the top marketing management level of those OISs and thus had knowledge on the branding of Alexandria and other tourist destinations.

They were also in a position to implement the findings of this research because they are the official destination marketing organizations in Alexandria.

The interview protocol consists of four groups of questions: (A) basic questions aiming to identify the main OISs in charge of developing 'Brand Alexandria' and their specific role(s). Also, they aimed to identify the major communication channels among them and to find out other related stakeholders. (B) Interviewees were asked to evaluate via storytelling and collage the perceived brand identity of Alexandria and if there is any official brand for Alexandria enough to enhance its competitiveness. It identified the potential 'Brand Alexandria' and how it is communicated from the OISs viewpoints. (C) Interviewees were asked to select slogans, pictures and poster backgrounds about their perspectives of 'Brand Alexandria' from a slide show. (D) This part of the interview investigated the associated emotions of the OISs with Alexandria.

## Findings

The purpose of this chapter is to explore the perception of the OISs about 'Brand Alexandria' and whether different stakeholders have varying destination perceptions or not. The collage technique helped to identify these different interpretations of 'Brand Alexandria'. Pictures, logos and slogans were based on internet surveys and the researchers' photographs.

### *Major outcomes of interviews*

The interviewed OISs included:

- The Ministry of Tourism Head Office in Alexandria (Respondent 1);
- the Regional Authority for Tourism Promotion (Respondent 2);
- Egyptian General Tourist Authority in Alexandria (Respondent 3).

Respondents agreed that the following is the order of the three OISs in terms of their importance in marketing Alexandria:

1   Ministry of Tourism Head Office in Alexandria.
2   The Regional Authority for Tourism Promotion.
3   Egyptian General Tourist Authority in Alexandria.

The results showed that OISs are well aware of the importance of developing 'Brand Alexandria'. Typical quotes were: 'we know that branding could help communicating the identity of Alexandria to the world' (Respondent 3), '"Brand Alexandria" has to cope with the future evolution in marketing and branding … therefore we need to build this brand' (Respondent 2). They shared regular meetings to discuss the future of the tourism sector in Alexandria, such as: the Executive Council of the Regional Authority for Tourism Promotion in Alexandria governorate led by the governor; the Higher Committee of Tourism of Alexandria as the

Capital of Arab Tourism. However, Respondent 1 emphasized that they 'never discussed branding Alexandria and their meetings are superficial'.

The major role of the OISs in developing 'Brand Alexandria' was debated. Respondent 1 is in charge of achieving national income from tourism and accrediting and implementing the decisions of the Regional Authority for Tourism Promotion (Respondent 2) as a representative of the Egyptian Ministry of Tourism: 'We have got all the same administrative departments as the Ministry of Tourism in Cairo' (Respondent 1). Respondent 2 is responsible for marketing Alexandria internally. Respondent 3 is in charge of producing materials for marketing Alexandria externally. Occasionally, they involved other public or private stakeholders such as: hotel managers; tourist companies' managers; heads of Egyptian Hotel and Tourism Associations; Egyptian Commercial Association; Egyptian Tourism Establishments Association.

The respondents were asked to evaluate the current brand of Alexandria, if any. Although Respondent 2 communicates posters and other publications to promote tourism, there is no brand for Alexandria yet developed. These attempts encompassed many challenges in terms of: occasionality; sloganeering; bias to certain nationalities; lack of management control; low budget: 'there is no budget dedicated to developing "Brand Alexandria". The allocated budget is dedicated to marketing in general' (Respondent 3). Moreover, they were produced to promote particular events such as 'Alexandria, the capital of Arab Tourism 2010'. Moreover, it was clear that they were free from emotions which are considered a key factor towards the success of any destination brand development process.

Frequently used slogans encompass two 'common' slogans: 'Alexandria the Mermaid of the Mediterranean' (Respondent 1) and 'Alexandria Egypt' (Respondent 2), and one cultural tourism slogan: 'Explore Ancient Alexandria under water' (Respondent 3). The 'common' slogans do not reflect emotions which link minds and hearts of the potential tourists to Alexandria. However, the third slogan bears strong emotions for diving and viewing monuments under water. Besides, the word 'explore' indicates that there is something they are going to experience and discover in Alexandria. Frequently used photos included: Alexandria Lighthouse (3 times), *Pompays* Pillar and Sphinx (3 times), *Bibliotica Alexandriana* from outside at night (2 times), Diver and marine monuments (3 times).

Emotions associated with Alexandria were extensively debated with respondents and could be summarized in these three quotes: 'Alexandria is different from other 44 Alexandria towns in the world because of its extraordinary heritage' (Respondent 1). 'Alexandria is a piece of art and its people are full of pride' (Respondent 2). 'Diversity of nationalities living in Alexandria has created a unique type of people, known as Alexandrians' (Respondent 3).

## *OIS's perceptions of 'Brand Alexandria'*

The results showed that different OISs had different perceptions about 'Brand Alexandria'. A sole poster for 'Brand Alexandria' from the perception of each OIS has been developed (see Figure 7.2).

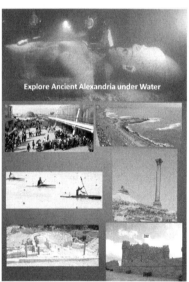

*Figure 7.2* Stakeholders' different perceptions of developing 'Brand Alexandria'. (a) Respondent 1: Ministry of Tourism – Head Office in Alexandria. (b) Respondent 2: The Regional Authority for Tourism Promotion. (c) Respondent 3: Egyptian General Tourist Authority in Alexandria. (Source of the underwater picture: Goddio, 2004: 79.)

Content analysis and collage technique were used to integrate these posters into one. Seventeen photos in the three posters out of 25 photos (68 per cent) identified Alexandria as a cultural destination which emphasizes the position of the city as a cosmopolitan town with varied art types, archaeological sites representing all historical periods, museums and most importantly as a marine monuments paradise, which can create a clear differentiation between Alexandria and its competitors.

Three out of 25 photos in the three models (12 per cent) identified Alexandria as a sport destination due to the existence of the only international rowing venues in Egypt. Furthermore, yachting and fishing are also common sport activities in Alexandria. Three out of 25 photos in the three posters (12 per cent) identify Alexandria as a leisure destination while two photos (8 per cent) identify Alexandria as a convention and conference destination which aligns with the policy of the government to build conference halls in Alexandria.

The selected background colour in the three posters was blue. This consensus was interpreted by the interviewees to have an association with the Mediterranean. Therefore, the composite poster in Figure 7.3 reflects and integrates the perceptions of the OISs in charge of developing 'Brand Alexandria'. There are eight photos: five for cultural tourism (62.5 per cent); one for sports tourism (12.5 per cent); one

*Figure 7.3* The developed 'Brand Alexandria' from the perception of the official internal stakeholders. (Source of the underwater picture: Goddio, 2004: 79.)

for leisure tourism (12.5 per cent); and one for convention/conference tourism (12.5 per cent). There is also one slogan for cultural tourism.

## Conclusion

The collage technique enabled the exploration and identification of OISs' perceptions of developing 'Brand Alexandria' through picture and word association that could differentiate Alexandria from its competitors. This chapter developed ideas for 'Brand Alexandria' as seen through the eyes of OISs in the form of different posters that were integrated into a composite poster for 'Brand Alexandria'. It is also concluded that different OISs reveal different identities of Alexandria as a tourist destination. However, this study is limited to the OISs' viewpoint; therefore, further research to develop other models from the viewpoints of visitors, local communities, and other related unofficial stakeholders studies could be conducted to attain a more appropriate 'Brand Alexandria' which resonates with all internal and external stakeholders.

## Acknowledgement

We would like to express our deepest appreciation to Professor Eleri Jones for her expert guidance.

## References

Anholt, S. (2003). *Branding places and nations: Brands and Branding.* London: Profile Books.

Barnes, S., Mattsson, J., & Sørensen, F. (2014). Destination brand experience and visitor behavior: Testing a scale in the tourism context. *Annals of Tourism Research*, *48*, 121–139.

Blain, C., Levy, S., & Ritchie, J. (2005). Destination branding: Insights and practices from destination management organizations, *Journal of Tourism Research*, *43*(4), 328–38.

Boo, S., Busser, J., & Baloglu, S. (2009). A model of customer-based brand equity and its application to multiple destinations. *Tourism Management*, *30*(2), 219–231.

Bornhorst, T., Ritchie, J., & Sheehan, L. (2010). Determinants of tourism success for DMOs & destinations: An empirical examination of stakeholders' perspectives. *Tourism Management*, *31*, 572–589.

Brodie, R. J., Whittome, J. R., & Brush, G. J. (2009). Investigating the service brand: A customer value perspective. *Journal of Business Research*, *62*(3), 345–355.

Buhalis, D. (2000). Marketing the competitive destination of the future. *Tourism Management*, *21*(1), 97–116.

Chen, C., & Phou, S. (2013). A closer look at destination: Image, personality, relationship and loyalty. *Tourism Management*, *36*, 269–278.

De Chernatony, L., & Segal-Horn, S. (2003). Building a service brand: Stages. *The Service Industry Journal*, *23*(3), 1–21.

Ferns, B., & Walls, A. (2012). Enduring travel involvement, destination brand equity, and travelers' visit intentions: A structural model analysis. *Journal of Destination Marketing & Management*, *1*, 27–35.

Flagestad, A. (2002). *Strategic success and organisational structure in winter sports destinations*. Bradford: University of Bradford.

Freire, J. R. (2009). 'Local people' a critical dimension for place brands. *Journal of Brand Management, 16*(7), 420–438.

García, J., Gómez, M., & Molina, A. (2012). A destination-branding model: An empirical analysis based on stakeholders. *Tourism Management, 33,* 646–661.

Goddio, F. (2004). *Egypt's Sunken Treasures.*

Hankinson, G. (2004). The brand image of tourism destinations: A study of the saliency of organic images. *Journal of Product and Brand Management, 3*(1), 6–14.

Haugland, S., Grønseth, H., & Aarstad, J. (2011). Development of tourism destinations: An integrated multilevel perspective. *Annals of Tourism Research, 38*(1), 268–290.

Hosany, S., Ekinici, Y., & Uysal, M. (2006). Destination image and destination personality: An application of branding theories to tourism places. *Journal of Business Research, 59*(2), 638–642.

Hudson, S. (2014). Selling America to the world: The case of brand USA. *Journal of Destination Marketing and Management, 3,* 79–81.

Jin, X., & Weber, K. (2013). Developing and testing a model of exhibition brand preference: The exhibitors' Perspective. *Tourism Management, 38,* 94–104.

Jones, R. (2005). Finding sources of brand value: Developing a stakeholder model of brand equity. *Journal of Brand Management, 13*(1), 10–32.

Kerr, G. (2006). From destination brand to local brand. *Brand Management, 13*(4/5), 276–83.

Kladou, S., & Kehagias, J. (2014). Assessing destination brand equity: An integrated approach. *Journal of Destination Marketing & Management, 3,* 2–10.

Konecnik, M., & Gartner, W. (2007). Customer-based brand equity for a destination. *Annals of Tourism Research, 34*(2), 400–421.

Konecnik, M., & Go, F. (2007). Tourism destination brand identity: The case of Slovenia. *Brand Management, 15*(3), 177–189.Kotler, P., & Gertner, D. (2004). Country as brand, product and beyond: A place marketing and brand management perspective. In N. Morgan, A. Pritchard, & Pride, R. (Eds.), *Destination branding* (pp. 40–56). 2nd ed., Burlington, MA: Elsevier Butterworth-Heinemann.

Marzano, G. & Scott, N. (2009). Power in destination branding. *Annals of Tourism Research, 36*(2), 247–267.

Merrilees, B., Getz, D., & O'Brien, D. (2005). Marketing stakeholder analysis: Branding the Brisbane goodwill games. *European Journal of Marketing, 39*(9/10), 1060–1077.

Morgan, N., & Pritchard, A. (2004). Meeting the destination branding challenge. In N. Morgan, A. Pritchard, & Pride, R. (Eds.), *Destination branding* (pp. 59–78). 2nd ed., Burlington, MA: Elsevier Butterworth-Heinemann.

Morgan, N., Pritchard, A., & Piggott, R. (2003). Destination branding and the role of the stakeholders: The case of New Zealand. *Journal of Vacation Marketing, 9*(3), 285–299.

Morgan, S., Pritchard, S., & Pride, R. (eds.) (2004). *Destination branding: Creating the unique destination proposition,* 2nd ed., Butterworth-Heinemann, Oxford.

Murphy, L., Moscardo, G., & Benckendorff, P. (2007). Using brand personality to differentiate regional tourism destinations. *Journal of Travel Research, 46,* 5–14.

Park, S.Y., & Petrick, J.F. (2006). Destinations' perspectives of branding. *Annals of Tourism Research, 33*(1), 262–265.

Pike, S. (2002). Destination image analysis–A review of 142 papers from 1973 to 2000. *Tourism Management, 23*(5), 541–549.

Pike, S. (2005). Tourism destination branding complexity. *Journal of Product and Brand Management, 14*(4), 258–259.

Pike, S. (2012). *Destination marketing: An integrated marketing communication approach.* Burlington, MA: Butterworth-Heinemann.

Prebensen, N.K. (2007). Exploring tourists' image of a distant destination. *Tourism Management, 28*(3), 747–754.

Pride, R. (2004). A challenger brand: Wales, golf as it should be. In N. Morgan, A. Pritchard, & Pride, R. (Eds.), *Destination branding.* 2nd ed., Burlington, MA: Elsevier Butterworth-Heinemann.

Qu, H., Kim, L., & Im, H. (2011). A model of destination branding: Integrating the concepts of the branding and destination image. *Tourism Management, 32*, 465–476.

Ritche, B.J., & Crouch, G.I. (2000) The competitive destination-a sustainable perspective. *Tourism Management, 21*, 1–7.

Sheehan, L., & Ritchie, J. (2005). Destination stakeholders: Exploring identity and salience. *Annals of Tourism Research, 32*(3), 711–734.

Sheehan, L., Ritchie, J., & Hudson, S. (2007). The destination promotion triad: Understanding the asymmetric stakeholder interdependencies between the city, the hotels and the DMO. *Journal of Travel Research, 46*(1), 64–74.

Tasci, A., & Kozak, M. (2006). Destination brands vs destination image: Do we know what we mean?, *Journal of Vacation Marketing, 12*(4), 299–317.

Vallaster, C., & de Chernatony, L. (2006). Internal brand building and structuration: The role of leadership. *European Journal of Marketing, 40*(7/8), 761–84.

Vargo, S.L., & Lusch, R.F. (2004). Evolving to a new dominant logic for marketing. *Journal of Marketing, 68*(1), 1–17.

Wagner, O., & Peters, M. (2009). Can association methods reveal the effects of internal branding on tourism destination stakeholders?, *Journal of Place Management and Development, 2*(1), 2009, 52–69.

# 8 Rebranding components towards developing a tourism destination

*Nurliana Jafar*

## Introduction

Destination branding plays a crucial role in bringing together various existing specializations that destinations can offer in terms of brand management strategy and policy development, in particular with a view to creating a new building, bringing together visionary strategies with hands-on implementation. It helps in developing a new image that is more interesting and attractive, making it a very important phenomenon which involves criteria of products, branding and services. It has been the basis for survival of a destination in a competitive global market by providing the means for it to create a unique identity in order to uncover niche opportunities and distinguish itself from its competitors (Morgan, Pritchard & Piggott, 2002). It is because higher tourist expenditure arises from a stronger feeling of attachment to a destination as well as preference for various kinds of high-quality products (Alegre & Juaneda, 2006).

Thus, the objective of this chapter is to identify the relationships between branding strategy components from various elements and their implications for tourism destination development. A descriptive research design using a quantitative approach was employed in this study. A cross-sectional study was also conducted. In this case, it is important to review how various key elements of tourism are currently viewed, potential improvements and how stakeholders' involvement will affect tourism destination development in Negeri Sembilan, Malaysia.

## Literature review

A more comprehensive definition of rebranding can simply be an effort to give a unique identity image to a particular product or service in order to add value to the existing brand and which may reflect a tourist's perception about the products or services. While De Chernatory, Christodoules and Roper (2008) identified that brand image improvement is a vital factor that may encourage firms to undergo rebranding, Miller and Muir (2005) added two motivating factors: that it can be either as a result of a change of organizational direction or due to an image crisis.

On the other hand, the ability of visitors to make sense of all the information collected will affect their decision process in choosing a particular destination

(Kotler & Gertner, 2004). This process becomes much easier when destinations focus on their own unique set of functional and tangible components (Woodside & Dubelaar, 2002). This statement is strengthened by Hankinson (2005) who comments that a stronger connection with the overall standard of quality and hence destination competitiveness is gained through functional attributes. In addition, a study conducted by Mowle and Merilees (2005) found that symbolic properties, rather than the functional qualities, are what the consumer prefers and what gives added value to a destination, as well as creating a greater sustainable competitive advantage.

However, customers who enjoy variety or a mix of elements with both functional and symbolic components will have an even higher level of satisfaction. It is a key driver for the decision-making process, and even if they do not revisit, there will be a higher possibility that they will try to recommend the destination to others (Castro, Armario & Ruiz, 2007). A recommendation can also play a role as a core for brand loyalty which in turn leads to higher destination performance (Reichheld, 2003). This is because the quality (Atilgan, Akinci & Aksoy, 2003), value (Sanchez, Callarisa, Rodriguez & Moliner, 2006), low risk (Aqueveque, 2006) and perceived attractiveness (Um, Chon & Ro, 2006) of a holiday destination can attract repeat visitors, leading to increased employment opportunities as well as modern infrastructure (Darnell & Johnson, 2001).

However, according to Hatch and Schultz (2003), a corporate brand needs to deal with the requirements of multiple stakeholders, especially in developing a successful brand. The importance of stakeholder involvement is to invest in the destination's physical environment, such as buildings, infrastructure (Hankinson, 2009) and the overall tourism product. Pike (2005), in a study on tourism destination branding complexity, argues that there is a fine balance to be struck between community consensus and brand theory because a top-down approach to destination brand implementation is likely to fail without buy-in from these stakeholders. The emphasis, therefore, should be on formulating the destination vision through a publicly driven process based on stakeholder values and consensus, rather than through a more private expert-driven process based solely on market forces (Morgan, Pritchard & Piggott, 2003). Based on the literature the study framework of this research is shown in Figure 8.1.

As shown in the study framework, this study aims to determine the components that best describe destination branding strategies associated with tourism development around Negeri Sembilan from both functional and symbolic perspectives. Thus, this study will place a major focus on three main objectives:

- to identify the functional attributes that best describe rebranding components in a tourism destination;
- to examine the key symbolic attributes that best describe rebranding components in tourism destination;
- to identify the relationship between rebranding components (functional elements and symbolic elements) and its implication towards tourism destination development.

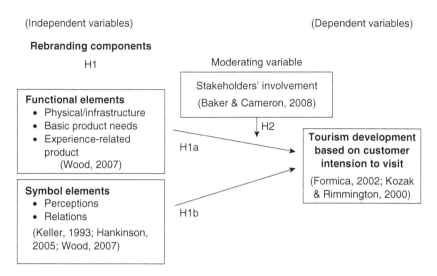

*Figure 8.1* Study framework.

In order to support the objectives of this study, the following research questions are posed:

- What are the functional attributes that best describe rebranding components in a tourism destination?
- What are the key symbolic attributes that best describe rebranding components in a tourism destination?
- What is the relationship between rebranding components (functional elements and symbolic elements) and its implications for tourism destination development?
- How does stakeholders' involvement affect rebranding components in developing a tourism destination?

## Methodology

A descriptive research design using a quantitative approach was considered as the most relevant to be employed. A cross-sectional study was also conducted. Thus, information requirements were obtained through self-reported and self-administered questionnaires conducted with tourists in Port Dickson, Pelenggong Homestay and Seri Menanti Royal Museum during four-week periods in September and October 2014. Every local visitor who stopped at the three selected tourism spots was approached to participate in answering the questionnaire in which a random starting number for each day was created. In order to interview respondents, a self-administered questionnaire was used, comprising five sections. Apart from demographic details as the first part (Part A) of the questionnaire, it also included other sections (Parts B and C) relating to the components of destination branding inclusive of both functional and symbolic elements which are important to customers in decidiing upon a destination from their wish list. This includes all the elements such as the issues and importance of basic physical infrastructure, basic product needs, experiences (related to product) and relationships, as well as the visitor's perception. Part D of the questionnaire related to the stakeholder involvement and its importance in rebranding and developing a tourism destination. Finally, Part E focused on overall rebranding components and their implications for tourism destination development. Approximately 600 domestic tourists were approached during this period; about 300 of them agreed to answer the questionnaires, but only 269 completed questionnaires were returned and collected due to time constraints. The data was then keyed for analysis using the Statistical Package for the Social Sciences (SPSS). By using a five-point Likert scale, factors important to the tourists were short-listed, identified and further analysed. Descriptives like standard deviation, mean and inferential statistics were employed whenever appropriate with the research objectives and questions of the study.

## Findings

The results of this study contain the analysis of the data obtained from the questionnaire. The data analysis was conducted under four research themes, as follows.

### Responses for functional branding components: basic physical infrastructure, basic product needs and experiences (related to product)

The magnitude of the mean scores ranges from 3.84 to 4.30, which indicates that the majority of the local tourists agreed with most of the items in this section of the analysis. As such, the majority of the tourists agree that experiences related to product are the most important in the functional rebranding components, compared with others. Out of these three components, it was found that the basic physical infrastructure was the least important functional rebranding component in developing a tourism destination.

### Responses for symbolic rebranding components: perceptions and relationships

The magnitude of the mean scores ranges from 4.2 to 4.0, which indicates that the majority of the local tourists agreed with most of the items in this section of the analysis. As such, the majority of the tourists agree that perception of the tourism destination is the most important in the symbolic rebranding components, compared with relationships.

### Responses for stakeholder involvement in accelerating tourism destinations

Results of multiple regressions of stakeholder involvement moderates the relationship between rebranding components and tourism destination (see Table 8.1)

*Table 8.1.* Multiple regressions of stakeholder involvement

| Predictors | Model 1 Std. $\beta$ | Model 2 Std. $\beta$ |
|---|---|---|
| Step 1: Model variables | 0.42*** | |
| Rebranding components | | |
| Step 2: Moderating variables | | 0.48*** |
| Stakeholder involvement | | |
| $R^2$ | 0.32 | 0.53 |
| Adj.$R^2$ | 0.31 | 0.52 |
| $R^2$ change | 0.32 | 0.21 |
| $F$-change | 123.868*** | 118.831*** |

Note: *p < 0.05, **p < 0.01, ***p < 0.001.

able to explain the 32 per cent ($R^2 = 0.32$, $F$-change $= 123.868$, $p < 0.001$) variation on the tourism development. The value of $\beta = 0.42$, $p < 0.001$ demonstrated that rebranding components have a significant impact on the tourism development among the local tourists. In the second step of hierarchical multiple regression, the stakeholder involvement as moderator was entered as another independent variable to influence the dependent variable. The stakeholder involvement is able to explain the additional 21 per cent ($R^2$ change $= 0.21$) as a moderator for rebranding components that influence the tourism development. The beta value ($\beta = 0.48$, $p < 0.001$) of stakeholder involvement moderate relationship between rebranding components and tourism development ($\beta = 0.42$, $p < 0.0001$).

### Responses for overall tourist intention to visit a particular place

To be precise, to evaluate the how well the rebranding components influence the tourism development. The independent variable (rebranding components) was entered into the equation at once against the dependent which is the tourism development. Results of multiple regressions of the rebranding components and tourism destination development (see Table 8.2) shows that the rebranding components (functional and symbolic) were able to clarify 32 per cent ($R^2 = 0.32$, $F$-change $= 123.868$, $p < 0.001$) of the variance in the tourism development. The outcomes demonstrated that the rebranding components significantly contributed to the prediction of its tourism development dimension. In determining the contribution of independent variable, it is essential to use the beta ($\beta$) values, ignoring any negative signs (Pallant, 2005). As the rebranding components significantly and positively influence tourism development ($\beta = 0.56$, $p < 0.001$), it can be said that the assumption about the influence of rebranding components on its tourism development is apparent.

*Table 8.2.* Multiple regressions of rebranding components and destination development

| Predictors | Model 1 Std. β |
| --- | --- |
| Step 1: Model variables | 0.56*** |
| Rebranding components | |
| $R^2$ | 0.32 |
| Adj. $R^2$ | 0.31 |
| $R^2$ change | 0.32 |
| $F$-change | 123.868*** |

Note: *$p < 0.05$, **$p < 0.01$, ***$p < 0.001$.

## Conclusion

There is no doubt that rebranding both functional and symbolic components is important in developing tourism destination in Negeri Sembilan. Rebranding of functional components in destination development is a growing concern as most destination branding attempts to remain competitive in the tourism market. This means the destination needs to portray positive images in the mind of tourists especially their domestic visitors. The perception of local tourists can be a benchmark that defines the level of destination attractiveness. If it is perceived as unattractive by the locals, this means that the destination is not competitive enough to attract international tourists. To be competitive, brands must be able to consider and adapt to tourists' changing needs and trends to do way better than only static brands (Jacobson & Mizik, 2008). Destination marketing organizations (DMOs) must communicate to customers that each place has its own unique value. From this study, Negeri Sembilan should be portrayed as a destination that offers a lot of tourism experiences such as sport and adventure activities, entertainment and recreational services, as well as its delicious local foods, since these components were found to be the most favorable by the local tourists. Low frequency of repeat visitation among tourists also indicated that tourists are still not aware of the tourism products in Negeri Sembilan, although this destination has a lot of potential to be one of the top destinations in Malaysia.

It is not an easy task to promote a destination; it takes a lot of preparation and cooperation from various bodies as well as agencies such as travel agencies, tour operators, government authorities and many others. High involvement from various stakeholders plays a vital role in enhancing tourism development. It is a prerequisite for DMOs to focus not only on the experience with one particular product or service at the destination, but also on the visitor experience as a whole. Similarly, the brand offers should not only be unique, but must also be valuable to visitors as consumers.

Usakli and Seyhmus (2011) explain that DMOs should put into effect programmes that highlight a destination's unique personality. However, one common mistake to avoid is combining too many features simultaneously in a promotional campaign. The existence of various elements being marketed may weakening the maximum degree of execution of the brand's core identity (Qu, Kim & Im, 2011). Only one or two important attributes should be concentrated on for rebrand positioning. The first step to be undertaken is to conduct market research frequently in order to create a unique and effective destination brand. This is because it is essential to explore and identify what visitors already know about the place. Only then can an effective mix of brand elements be chosen to promote a positive image (Prebensen, 2007).

In addition, DMOs should make effort to obtain hard visitor data such as the number of first-time visitors and repeat visitors because according to Gartner (2011), in his research, each group evaluates the place brand somewhat differently. With the information on repeat visitor versus first-time visitation rates, DMOs could fine-tune their rebranding approach accordingly to focus on reaching a specific group.

Collaboration from different organizations and stakeholder groups is also important as the next key step in creating a successful and unified destination brand. Proper involvement and relationships among these stakeholder groups will result in better understanding of the value each contributes to the brand, in order to achieve a consensus on a brand strategy (Prebensen, 2007). Along with the visitors, local residents and business suppliers or owners are also main players of the core brand (Gilmore, 2002). A brand must able to capture the spirit of its people. Thus, it is important to keep these stakeholders' values in mind; in particular, locals should never be ignored, as they symbolize the brand.

On the other hand, supportive attitudes and mutual agreement from other individual tourism suppliers (tourism attractions, accommodation, etc.) also play vital roles in rebranding a particular destination (Prebensen, 2007). Often, individual attractions or tourist spots do not have the resources to generate strong promotional campaigns (Morgan et al., 2002). It is a beneficial practice to be employed in order to create a 'critical mass' through pooling of resources that would be strong enough for a visitor to associate with a brand name. To ensure the success of the brand, Prebensen (2007) also emphasized the need of coming up with a unified agenda and goals that are measurable and actionable so that these make it more likely that the brand will actually be monitored and implemented successfully.

As a conclusion, the above highlighted issues could be resolved with the research conducted and agreement achieved between stakeholder groups to implement a destination branding strategy. However, they should first observe customer trends and visitors' changing needs frequently to remain competitive in the market. As different destinations have their own unique value, DMOs should identify the best attributes that may define their place branding strategies. García, Mar and Arturo (2012) strengthened the idea by suggesting that DMOs should develop a two-stage branding strategy, first, concentrating on the stakeholders associated with the place and second, focusing on visitors. The reason is that no one else will be attracted to it if there is no support and buy-in to the brand from locals (García et al., 2012; Lodge, 2002; Morgan et al., 2002).

As mentioned previously, this stakeholder group is the image of the brand with which visitors actually interact. It is important to taken into account that the brand

and destination image chosen for a country has to symbolize the people if it is to be believable. Locals can damage the brand if they are depressed or disillusioned with their own country's attractions, so it is important also to appeal positively to them to encourage a sense of pride about where they come from. In fact, the first stage is a necessary condition for the second.

## References

Alegre, J., & Juaneda, C. (2006). Destination loyalty: Consumers' economic behavior. *Annals of Tourism Research*, 33(3), 684–706.

Aqueveque, C. (2006). Extrinsic cues and perceived risk: The influence of consumption satisfaction. *Journal of Consumer Marketing*, 23 (5), 237–247.

Atilgan, E., Akinci, S., & Aksoy, S. (2003). Mapping service quality in the tourism industry. *Managing Service Quality*, 13 (5), 412–422.

Baker, M.J., & Cameron, E. (2008). Critical success factors in destination marketing. *Tourism and Hospitality Research*, 8(2), 79–97.

Castro, C.B., Armario, E.M., & Ruiz, D.M. (2007). The influence of market heterogeneity on the relationship between destination image and tourists' future behaviour. *Tourism Management*, 28 (1), 175–187.

Darnell, A., & Johnson, P. (2001). Repeat visits to attractions: A preliminary economic analysis. *Tourism Management*, 22 (2), 119–125.

De Chernatory, L., Christodoules, G., & Roper, S. (2008). Brand management. *European Journal of Marketing*, 42, 5–6.

Formica, S. (2002). Measuring destination attractiveness: A proposed framework. *Journal of American Academy of Business,* 1 (2), 350–355.

García, J. A., Mar, G. & Arturo, M. (2012). A destination-branding model: An empirical analysis based on stakeholders. *Tourism Management*, 33, 646–661.

Gartner, William C. (2011). Tourism destination brand equity dimensions: Renewal versus repeat market. *Journal of Travel Research*, 50 (5), 471–481.

Gilmore, F. (2002). A country – can it be repositioned? Spain – the success story of country branding. *Brand Management,* 9, 281–293.

Hankinson, G. (2005). Destination brand image: A business tourism perspective. *Journal of Services Marketing*, 19 (1), 24–33.

Hankinson, G. (2009). Managing destination brands: Establishing a theoretical foundation. *Journal of Marketing Management*, 25(2), 97–115.

Hatch, M.J., & Schultz, M. (2003). Bringing the corporation into corporate branding. *European Journal of Marketing*, 37(8), 1041–1064.

Jacobson, R. & Mizik, N., (2008). The financial value impact of perceptual brand attributes. *Journal of Marketing Research*, 45, 15–32.

Keller, K. (1993). Conceptualizing, measuring and managing customer-based brand equity. *Journal of Marketing*, 57 (3), 1–22.

Kotler, P., & Gertner, D. (2004). Country as a brand product and beyond. In N. Morgan (ed.), *Creating the unique destination proposition* (pp. 40–56). Oxford: Butterworth Heinemann.

Kozak, M., & Rimmington, M. (2000). Tourist satisfaction as an offseason holiday destination. *Journal of Travel Research*, 38 (2), 260–269.

Lodge, C. (2002). Success and failure: The brand stories of two countries. *Brand Management*, 9, 372–384.

Miller, J., & Muir, D. (2005). *Business of brands.* New York: John Wiley.

Morgan, N., Pritchard, A., & Piggott, R. (2002). The creation of a powerful niche destination brand. *Brand Management,* 9 (4), 335–354.

Morgan, N. J., Pritchard, A., & Piggott, R. (2003). Destination branding and the role of stakeholders: The case of New Zealand. *Journal of Vacation Marketing,* 9(3), 285–299.

Mowle, J., & Merrilees, B. (2005). A functional and symbolic perspective to branding Australian SME wineries. *Journal of Product & Brand Management,* 14 (4), 220–227.

Pallant, J. (Ed.). (2005). *SPSS survival manual: A step by step guide to data analysis using SPSS for windows (Version 12).* Maidenhead: Open University Press.

Pike, S. (2005). Tourism destination branding complexity. *Journal of Product & Brand Management,* 14 (4), 258–259.

Prebensen, N. K. (2007). Exploring tourists' images of a distant destination. *Tourism Management,* 28, 747–756.

Qu, H., Kim, L.H., & Im, H.H. (2011). A model of destination branding: Integrating the concepts of the branding and destination image. *Tourism Management,* 32, 465–476.

Reichheld, F.F. (2003). The one number you need to grow (Review of the book *Providing branding elements*) by Girch, S. *Harvard Business Review,* 81, 46–54.

Sanchez, J., Callarisa, L., Rodriguez, R., & Moliner, M. (2006). Perceived value of the purchase of a tourism product. *Tourism Management,* 27 (3), 394–409.

Um, S., Chon, K., & Ro, Y. (2006). Antecedents of revisit intention. *Annals of Tourism Research,* 33 (4), 1141–1158.

Usakli, A., & Seyhmus, B. (2011). Brand personality of tourist destinations: An application of self-congruity theory. *Tourism Management,* 32, 114–127.

Wood, L. (2007). Functional and symbolic attributes of product selection. *British Food Journal,* 109 (2), 108–118.

Woodside, A.G., & Dubelaar, C. (2002). A general theory of tourism consumption systems: A conceptual framework and an empirical examination. *Journal of Travel Research,* 41 (2), 120–132.

# 9 Analysing destination readiness for branding

## A case study of Croatia

*Neda Telišman-Košuta and Neven Ivandić*

## Introduction

Reflecting broader trends, Croatia has over the past decade witnessed a steadily growing interest in destination branding both among the country's academic community and the destination marketing practitioners. This surge of interest is being driven by Croatia's dependence on tourism, the industry having generated 8.6 billion euros in tourism expenditure in 2013 (Croatian National Bank, 2014) and directly contributing 10.4 per cent of the GDP in 2011 (Ivandić, Marušić, Šutalo & Vuglar, 2014), while, at the same time, the country's persisting image as a 'sea, sun and summer only' destination limits its competitive edge in a hypercompetitive global tourism marketplace.

Although tourism in Croatia originated in the mid-1880s as a seaside, health-oriented winter pastime mostly for Austro-Hungarian nobility and wealthy entrepreneurs, the mid-1960s, with summer vacation travel having become a middle-class 'right' and the Adriatic coast being close, warm and affordable, namely for large West German and Austrian markets, ushered the transformation of Croatia into a mass tourism, coastal summer destination. This is how it essentially remains; despite its astonishing diversity of natural and cultural heritage as a country on the crossroads of Alpine, Pannonian, Balkan and Mediterranean Europe, tourism activity has always been concentrated along a narrow coastal sliver, from mid-June to mid-September. Remaining essentially unchanged over the years, the Adriatic coast attracted 96 per cent of total overnight stays registered in Croatia in 2013, with 90 per cent of those occurring during the summer months (Croatian Bureau of Statistics, 2014).

Aside from stretching the limits of coastal capacity during the summer, the existing concentration of tourism activity leaves the huge potential of the adjoining seasons and inland parts of Croatia untapped. Extending the tourism season and extending the spatial distribution of tourism activity has thus become a 'mantra' in strategic tourism development and marketing planning across the country. On the national level, both Croatia's recently adopted *Strategy of Tourism Development of Croatia up to 2020* (Ministry of Tourism of Republic of Croatia, 2013) and the new *Strategic Marketing Plan of Croatian Tourism* (Croatian National Tourist Board, 2014) emphasize seasonal and spatial distribution as their principal goals.

This is the context within which branding has come to be seen as a key strategy of change, bringing about change in image and change in visitation patterns.

Even though much of the recent destination development and marketing planning in Croatia deals with branding to some extent, often recommending further brand work, the implementation side of the process seems to be largely missing. At this point, destination branding in Croatia is for the most part strategy on paper. Attempting to detect factors which may be deterring brand implementation, this research effort focused on stakeholder understanding of destination brands and the branding process, as well as on their perception of barriers to destination branding in Croatia today.

## Literature review

Building on a significant body of literature exploring the correlation between destination image and likelihood of visitation and, further, drawing on the experiences testifying to the power of brands in increasing the values of goods and services, first academic papers, discussions and books on destination branding appeared in the late 1990s (Pike, 2005). The argument was that in a globalized world, with increasing competition among in many ways similar destinations and visitors often making their travel choices based on simplified perceptions of places, the brand, and no longer just the price or the product, is the key factor of destination success (Morgan, Pritchard & Pride, 2004). A number of influential authors in the field, including Anholt (2009), Olins (2004), Kotler and Gertner (2002), argued that, similar to branding of goods and services, tourism destinations can be branded to differentiate themselves by projecting memorable, powerful and convincing brand images. Anholt (2009) went further, stating that a destination's brand equity 'becomes an asset of enormous value – probably more valuable … than all its tangible assets, because it represents the ability of the place … to continue to trade at a healthy margin for as long as its brand image stays intact' (p. 8).

Destination branding very quickly developed into one of the hottest subjects in tourism marketing. It also continues to be a controversial one. Reacting to the ensuing view, all too often held by destination marketing organizations (DMOs) and especially by the political establishment, of branding as a 'quick fix' for destination ambiguity or even anonymity, pioneering authors on the subject were quick to point out that branding is not something that can be 'done to' or invented about a destination and that images, being constructs created from information gathered from numerous sources, cannot be influenced through marketing communication such as advertising or public relations alone (Anholt, 2009). Thus Olins (2007) writes of the need for destinations to discover the 'truth' about themselves and communicate it through everything they do, while Anholt (2007) introduces the notion of 'competitive identity' meaning a joint, coordinated effort by diverse stakeholders to transmit a destination's fundamental and permanent values. Buncle (2009) describes a destination brand as 'the DNA that defines the destination' (p. 31) and, while a destination can present itself in a different light, adapting the message to different market segments, this underlying, core characteristic is always the same. In their view, branding must be based on the reality of a place which is relevant for potential visitors and concisely communicated to them in, what can be expected to be, a long-term process of image building.

Discerning a destination's true identity, relevant to both hosts and guests, is undoubtedly a difficult task. The delivery of that core brand concept by all the different destination stakeholders in a coordinated manner over the longer term is, however, the real challenge. As Buncle (2009) notes, 'living the brand' through marketing communication, through the products and services being delivered or through contacts with the local population, not to mention delivery in the Web 2.0 environment, so that a visitor's experience matches the brand's promise, is the most critical element of destination branding. Acknowledging these difficulties, and without disputing the importance of image to destination competitiveness, there is growing questioning of the feasibility of branding in a destination context.

Several problem areas, or at least areas requiring further research, have been identified. First of all, there is the issue of limitations of reduction or, in other words, the question of whether something as complex as a destination can be reduced to a clear, simple core? While traditional product or service brands have clear cores, the essence of a destination is seldom so clear since these are socie-ties possessing layers of history and constantly changing (Morgan, Pritchard & Pride, 2004). Pike (2008) furthermore voices concern about the possibilities of destinations to generate effective brand positioning strategies in markets as het-erogeneous as those encompassed by tourism. Second, what are the stakeholder dynamics in defining the core and in delivering the destination brand among a group as diverse as large public sector institutions and a myriad of entrepreneurs, and does the local community even participate? Can DMOs be a cohesive force when they have limited control over the marketing mix and are, thus, likely to equate branding with promotion (Nicholaisen & Blichfeldt, 2012)? Finally, further research is needed in the area of measuring brand equity as related to (re)shaping destination image or generating customer loyalty (Pike, 2008). Ultimately, the question arises of whether branding is too complex a task in a tourism destination context (Blichfeldt, 2005; Nicholaisen & Blichfeldt, 2012).

## Methodology

The undertaking of this study on Croatian stakeholder understanding of desti-nation branding was envisioned as exploratory work intended to guide future research into challenges of brand implementation in a tourism destination context. The study scope was limited to a group of 20 regional (county) and local (town or municipality) tourist board directors from diverse parts of Croatia selected on the basis of their experience with the national tourist board system, as well as their experience in destinations branding. Data was collected through structured, 'one-on-one' interviews lasting between 30 and 60 minutes. The interviews were conducted in the course of May 2014.

Three main research topics were addressed, namely:

1 understanding of scope and value of destination branding, with subtopics probing the respondents' understanding of branding as a promotional versus a destination management tool, as well as their opinions on current practice regarding destination branding in Croatia;
2 understanding of the destination branding process, which also entailed a discussion on the extent of exploratory research being conducted in preparation of destination branding, the extent and the quality of destination stakeholder participation in the process and the allocation of responsibility for brand delivery;
3 barriers to destination branding, particularly focusing on differing interests among the complex structure of destination stakeholders.

The interviews were taped and the information gathered in the interviews was analysed using content analysis tools.

## Findings

The Croatian tourist board system, spanning national, regional (county) and local (town or municipality) levels, has thus far functioned in the capacity of DMOs, while the intention of pending new regulation is to increase the system's involvement in destination management, transforming it, in fact, into a destination marketing and management entity. Even though the extent of the system's management function is still undefined and it remains to be seen as to what duties and responsibilities it can take over from other destination stakeholders, the tourist boards, particularly at the local level, remain one of the 'few points of unity' representing a destination's interest. As such, they could evolve into brand leaders and their understanding of destination branding is crucial. The results of a brief exploratory research study carried out among 20 regional and local tourist board directors provide interesting insights into the state of destination branding awareness in Croatia.

### *Understanding the scope and value of destination branding*

A destination brand is seen by the interviewed tourist board members to be some distinguishing feature which is key to generating the destination's market visibility and recognizability. However, their beliefs or opinions on what actually constitutes a destination brand differ. Most respondents consider it a unique physical feature, such as a beach or a monument, allowing the destination to be branded as the place with '*the* beach', '*the* church', '*the* aquarium', etc. A fewer number of respondents see the brand as something intangible, such as 'a promise' or 'a story', at the same time considering this very difficult to find. Some believe that destination branding is ensuring quality products and services, while some expressed the opinion that destinations can have more than one brand, although in such cases it is important that they are of the same quality.

There are outright sceptics among the respondents regarding the effects of desti-nation branding, albeit with different degrees of suspicion. A few voiced their opinion that destination branding is simply a 'trendy' thing to be doing at this time and that it is ... *just a fancy new name for something we have been doing all along and which encompasses finding and asserting a destination's most valuable asset.* It is seen as 'a fashion' started by consulting, advertising and promotion agencies. Finally, issues were raised as to whether it is branding that makes places recognizable or whether they gained their reputations and came to be widely known by some other 'natural' process which had nothing to do with a branding strategy. This sentiment is echoed in the question ... *did Paris naturally evolve into a brand or was it branding strategy?*

Current destination branding practice in Croatia is regarded as being exclusively promotional in nature. Branding ... *is equated with destination logos, slogans and promotional materials* ... even though it is clear that these elements alone cannot create awareness of a destination. At the same time, tourism promotion is the only aspect of destination branding which is dealt with consistently.

### Understanding the destination branding process

The destination branding process is understood to encompass steps such as the identification of a destination's distinguishing features, research into guest per-ceptions, brand delivery backed up by a clear allocation of responsibility for implementation and the creation of brand hierarchies. Although there is a general understanding of the process itself, a certain degree of defensiveness as to the tourist boards' own role in it should be noted.

Namely, the tourist boards do not see themselves as being the ones in position to play the leading role in the destination branding process. Thus, for example, the respondents perceive existing guests as arbiters determining the differentiating features of the destination since ... *we ourselves are very critical and cannot agree on what about us is most important.* The local government is believed to have the responsibility and ... *must take the lead* ... in destination branding since the tourist boards ... *cannot be responsible for branding as they do not have the finances, the manpower, nor the knowledge to do so.* Similarly, brand delivery is outside the boards' realm as they do not own or manage the facilities and services offered to visitors and thus ... *do not have any real influence over the visitor experiences that make up the brand.* Doubt is also expressed as to the possibility of ... *every little town being branded* ..., followed by the opinion that ... *the National Tourist Board is not doing a good job in creating a strong national and regional brands* ... which smaller destinations could become a part of.

### Barriers to destination branding in Croatia

The multiple barriers to destination branding being perceived by tourist board directors interviewed for this study fall into two main groups of related issues. Uppermost is the lack of 'destination thinking'. The respondents feel that what is being proclaimed publicly is contrary to the actual thinking in which ... *everyone is pushing their own interests.* In addition, they note the lack of a longer time perspective as a critical issue. Thus, the political elite are seen as ... *having only an election-to-election, four year horizon* ... during which they are interested mainly ... *in pushing their party's political agenda and in keeping the opposition at bay or discredited.* The private sector is ... *short tempered ... and does not understand long processes.* The resulting lack of unity, continuity and perseverance are counterproductive to any attempts of destination branding, but are ... *symptomatic of Croatia and both very difficult and slow to change.*

At the same time, there is no clear leader of the branding process. Seeing destinations as complex, multi-layered systems, the respondents do not presently recognize a natural brand leader within this structure. In their view, the tourist boards are in charge of promoting destinations, companies are focused on their business results and, in fact, only the ... *local government could have the legitimacy for a process as all-encompassing as branding.* Yet, local governments are seen to be all too often basically incapable of sustaining a longer-term and broad-based effort such as branding due to their short-term and partisan political agendas.

## Conclusion

This research study attempted to ascertain the understanding of and views on destination branding within the Croatian tourist board system which, due to its destination marketing and management functions, is key to the implementation of destination branding in practice. While destination branding is generally understood by the interviewed respondents from selected regional and local tourist boards included in the study both in terms of scope and process and is seen as a modern and useful tool in differentiating destinations, thus being a key factor of their competitiveness, the thinking is also characterized by a certain lack of conviction.

Reaffirming some of the issues raised in the literature, the respondents emphasized limitations to destination branding stemming from the lack of 'destination thinking' due to divergent stakeholder interests, lack of brand-directed leadership within destinations and the incapability of tourist boards to act as destination branding champions and managers due to insufficient finances, manpower, knowledge and authority. Whether because of the above issues or even disbelieving the power of the brand in the destination context all together, branding seems to be seen in Croatia more as a promotional tool rather than a strategic one.

Destination branding is undoubtedly a challenging process for all destination stakeholders. Due to the inherent complexity of tourism destinations, it is a process which relies on consensus building and for which new management procedures and skills need to be developed focusing particularly on the competencies and responsibilities of tourist boards or destination marketing and management organizations. Increasing their capabilities is an area requiring further research and development.

## References

Anholt, S. (2007). *Competitive identity: The new brand management for nations, cities and regions.* New York: Palgrave Macmillan.
Anholt, S. (2009). Introductory essay: Why national image matters. In ETC & UNWTO *Handbook on tourism destination branding* (pp. 8–17). Madrid: UNWTO.

Blichfeldt, B.S. (2005) Unmanageable place brands. *Place Branding*, 1(4), 388–401.

Buncle, T. (2009). Introduction. In ETC & UNWTO *Handbook on tourism destination branding* (pp. 23–30). Madrid: UNWTO.

Croatian Bureau of Statistics (2014). *Statistical databases–Tourism 2013*. Zagreb. Retrieved from http://www.dzs.hr/default_e.htm

Croatian National Bank. (2014). *Annual report 2013*. Zagreb. Retrieved from http://www.hnb.hr/publikac/godisnje/2013/e-god-2013.pdf

Croatian National Tourist Board. (2014). *Strategic marketing plan of Croatian tourism 2014–2020*. Zagreb. Retrieved from http://www.mint.hr/UserDocsImages/SMPHT-2014–2020-Sazetak.pdf

Ivandić, N., Marušić, Z., Šutalo, I., & Vuglar, J. (2014). *Tourism satellite account of Croatia for 2011 and calculation of indirect and total contribution of tourism to Croatian economy*. Zagreb: Ministry of Tourism of Republic of Croatia and Institute for Tourism.

Kotler, P., & Gertner, D. (2002). Country as brand, product and beyond: A place marketing and brand management perspective. *Brand Management*, 9(4–5), 249–261.

Ministry of Tourism of Republic of Croatia (2013). *Strategy of tourism development of Croatia up to 2020*. Zagreb. Retrieved from http://www.mint.hr/UserDocsImages/130426–Strategija-turizam-2020.pdf

Morgan, N., Pritchard, A., & Pride, R. (2004). *Destination branding: Creating the unique destination proposition*. Oxford: Elsevier Butterworth-Heinemann.

Nicholaisen, J., & Blichfeldt, B.S. (2012). Destination branding: Mission impossible? TRU Progress Working paper no. 9. Aalborg University Denmark. Retrieved from http://vbn.aau.dk/files/68473670/TRUprogress_9.pdf

Olins, W. (2004). Branding the nation: The historical context. In Morgan, N., Pritchard, A. & Pride, R. (Eds.) *Destination branding: Creating the unique destination proposition*. (pp. 18–25).

Olins, W. (2007). *On br@nd*. London: Thames and Hudson.

Pike, S. (2005). Tourism destination branding complexity. *Journal of Branding and Brand Management*, 14(4), 258–259.

Pike, S. (2008). *Destination marketing: An integrated marketing communication approach*. Oxford: Elsevier Butterworth-Heinemann.

# Part III

# Supporting elements of destinations

# 10 Exploring film-induced tourism

## Implications for on-site heritage interpretation

*Justyna Bąkiewicz, Anna Leask, Paul Barron and Tijana Rakić*

## Introduction

While the phenomenon of film-induced tourism has been explored for over three decades by different authors, and from many different perspectives (e.g. see Beeton, 2005, 2010; Busby & Klug, 2001; Buchmann, Moore & Fisher, 2010; Connell, 2005, 2012; Connell & Meyer, 2009; Croy & Buchmann, 2009; Hudson & Ritchie, 2006; Kim, 2012; Macionis, 2004; Macionis & Sparks, 2009; Riley, Baker & Van Doren, 1998; Rittichainuwat & Rattanaphinanchai, 2015; Su, Huang, Brodowsky & Kim, 2011; Tooke & Baker, 1998), these studies have paid limited attention to the impact of film-induced tourism on visitors' prior expectations and preferences for heritage interpretation at heritage sites. Previous studies that have examined visitors' interactions or experiences with heritage interpretation were conducted either at National Parks in New Zealand (e.g. see Carr, 2004; Stewart, Hayward, Devlin & Kirby, 1998) or at sacred and dark tourism sites (Biran, Poria & Oren, 2011; Poria, Biran & Reichel, 2009) and have overlooked the influence of film-induced tourism on heritage interpretation. This being the case, this chapter focuses on visitors' prior expectations of engagement with various heritage interpretation methods at Alnwick Castle, a heritage site that has been used as a backdrop for a number of films and is closely associated with the Harry Potter film series.

## Literature review

Images and representations of places in various films have an important position in constructing and forming tourism spaces, raising awareness and making them emblematic attractions (Kim & O'Connor, 2011). Therefore, travelling to locations featured in films has become a global phenomenon, creating a tourism niche known as film-induced tourism (Beeton, 2005; Macionis & Sparks, 2009). Film-induced tourism has become visible at various heritage sites in the UK, such as Rosslyn Chapel in Scotland, Alnwick Castle in Northumberland, the Old Royal Naval College in London and the eighteenth-century Antony House in Cornwall, making the past and heritage omnipresent and widely accessible for people's consumption (Butler, 2011; Ozdemir & Adan, 2015).

Film-induced tourism, which can be seen as a sub-category of pop culture tourism (Gyimóthy, Lundberg, Lindström, Lexhagen & Larson, forthcoming in 2015;

Larson, Lundberg & Lexhagen, 2013), is essentially a form of cultural and heritage tourism (Hoppen, Brown & Fyall, 2014; Martin-Jones, 2014; Rewtrakunphaiboon, 2009). It is a phenomenon which has been explored since the early 1990s, with the early scholarly debates focusing on economic aspects and visitor numbers (Riley & Van Doren, 1992; Tooke & Baker, 1996; Riley et al., 1998). In recent years, the focus has shifted to further exploration of the intricacies of visitors' expectations, experiences, interactions with and constructions of places, drawing on a variety of disciplines and fields of study beyond tourism, such as sociology, anthropology, human and cultural geography, media and film, as well as language studies (e.g. see Carl, Kindon & Smith, 2007; Couldry & McCarthy, 2004; Hao & Ryan, 2013; Karpovich, 2010; Kim, 2010; Martin-Jones, 2014; Mazerska & Walton, 2006). In her overview of film-induced tourism literature from a cross-disciplinary perspective, Connell (2012), among others, also argues that visitors' expectations, interactions and experiences of locations featured in films is an area which has still not been widely explored.

Expectations are an integral part of tourism as they motivate travel and economic practices, movement and performance in a space, as well as social and cultural changes (Gnoth, 1997; Skinner & Theodossopoulos, 2011). The representation of a specific location or place through the visual lens of film creates perceptions that influence an individual's understanding of that place, which further informs their expectations and imaginings of what can be experienced at the place during a visit (Beeton, 2005; Connell, 2012; Kim, 2012; Ward & O'Regan, 2009). In other words, and as Hughes (1995, p. 791) suggests, films have an influence on their interaction with tourism through 'encoding within tourism, a range of partialities and expectations' which, according to Urry (2002, p. 151), when expressed, contribute to the cultural construction of place where place acquires a 'mediated nature'. This mediatisation of place may change people's view of particular locations, destinations or heritage sites, consequently influencing the expectations that shape touristic practices (Jansson, 2006). Indeed, visitors to film-induced visitor attractions carry with them a multitude of expectations, many of which are influenced by their prior exposure to images from the film associated with the attraction (Buchmann et al., 2010; Carl et al., 2007; Connell & Meyer, 2009).

Consequently, it has been argued that films simulate representations of places to such an extent that the audience may identify destinations and sites with the film's director or plot rather than with the historical importance of the place (Mazierska & Walton, 2006; Ward & O'Regan, 2009). As a result, visitors are very likely to perceive places as they remember them from the media exposure (Beeton, 2005). A significant outcome of this influence is that people who visit places that they have seen and remember from films may still refer to the film's stories in describing their visit to the location (Månsson, 2011). In addition, Urry (2002) and Beeton (2005) both argue that places featured in a film which are consequently visited do not usually live up to tourists' expectations. This demonstrates that a strong perception of a location gained from media exposure may create unrealistic visitor expectations to such an extent that tourists may feel disappointed when the site does not live up to those expectations (Beeton, 2005; Ward & O'Regan, 2009).

Representation of heritage sites in media such as films may, therefore, be problematic for heritage interpretation, which may not necessarily relate to the cinematic representation, and could thus provide an unappealing experience (Puczko, 2006; Dueholm & Smed, 2014) and cause visitors disappointment (Kim, 2012).

Heritage interpretation plays a crucial role in developing and managing heritage visitor attractions (Howard, 2003; Hughes, Bond & Ballantyne, 2013; Veverka, 2013) and is an integral part of the visitor experience (Calver & Page, 2013; Moscardo & Ballantyne, 2008; Weiler & Walker, 2014). Studying visitors' engagement with, and preference for, heritage interpretation is of crucial significance in the context of understanding visitors' expected experiences (Poria, 2010). It is also an essential element in the management of heritage sites (Hughes et al., 2013).

Visitors to heritage sites actively participate in shaping the experiential product by using their preconceptions, prior expectations and familiarity with history (Moscardo, Ballantyne, & Hughes, 2007). Through their engagement with various interpretative media and activities available at the site, they re-conceptualise their experiences (Chronis, 2008) and co-create new more personal ones (Binkhorst & Den Dekker, 2009). In this regard, visitors' personal thoughts, perspectives, emotions, imaginations and reactions are a critical concern for the heritage management of on-site interpretation as they are deemed to be a significant factor in achieving a symbiotic and sustainable relationship between visitors and heritage site resources (Chan, 2009).

Interestingly, Hughes et al. (2013) revealed that the majority of visitors to built heritage sites were 'experience seekers', who visited because the site was famous and thus considered it as an important destination to visit, so by visitors having 'been there and done that' had already contributed to a satisfying experience. This demonstrates that visitors to heritage sites are not necessarily looking for firm historical proof, thus an interest in history might not be the primary reason for their visit (Poria, 2010; Schouten, 1995). Visitors may instead be seeking a new symbolic experience of the site's features and its past (Sheng & Chen, 2012). Some visitors may desire to experience the social and industrial aspects of the site's history, whereas others visit to relax and enjoy a day out (Beeho & Prentice, 1997; Sheng & Chen, 2012). This indicates that visitors to heritage sites may, therefore, be engaging with interpretation that is not necessarily related to history or antiquity, but rather to emotion or imaginary.

Heritage managers, thus, increasingly need to recognise the additional needs of visitors and provide diverse interpretational perspectives as visitors seek different meanings and experiences at the same heritage sites (Biran et al., 2011; Chronis, 2008; Ung & Vong, 2010). As a result, managers of heritage sites should take into account visitors' motivations, perceptions and expectations before deciding on the implementation of interpretative programmes and thus enrich the visitor experiences and enhance the likelihood of a satisfying visit. So there is a need for the focus of heritage interpretation to emphasise the need for 'mass customisation' of visitors' experiences of heritage sites, rather than providing solely 'monolithic experiences' (Poria et al., 2009, p. 1).

## Methodology

This chapter draws on the findings from the primary research conducted at Alnwick Castle heritage visitor attraction – which has featured in many different films and television series – focusing particularly on its relationship with the Harry Potter films. Alnwick Castle, often referred to as the Windsor of the North, is the second largest inhabited castle in England and is located in a small town close to the North Sea in Northumberland. The lead author spent three weeks at the site in the summer of 2013 and relied on semi-structured interviews with managers, visitors and guides to collect data.

This data was further enriched through sessions of textually and visually recorded observation, focusing on the documentation of the various heritage interpretation methods at Alnwick Castle, as well as on the visitors and their participation and engagement with the different heritage interpretation propositions available at the site. Altogether, four interviews with managers, three with guides and thirty short interviews with both domestic and international visitors were conducted at Alnwick Castle. This allowed a better understanding of visitors' experiences with heritage interpretation from multiple perspectives.

## Findings

Many different parts of Alnwick Castle were filmed and featured in the first two Harry Potter films. The castle was one of several locations which served as Hogwarts, the School of Witchcraft and Wizardry. In fact, Hogwarts is an amalgam of an excellent studio set against the backdrop of the Scottish Highlands, with interiors comprising Durham Cathedral, Lacock Abbey and no less than three Oxford locations, in addition to CGI enhancements combined with special effects.

The findings obtained from the fieldwork revealed that the Harry Potter films played a significant role in the creation of visitors' expectations of what could be seen or experienced at Alnwick Castle. While some of these expectations were revealed through the interviews with managers and guides, sessions of observations and interviews with visitors also revealed this correlation. Indeed, when visitors were asked about their expectations during interviews, many of them regularly mentioned Harry Potter images from the films. For example, Benjamin and his son Ezra from Israel were among the visitors influenced by the Harry Potter films. The following excerpt illustrates some of the common visitors' views on that particular aspect.

BENJAMIN [*mid-forties, from Israel*]: actually there are some scenes from the movie that I expect to see still inside […] Hopefully we will get to see some of the rooms, some of the settings for the movie but it is also the beauty of the castle regardless of the movie.
EZRA [*early twenties, from Israel*]:  In the movie you don't get to see that much of the outside of the castle there is more inside.

BENJAMIN: I think some of the movies were actually not filmed here, they were filmed in other places. Before the kids walk inside they can't know which part of the movie was filmed here.

EZRA: I think when we go inside it will be easier to recognise it.

This particular issue was confirmed by the interviewed managers, who stated that some visitors believe that they will see the interior of Hogwarts inside Alnwick Castle. As the marketing manager commented:

> If is not explained to people that the castle was only used for exterior filming, people may come in to the castle and expect it. I have heard a visitor saying I came in and expected to see Great Hall from Hogwarts and of course that wasn't here that was in a studio. So I think some people when they go inside are surprised that it doesn't look like Hogwarts on the inside but it's difficult to manage those expectations.
>
> (Marketing Manager, August, 2013)

Therefore, Alnwick Castle's representation in the Harry Potter films had a significant influence on the visitors' expectations in relation to what they would see at the castle during their actual visit. This reveals an issue highlighted in the literature by Beeton (2005) and later by Kim (2012), that cinematic representation of a place may create new, or even unrealistic, expectations.

Another interesting finding that was revealed during this research was that due to the dramatic increase in the numbers of new, and sometimes difficult to please, visitors, the castle had to adapt itself to new needs and expectations, which were partially derived from the Harry Potter images seen on screen as well as those used in different marketing campaigns that advertised Alnwick Castle as Hogwarts. Aware of the success of Harry Potter and the power of film in creating strong perceptions and expectations, the managers at Alnwick Castle decided to develop new, Harry-Potter-informed, heritage interpretation, demonstrating a move away from the existing interpretation which is exclusively rooted in the history of the place (see Table 10.1).

When discussing visitors' preferences for heritage interpretation available on-site, it has become apparent that the majority of the interviewed visitors expected to see interpretation based on content from the Harry Potter films. Interestingly, a majority of those visitors not only expected or preferred interpretation inspired by the Harry Potter films, but also commented on the fact that they were satisfied with the Harry-Potter-inspired interpretation methods and found that these did not detract from the castle's historical significance. While Alnwick Castle served solely as a backdrop for the first two Harry Potter films, the findings of this study revealed that it still created strong emotional feelings in the minds of the potential visitors. This emotional engagement was particularly visible in the visitors' preferences for heritage interpretation.

All three interviewed guides confirmed that some visitors actually preferred to engage with Harry-Potter-inspired interpretative media. The guides stated that

*Table 10.1* Heritage interpretation at Alnwick Castle

| History-and-architecture-informed interpretation | Harry-Potter-informed interpretation |
| --- | --- |
| Visitor proclamation | Battleaxe to Broomstick Tour |
| Information boards | Harry-Potter-inspired characters |
| What's On Today information boards | Broomstick Training |
| Information boards with a historical timeline | Dragon Quest |
| Historical guided tours in the state rooms | Harry-Potter-related products |
| and the grounds | Harry-Potter-based brochure |
| Fusiliers' Museum | Knight's Quest |
| Percy Tenantry Museum | The Lost Cellars performances |
| Castle Museum | Harry-Potter-related products |
| Battle of Flodden Exhibition | |
| Harry Hotspur Exhibition | |
| Coach house | |
| First Duchess Collection | |
| Historical books and guidebooks | |

even visitors who joined the historical guided tours (tours based specifically and exclusively on the castle's history) were still interested in the Harry Potter connection, despite the availability of many different Harry-Potter-inspired interpretations, including a regular Harry-Potter-specific tour. Indeed, as indicated by the guides, visitors who joined historical tours more often expected to hear about Harry Potter than Harry Hotspur (an important character from the castle's history) or other historical aspects of the castle. For example, when asked if visitors still wanted to hear about Harry Potter during the historical tour, despite having other activities related to Harry Potter available to them, the guides, Ela and David, commented:

> Yeah, all the time, I would say probably every time there is someone who asks about Harry Potter. That's good for me because I love Harry Potter so I know everything about it.
>
> (Ela, historical guide at Alnwick Castle, August, 2013)

> Sometimes they go all the way around and then they ask when you are going to tell us about Harry Potter [...] If people are interested or ask about it obviously, I will tell them but it doesn't tend to be part of the historical tour.
>
> (David, historical guide at Alnwick Castle, August, 2013)

This engagement with, and preference for, Harry-Potter-inspired interpretation was also evident during observation of visitors' explorations of the gift shop. Many visitors were particularly interested in the Harry Potter products and a number of them bought Harry Potter souvenirs in the castle shop, despite the fact that the same products could be found at a better price online or elsewhere. What is more, some visitors took their engagement with Harry Potter further by wearing the masks of Harry Potter characters during their exploration of the site (see Figure 10.1).

*Figure 10.1* Visitors wearing Harry Potter masks bought in the gift shop. (Photos by J. Bąkiewicz.)

For many interviewed visitors, Harry-Potter-inspired interpretation played an important role in constructing their experience, so they were very likely to favour these interpretative methods over traditional methods based on historical fact. Paul and his wife Ute were among the visitors who expressed a preference for experiencing Alnwick Castle in the context of its association with Harry Potter rather than purely as a medieval castle:

UTE [*mid-forties, from Germany*]: We were deciding whether to come here today or yesterday but we found out from the leaflet that you have different topics and yesterday was medieval and today is Harry Potter so that's why we came today.

PAUL: We have a lot of medieval things in our area so we come from Magdeburg and its medieval town.

This conversation reveals that Paul and Ute were not interested in visiting just another medieval castle, as they had seen many of them in their home country. Paul and Ute were looking for something different; therefore, they decided to visit after discovering the castle's connection with Harry Potter. What is more, Paul and Ute wanted to make sure that they would be able to experience the Harry Potter associations, so they chose to visit on a day they knew there would be something related on offer. In this particular case, Harry Potter triggered a desire to visit Alnwick Castle to experience something that differed from their past experiences; they expected an association with Harry Potter films in their engagement with the site and the interpretation provided.

Emma and Anna were other visitors who expressed a preference for the stories from Harry Potter rather than stories from the castle's history, additionally suggesting that there was not enough of the Harry Potter magical world for them to experience:

JUSTYNA: Did you expect to see any exhibits, activities which would present association with the film?
ANNA [*early twenties, from Consett, England*]: Actually I thought it would be more.
EMMA [*early twenties, from Consett, England*]: Yeah, I thought it would be more.
JUSTYNA: So you would like to see more?
EMMA: Yeah, maybe the bit about the films and where they were shot.
ANNA: Yeah and maybe like they've got the museum there [*talking about one of the three museums which are on-site*] they could have a little bit with pictures and stuff that would have been good, like where scenes were shot so you can go and have a picture taken in the right place.
EMMA: Yeah, it would be nice.

Emma and Anna also felt that the site could make even more of the association with Harry Potter and develop more Harry-Potter-inspired interpretation. Emma and Anna were visitors for whom the presence of interpretation based on the magical world of Harry Potter played an important role in their experience of the site. What is more, both of them had a good idea of what else they had expected to see and experience through engagement with different interpretative media. They wanted to know exactly where all the Harry Potter scenes were filmed at the site – so a sign, information board or poster at the actual location of filming would have helped them take a picture at the 'right place'. The new narratives created by the Harry Potter stories influenced and shaped visitors' practices at the site, in particular the way visitors engaged with the site and the different interpretation methods. This means that pre-visit influences shaped their engagement with the heritage interpretation available at the site (Hughes et al., 2013).

As demonstrated, some visitors were keen to engage with the new narratives when visiting the site as a result of its exposure in the Harry Potter films. Through their engagement with interpretation, visitors at Alnwick Castle were provided with a variety of narratives based primarily on entertainment and the Harry Potter films. Accordingly, visitors to Alnwick Castle were looking for something different from that experienced visiting similar heritage sites: something whimsical, carefree, and that provided an opportunity to play in a safe environment. In many cases, the castle was not perceived by visitors as something monumental or as an important heritage site, but rather as an imaginary playground where the interpretative media based on Harry Potter created a form of theatre in which they could actively participate.

## Conclusion

This chapter has provided a greater insight into visitors' prior expectations and their influence on the multidimensional nature of their engagement with the various heritage interpretation methods available at Alnwick Castle. It has demonstrated how visitors' preferences amongst different types of interpretation were mediatised by the Harry Potter films. In addition, this chapter has also explored the potential changes that may occur at a heritage site involved in film-induced tourism. This exploration provided a greater understanding of the site's exposure in the Harry Potter films in terms of its impact on visitor expectations in relation to heritage interpretation, as well as the consequent application of Harry-Potter-informed interpretation.

These findings have important implications for heritage site management, namely, if managers focus predominantly on the education, conservation and preservation of the site – omitting the site's contemporary dimensions – the clash between the site and visitors' expectations may affect visitors' experience of the site. On the other hand, a reliance solely on the more imaginative narratives may overshadow the historical importance of the site, causing dissatisfaction among more traditional visitors interested in the historical aspects of the site. In the context of Alnwick Castle, the balance can be achieved through the application of, and an emphasis on, heritage interpretation methods based solely on historical aspects of the castle, in addition to Harry-Potter-informed interpretation. This chapter, thus, argues that heritage interpretation should be considered as a valuable management tool for developing and managing film-induced tourism heritage attractions.

## References

Beeho, A. J., & Prentice, R. C. (1997). Conceptualizing the experiences of heritage tourists. A case study of New Lanark World Heritage Village. *Tourism Management, 18*(2), 75–88.

Beeton, S. (2005). *Film-induced tourism.* Clevedon, UK: Buffalo, NY: Channel View Publications.

Beeton, S. (2010). The advance of film tourism. *Tourism and Hospitality Planning & Development, 7*(1), 1–6.

Binkhorst, E., & Den Dekker, T. (2009). Agenda for co-creation tourism experience research. *Journal of Hospitality Marketing & Management, 18*(2–3), 2–3.

Biran, A., Poria, Y., & Oren, G. (2011). Sought experiences at (dark) heritage sites. *Annals of Tourism Research, 38*(3), 820–841.

Buchmann, A., Moore, K., & Fisher, D. (2010). Experiencing film tourism – Authenticity & fellowship. *Annals of Tourism Research, 37*(1), 229–248.

Busby, G., & Klug, J. (2001). Movie-induced tourism: The challenge of measurement and other issues. *Journal of Vacation Marketing, 7*(4), 316–332.

Butler, R. (2011). It's only make believe: the implications of fictional and authentic locations in films. *Worldwide Hospitality and Tourism Themes, 3*(2), 91–101.

Calver, S. J., & Page, S. J. (2013). Enlightened hedonism: Exploring the relationship of service value, visitor knowledge and interest, to visitor enjoyment at heritage attractions. *Tourism Management, 39*(3), 23–36.

Carl, D., Kindon, S., & Smith, K. (2007). Tourists' experiences of film locations: New Zealand as 'Middle-Earth'. *Tourism Geographies, 9*(1), 49–63.

Carr, A. (2004). Mountain places, cultural spaces: The interpretation of culturally significant landscapes. *Journal of Sustainable Tourism, 12*(5), 432–459.

Chan, K. L. (2009). The consumption of museum service experiences: benefits and value of museum experiences. *Journal of Hospitality Marketing and Management, 19*, 173–196.

Chronis, A. (2008). Co-constructing the narrative experience: staging and consuming the American Civil War at Gettysburg. *Journal of Marketing Management, 24*(1), 5–27.

Connell, J. (2005). Toddlers, tourism and Tobermory: Destination marketing issues and television-induced tourism. *Tourism Management, 26*(5), 763.

Connell, J. (2012). Film tourism – Evolution, progress and prospects. *Tourism Management, 33*(5), 1007–1029.

Connell, J., & Meyer, D. (2009). Balamory revisited: An evaluation of the screen tourism destination-tourist nexus. *Tourism Management, 30*(2), 194–207.

Couldry, N., & McCarthy, A. (2004). Orientations: Mapping MediaSpace. In N. Couldry & A. McCarthy (Eds.), *Mediaspace. place, scale and culture in a media age* (pp. 1–18). London: Routledge.

Croy, W. G., & Buchmann, A. (2009). Film-induced tourism in the high country: Recreation and tourism contest. *Tourism Review International, 13*(2), 147–155.

Dueholm, J., & Smed, K. M. (2014). Heritage authenticities – A case study of authenticity perceptions at a Danish heritage site. *Journal of Heritage Tourism, 9*(4), 285–298.

Gnoth, J. (1997). Tourism motivation and expectation formation. *Annals of Tourism Research, 24*(2), 283–304.

Gyimóthy, S., Lundberg, C., Lindström, K. N., Lexhagen, M., & Larson, M. (forthcoming in 2015). Popculture tourism research manifesto. In D. Chambers & T. Rakić (Eds.), *Tourism Research Frontiers*: Elsevier.

Hao, X., & Ryan, C. (2013). Interpretation, film language and tourist destinations: A case study of Hibiscus Town, China. *Annals of Tourism Research, 42*(2), 334–358.

Hoppen, A., Brown, L., & Fyall, A. (2014). Literary tourism: Opportunities and challenges for the marketing and branding of destinations? *Journal of Destination Marketing & Management, 3*, 1, 37–47.

Howard, P. (2003). *Heritage: Management, interpretation, identity*. London; New York: Continuum.

Hudson, S., & Ritchie, J. R. B. (2006). Film tourism and destination marketing: The case of Captain Corelli's Mandolin. *Journal of Vacation Marketing, 12*(3), 256–268.

Hughes, G. (1995). Authenticity in tourism. *Annals of Tourism Research, 22*(4), 781–803.

Hughes, K., Bond, N., & Ballantyne, R. (2013). Designing and managing interpretive experiences at religious sites: Visitors' perceptions of Canterbury Cathedral. *Tourism Management, 36*, 210–220.

Jansson, A. (2006). *Specialized spaces: Touristic communication in the age of hyper-space-biased media*. Århus: Center for Kulturforskning, Aarhus University.

Karpovich, A. I. (2010). Theoretical approaches to film-motivated tourism. *Tourism and Hospitality, Planning and Development, 7*(1), 7–20.

Kim, S. (2010). Extraordinary experience: Re-enacting and photographing at screen tourism locations. *Tourism and Hospitality, Planning and Development, 7*(1), 59–75.

Kim, S. (2012). Audience involvement and film tourism experiences: Emotional places, emotional experiences. *Tourism Management, 33*(2), 387–396.

Kim, S., & O'Connor, N. (2011). A cross-cultural study of screen-tourists' profiles. *Worldwide Hospitality and Tourism Themes, 3*(2), 141–158.

Larson, M., Lundberg, C., & Lexhagen, M. (2013). Thirsting for vampire tourism: Developing pop culture destinations. *Journal of Destination Marketing & Management, 2*(2), 74–84.

Macionis, N. (2004). Understanding the film-induced tourist. In W. Frost, G. Croy, & S. Beeton (Eds.), *International Tourism and Media Conference Proceedings, 24–26* November. Melbourne: Tourism Research Unit, Monash University. 86–97.

Macionis, N., & Sparks, B. (2009). Film-induced tourism: An incidental experience. *Tourism Review International, 13*(2), 93–102.

Månsson, M. (2011). Mediatized tourism. *Annals of Tourism Research, 38*(4), 1634–1652.

Martin-Jones, D. (2014). Film tourism as heritage tourism: Scotland, diaspora and The Da Vinci Code(2006). *New Review of Film and Television Studies, 12 (*2), 156–177.

Mazierska, E., & Walton, J. (2006). Tourism and the moving image. *Tourist Studies, 6*(1), 5–11.

Moscardo, G., & Ballantyne, R. (2008). Interpretation and attractions. In A. Leask, B. Garrod, S. Wanhill, & A. Fyall (Eds.), *Managing visitor attractions: New directions*. Elsevier Science & Technology.

Moscardo, G., Ballantyne, R., & Hughes, K. (2007). *Designing interpretive signs: Principles in practice*. Golden, Colo.: Fulcrum Pub.

Ozdemir, G., & Adan, O. (2014). Film tourism Triangulation of destinations. *Procedia–Social and Behavioral Sciences Procedia–Social and Behavioral Sciences, 148*(3), 625–633.

Poria, Y. (2010). The story behind the picture: Preferences for the visual display at heritage sites. In E. Waterton & S. Watson (Eds.), *Culture, heritage and representation: Perspectives on visuality and the past* (pp. 217–228). Ashgate Publishing.

Poria, Y., Biran, A., & Reichel, A. (2009). Visitors' preferences for interpretation at heritage sites. *Journal of Travel Research, 48*(1), 92–105.

Puczko, L. (2006). Interpretation in cultural tourism. In M. Smith & M. Robinson (Eds.), *Cultural tourism in a changing world : politics, participation and (re)presentation* (pp. 239–256). Clevedon, UK; Buffalo, NY: Channel View Publications.

Rewtrakunphaiboon, W. (2009). Film-induced tourism: Inventing a vacation to a location *Academic Review*, 1–10.

Riley, R. W., & Van Doren, C. S. (1992). Movies as tourism promotion: A 'pull' factor in a 'push' location. *Tourism Management, 13*(3), 267–274.

Riley, R., Baker, D., & Van Doren, C. S. V. (1998). Movie induced tourism. *Annals of Tourism Research, 25*(4), 919–935.

Rittichainuwat, B., & Rattanaphinanchai, S. (2015). Applying a mixed method of quantitative and qualitative design in explaining the travel motivation of film tourists in visiting a film-shooting destination. *Tourism Management, 46*, 136–147.

Schouten, F. (1995). Improving visitor care in heritage attractions. *Tourism Management, 16*(4), 259.

Sheng, C. W., & Chen, M. C. (2012). A study of experience expectations of museum visitors. *Tourism Management, 33*(1), 53–60.

Skinner, J., & Theodossopoulos, D. (2011). *Great expectations: Imagination and anticipation in tourism*. New York: Berghahn Books.

Stewart, E., Hayward, B. M., Devlin, P. J., & Kirby, V. G. (1998). The "place" of interpretation: A new approach to the evaluation of interpretation. *Tourism Management., 19*(3), 257.

Su, H. J., Huang, Y. A., Brodowsky, G., & Kim, H. J. (2011). The impact of product placement on TV-induced tourism: Korean TV dramas and Taiwanese viewers. *Tourism Management, 32*(4), 805–814.

Tooke, N., & Baker, M. (1996). Seeing is believing: The effect of film on visitor numbers to screened locations. *Tourism Management, 17*(2), 87–94.

Ung, A., & Vong, T. N. (2010). Tourist experience of heritage tourism in Macau SAR, China. *Journal of Heritage Tourism, 5*(2), 157–168.

Urry, J. (2002). *The tourist gaze*. London: Thousand Oaks, California: Sage.

Veverka, J. (2013). Interpretation as a management tool. [online] available at:http://www. heritageinterp.com/interp_.htm [accessed: 02.04.2013].

Ward, S., & O'Regan, T. (2009). The film producer as the long-stay business tourist: Rethinking film and tourism from a Gold Coast perspective. *Tourism Geographies, 11*(2), 214–232.

Weiler, B., & Walker, K. (2014). Enhancing the visitor experience: Reconceptualising the tour guide's communicative role. *Journal of Hospitality and Tourism Management, 21*, 90–99.

# 11   *Ançã* stone in the building of a tourist destination

*Rita Gomes and Vivina Carreira*

## Introduction

The theoretical framework that permeates the present study draws on two fundamental ideas. One is that the transversal nature of tourism promotes contiguity between localities and municipalities, that urban central places, urban peripheries and rural areas function more as a system together than independently (Fernandes, 2008, p. 73) and that breaking geographical barriers and imagined boundaries and stigmas of concentration of goods and services promotes territorial sustainability. The other concerns the concept of geo-tourism considered in its broadest sense, that is, comprehending tangible and intangible cultural heritage of the areas concerned and, as a knowledge-based concept, integrating the tourism industry with conservation and education through interpretation of geological natural resources.

This chapter aims at demonstrating the ways in which a geological resource, *Ançã* stone, a limestone common to the counties of Coimbra and Cantanhede, in central Portugal, can, as a key element in the implementation of a tourist route, both enhance the role of Coimbra as an anchor-city for the development of eco-tourism in the peripheral, more rural region while boosting tourism in Coimbra itself by offering tourists one more reason to stay in the city for a longer period of time. Since geo-tourism aims to highlight not only the geological aspects of the destination, but also its landscape, culture, values, heritage and the well-being of populations, this tourism product benefits destinations by allowing access to knowledge and interpretation of the characteristics and natural resources of localities, also promoting their natural, cultural and human integrity.

*Ançã* stone was once a very important regional resource and one of the reasons for the establishment of the first peoples in the lands around these regions. There is evidence of its extensive use over the centuries, from the Middle Paleolithic to the Roman period, with a particularly strong usage in sculpture in the sixteenth and seventeenth centuries, and in the nineteenth century architecture throughout the country and abroad. The activity still goes on in the region, represented by some small businesses that extract the stone mechanically and manually for various usages as in door and window lintels, stonemasonry, street paving, staircases, columns, handrails, sinks, sculptures, altars, cloisters, portals, pulpits, tombs, etc.

Quarries and the quarrying activity associated with them are not free of negative impacts on the various phases of its operation, including the 'state of abandonment' (Martins, 2005, p. 20).

One of the most visible environmental impacts of extractive activity is landscape change. The project presented here consists in creating a geo-tourism route using *Ançã* stone as a tourism resource with four objectives in mind: (1) to call attention to the stone itself and all the customs and traditions associated with it; (2) to attract more tourists to the peripheral region and encourage them to stay longer in Coimbra; (3) to provide tourists with knowledge about geology and the use of the stone over the centuries; and (4) to call their attention to issues related to environmental impacts of stone extraction such as landscape change and how to avoid or remedy them.

## Literature review

The very definition of tourism includes its 'spatial dimension' related to the movement of people and the physical transformations of territories resulting from these movements (Vieira, 2007, pp. 16–22), giving rise to a complex web of interdependencies and linkages. This webbing should be analysed as a whole, so as to have a view of all the components and their relationships (Cunha & Abrantes, 2013, p. 96). The emergence of this phenomenon in Portugal without any basic planning for its development and too focused on the exploration of resources linked to the sun and sea, allowed the spatial distribution, both in terms of supply and demand, to be characterized today by profound asymmetries and spatial inequalities that lead not only to negative impacts, but also reduce the competitiveness of the territory. This fact becomes even more worrying if one thinks of the opposite capacity that tourism has on mitigating regional disparities within a country (Cabugueira, 2005, pp. 97–104).

Being an enhancer of relations, tourism establishes connections with not only all human activities as well as with the physical environment itself, since it is a spatial sector, which depends strongly on the physical environment and geographic phenomena. Approaching tourism as a system means that it comprises 'subsystems' as the tourist and the tourist object in interaction with the 'economic, social, political, legal, technological, and ecological systems' (Cunha & Abrantes, 2013). The systemic model of tourism entails a complexity of relationships and dependencies sometimes difficult to define. It is a network of multidisciplinary connections, where tourism is just another industry, but one that has the ability to influence all others and vice versa.

Within the scope of a tendency that reflects a growing concern about the environmental changes caused by various factors, alternative tourism arises, first, by the very 'way the traveller behaves and relates to the natural, social and cultural environment' (Brito, 2000, p. 5). Also according to Lockwood & Medlik (2001), the consumers of the future not only will want to deepen their personal knowledge but will also become more demanding, hence we can say that in the future, consumers will be the centre of the new market. This type of tourist privileges the individual and authentic, local production and direct contact with the communities and their traditions.

Alternative tourism is then associated with a multitude of tourist practices such as nature tourism, adventure tourism, green tourism, ecotourism, rural tourism, white or snow tourism, blue or sea tourism (Brito, 2000, p. 5). As it acts more locally, this type of tourism can function as a facilitator for the development of depressed areas, since 'alternative, responsible and sustainable tourism practices establish the connection between development and the promotion of the place through the combination of the natural and the human factors' (Brito, 2000, p. 7). This 'responsible tourism' is understood as a promoter of sustainable economic growth by favouring the contact with the cultural and environmental characteristics of the places, and differentiating itself from traditional forms of tourism by presenting itself without a distinctly marked seasonality (Brito, 2000, p. 10).

Batouxas (2002, p. 2) states that the progress of environmental issues and tourism industry brought this sector close to conservation practices of nature, culture and heritage, giving rise to other forms of tourism that are characterized by the practice of activities in close contact with nature, respecting the natural heritage and cultural values of certain regions. Among the various forms that can be called alternative tourism, as already mentioned, ecotourism and geo-tourism are emphasized here by the importance they pose to the subject approached in this study.

Fennell (2008, p. 17), who states that it was Hetzer who presented the concept of ecotourism to explain the relationship between tourists, environments and cultures, identifies four key pillars for this type of responsible tourism: minimum environmental impact, minimum impact on – and maximum respect for – host cultures, maximum economic benefits to host communities and maximum recreational satisfaction to participating tourists. He also adds that Ceballos-Lascuráin was the first to use the term in the early 1980s, which he defined as a form of 'traveling to relatively undisturbed or uncontaminated natural areas with the specific objective of studying, admiring and enjoying the scenery and its wild plants and animals, as well as any existing cultural manifestations (both past and present) found in these areas' (quoted in Fennell, 2008, p. 17).

The International Ecotourism Society defines ecotourism as responsible travel to natural areas that conserves the environment and improves the well-being of local people.

The Quebec Declaration on Ecotourism recognizes that ecotourism comprehends the principles of sustainable tourism as far as economic, social and environmental impacts of tourism are concerned, but it also includes other specific principles which distinguish it from the wider concept of sustainable tourism, namely, the conservation of natural and cultural heritage; safeguarding the welfare of local and indigenous communities; and interpretation of natural and cultural heritage sites for visitors.

Landscape is the basis for tourism and this is even truer for ecotourism. Portugal is not rich in natural landscapes, because the territory was transformed by man but, on the other hand, it is rich in cultural landscapes that reveal the human interaction with the environment. Agricultural activities, customs and traditions, flora and fauna that resulted from that interaction and, as mentioned by Oliveira (2009, p. 49), the stories recorded in the stones are sets of attractions for ecotourists. Considered the basis of the landscape, geology is one of the most important factors in its interpretation because the geological substrate creates soils with particular characteristics, which give rise to particular communities as well (Vieira & Cunha, 2002).

Although a new tourism sector in Portugal, geo-tourism has long been a common practice among tourists and only very recently did it begin to be understood as a specific featured tourist offering with particular market requirements. According to Manrique (quoted in Rodrigues, 2009, p. 39) this tourist product 'is the convergence of ecotourism, experiential tourism and cultural tourism' that, while not overlapping nature tourism, instead adds to it specific concepts, such as geology, that make it possible to observe a landscape 'from the inside' (Barbosa, Ferreira & Barra, 1999, p. 24). It also presupposes a set of measures relating to conservation, aiming to not only protect, but also to determine the 'potential use' of geo-sites (Rodrigues, 2009, p. 38), as well as to provide the public with scientific knowledge of geology in order to achieve the goals inherent in geo-science and geo-conservation education and simultaneously promoting experiences that enrich the traditional 'tourism' (Rodrigues; Carvalho, 2010, p. 2).

Hose (1997) first defined geo-tourism as the provision of services and facilities that allow tourists to understand the geomorphology of a place beyond mere aesthetic appreciation. As such, geo-tourism aims to highlight not only the geological aspects of the destination, but also its landscape, culture and heritage and the well-being of populations. According to recent tourist trends in demand for new locations and products, it can be an asset to destinations, thus allowing access to knowledge and interpretation of the natural features and resources of places, promoting at the same time its natural, cultural and human integrity.

Buckley (2003) notes that definition of the term geo-tourism varies and its practice is combined with the principles of another tourist segment, ecotourism, where there is also a concern to value, understand and conserve the natural areas involved. As such, the geological processes of scientific interest must be interconnected with the scenic beauty and the geo-cultural aspects that prove the close relationship established between man and the geology of the region. A particularly strong example of this relationship of man with the geological substratum is the mining culture which leaves deep marks both on the landscape and on memory.

The distinct territorial physical features, be they climatic, geomorphological, hydrological or speleological, together with the biological diversity and the combination of various elements of the environment may contribute to or even determine the occurrence and distribution of certain species of wild fauna and flora (Manosso, 2009, p. 103). In addition to this important function of being part of natural ecosystems and supporting life, the diversity of physical environments, or geo-diversity, can also in some cases provide important records that help to witness the history of our planet Earth. Geo-sites are the main attraction of geo-tourism destinations, and the combining of visits to geological heritage with educational and pedagogical activities can help minimize the negative impacts of tourism activities in these spaces. The geo-products design inspired by geological features may not only contribute to educational activities, but may increase the income of the agents of local services such as catering, accommodation and crafts (Farsani, Coelho, Costa & Carvalho, 2012, pp. 45–47).

Inácio & Patuleia (2008, p. 95) state that geo-tourism is a tourism niche that 'seeks to enhance and complement the existing tourist products', giving the opportunity for tourists to take 'a fresh look at what surrounds us' in natural, rural and urban spaces, differentiating and valuing these spaces. The authors argue that geo-tourism can be practised in any of these areas, since geological heritage is not limited to natural spaces. 'It is cultural tourism' because it integrates both natural and cultural heritage, 'it can present itself either in a nature trail or in the interpretation of the stones that build a church or a village'.

The national territory of Portugal has regions with different levels of development, which leads to the existence of several centres and various peripheries. To be peripheral is associated with low-density economies and the endogenous potential development of a region, together with 'the cultural, psychological and physical distance from other central regions'. However, as Fernandes (2008, p. 73) refers, 'In the current context of planning development and land use, there is a perception that central urban areas, urban peripheries and rural areas work better together as a system than each *per se*'. This means that despite any imaginary boundaries between the rural and the urban, between the central place and the periphery, the numerous interconnections and interdependencies between these areas of mutual influence tend to an inevitable union in their various and different functions.

Post-Fordism led cities to acquire, in addition to the functions of economic value, sociocultural value functions aimed at residents and tourists. Until then, cities were only seen as generators of tourism demand, a consequence of adversity to urbanism, seen as synonymous with poor quality of life, as opposed to the desire to escape and contact with nature. Tourism emerged in cities as a process of reversing the decline into which many cities fell in the 1970s, now assuming a place of importance as tourist destinations (Henriques, 2003, pp. 36–39). The very inclusion of tourism in the economic agendas of municipalities demonstrates the recognition of the potential of this sector for the conversion of the image of cities. Old spaces and equipment are re-used, areas of old industries are transformed into recreational spots, hotels and shops, the heritage and historical areas are valorized for tourism. Henriques (2003, p. 43) refers to this phenomenon as 'touristification of the city'.

Urban tourism is a tourism segment with one of the highest reputations and the ability to move large global tourist flows, and is considered as an impeller of a potential inter-relational dynamics and complementarity with rural areas, particularly those located around urban tourism destinations, helping to reduce territorial inequalities. The new consumer perceives as the best tourist destination one that provides a concentrated product and service offering. Thus, a destination that offers in the same space or in adjacent spaces a wide range of attractions and facilities to visitors, increasing efficiency in terms of time, travel and costs will see its attractiveness also increased.

The current technological innovations and networks also favour contiguity between localities and municipalities, working towards the diversity of supply and differentiation, increasing the power of attractiveness on demand and strengthening cohesion with the establishment of production clusters that streamline the regional economy. Therefore, tourism can present itself as a sector capable of breaking geographical barriers and stigmas of concentration of goods and services, i.e., tourism can promote territorial sustainability, combining harmoniously the economic, environmental and social dimensions.

Coimbra, a town in central Portugal, is a consolidated destination for urban tourism, city breaks and cultural touring. However, tourists don't spend much time in the city, in spite of its good cultural assets, hospitality services and interesting night life. There is therefore an inconsistency regarding the city of Coimbra, and many others, caused by static organization of tourist paths. It is a kind of hierarchy of tourist places, which limits the enjoyment that tourists can have of a place which is organised to the style of the rushed tourist who spends only a few hours in the city rather than a few days.

As a tourist city, Coimbra is focused on the University, a symbol of its origins. More recently, the international recognition of the brand Coimbra through the Nomination to World Heritage of 'University of Coimbra, Alta and Sofia' could be used strategically not only to attract more tourists but to make them stay longer and enjoy other cultural and natural assets of tourist interest. The heterogeneous nature of the tourism product requires taking into consideration all resources of a region, not just those that are easily identified as such, since tourism demand is constantly changing and a tourist destination quickly loses appeal and is replaced by another, and so, from the standpoint of sustainable tourism of the city itself, 'the successive incorporation of new places, new elements, new attractions is a condition for success' (Gomes, 2011, p. 147).

Having the above in mind, it can be said that the tourism potential of Coimbra is underused and limited. As a destination, Coimbra can be better utilized and marketed, with potential to extend its influence over markets to neighbouring towns and cities. If urban tourism continues to expand and the highest rates of business growth are recorded in niche markets such as ecotourism and adventure tourism, a destination such as Coimbra, together with its peripheral region must reconcile the various types of tourism resources and turn them into an integrated, diverse and functional offering.

There is evidence of the extensive use of *Ançã* stone over the centuries, from the Middle Paleolithic to the Roman period. As to fossils in this area, the ammonites stand out for their good preservation state. Ammonites of the Boiça quarry, for example, about 174 million years old, are an important source of scientific information to the geology of the country (Oliveira, 2000). *Ançã* limestone was used in the construction of the Roman cities of Aeminium and Conímbriga (Bento & Ribeiro, 1990, p. 104). The abundance of limestone in Cantanhede led to the establishment of a School of Arts and sculpture workshops in Coimbra, and the creation of numerous works of art and the dissemination of a style known as 'The Coimbra Renaissance', mentored by great masters such as Jean de Rouen or

Nicholas Chanterenne. Some of our most famous monuments and sculptures used the limestone of these lands. The importance of this natural resource for the people is reflected in the very names of associations, places, streets and restaurants as in 'The Royal Quarry Alley', or 'The Quarry Restaurant'.

Inácio & Patuleia (2008, pp. 96–97) classify 'the ornamental stones used in construction properly classified and identified' as urban geological resources, which can be used to integrate itineraries involving different territorial levels 'ranging from a path in a city, village or a neighbourhood in urban centres to a whole region'. In this sense, geo-tourism should be understood not as an alternative tourism, but rather as a complementary tourist offering bringing together science and heritage and, thus, promoting the understanding of what makes us unique and different.

## Methodology

'The *Ançã* stone geo-tourism route: from the city to the periphery' is a route based on a building element used in many monuments of the city of Coimbra and is intended to make tourists leave the city towards the peripheral region where *Ançã* stone is quarried. A survey was conducted which consisted of direct contact with both the population and tourists visiting Coimbra and Cantanhede through semi-structured interviews intended to find out about the interest raised by such a tourist product.

Tourists visiting Coimbra were asked whether they had heard of *Ançã* stone, if they knew that it was a geological component used in most visited monuments and sculptures. They were also asked if they knew that the stone had its origins in a place very close to Coimbra and finally, if they would be interested in visiting the extraction site and participating in a geo-tourism experience consisting of walks on rural footpaths, visiting quarries and a sculpture atelier, sampling the local cuisine and having contact with some local traditions. Tourists visiting Cantanhede were asked whether they were interested in participating in an experience of urban tourism that included a visit to some of the most interesting monuments and sculptural pieces made with *Ançã* stone and also having the opportunity to participate in a different cultural urban experience.

Contact with key regional public and private tourism entities and municipalities was established, and museums and local accommodation representatives were also approached and interviewed in order to ascertain their willingness to be involved in the implementation and the promotion of the tourist route. Having the aforementioned contacts proved successful; 'The *Ançã* stone geo-tourism route: from the city to the periphery' began to be designed according to the regulations issued by the Portuguese entity responsible for the approval and registration of walking trails. A partnership was created with the Museum of Stone, which stood as the official promoting entity.

The route is based on a geological resource; however, it is intended to comprehend a number of other attractions, ranging from the local architecture, lifestyles and traditions, classified monuments, characteristic and observable flora and fauna as well as other geological elements. The walking trail was traced on a military map and all its characteristic features (typology, point of departure, point of arrival, distance, maximum and minimum altitude, duration, difficulty, etc.) were identified. All the elements of natural and cultural material and immaterial heritage that could be associated in some way and integrated into the route were identified. All sections of the paths that require intervention were also pinpointed as well as the places where signposts and information boards could be installed. A logo and a promotional brochure were also created. The promoting entity, the Museum of Stone, will disclose the route from its website, as well as with its partners. Schools, universities, tourist offices, shops and restaurants, local, regional and national media will also be privileged places to perform promotional actions. The complete file is ready to be submitted to the official entity for registration and approval.

## Findings

'The *Ançã* stone geo-tourism route: from the city to the periphery' seeks to call attention to and dignify a geological feature, *Ançã* stone, and all the other cultural, historical, artistic and ethnographic aspects associated with it. It also intends to highlight the importance of restoration of areas that have been degraded due to extractive activities. This route may serve as a catalyst element for all the activities and businesses involving *Ançã* stone. As it is recognized by the people and organizations involved, it is a starting point for the development of ecotourism and other synergies that bring social, environmental and economic gains as it can trigger other ideas and projects that may lead to the creation of new products and related settings, for example, gastronomy, wines, crafts, accommodation and other regional links will be generated.

The involvement of the population in this project is fundamental. It was intended that this involvement should occur from the earliest stages, in order to inform inhabitants about its benefits, avoid future constraints and facilitate the development of the idea of the common good and collaboration at different stages. This route is associated with the concept of geo-tourism, in its broadest sense as, in addition to the scientific and educational motivations, it also includes heritage resources. Geo-tourism is a growing tourism segment, which encompasses the concepts of sustainable tourism and ecotourism and articulates geological values with biodiversity, culture and landscape that are associated with them. Geological heritage as a tourist resource must be fostered in its educational, scientific and tourist aspects, highlighting their cultural and social links and functions.

## Conclusion

This chapter has aimed at greatly contributing to the articulation of the tourist offering of the two counties, Coimbra and Cantanhede, bringing benefits to both in a perspective of networking and integrated promotional strategies. The project includes the rehabilitation of degraded and abandoned spaces with cultural value.

In environmental and landscape terms the extraction of the stone leaves marks that make the locations less attractive. Ecotourism and geo-tourism may represent a viable alternative for the restoration and use of these spaces, making them more pleasant.

The inclusion of pedestrian paths on the itinerary aims to diversify the regional tourism offering as well as take advantage of the work undertaken by several entities, in particular the Museum of Stone, as well as encouraging the revitalization of the spaces which have intimately marked the lives of local people. The itinerary 'The *Ançã* stone geo-tourism route: from the city to the periphery', which is in the hands of the official entities responsible for its implementation is, therefore, a contribution to strengthening the viability of a region as a tourist destination through a geological and cultural resource that is also important to preserve and honour.

## References

Barbosa, B., Ferreira, N., & Barra, A. (1999). Importância da geologia na defesa do património geológico, no geoturismo e no ordenamento do território. *Geonovas: Revista da Associação Portuguesa de Geólogos, 13,* 22–33.

Batouxas, M. (2002). Turismo ambiente e desenvolvimento regional. *1.º Congresso de Estudos Rurais – Ambiente e usos do território.* Vila Real: Universidade de Trás-os-Montes e Alto Douro.

Bento, M. P., & Ribeiro, E. C. (1990). *Pedra de Ançã: o meio, o homem, a arte.* Coimbra: GAAC – Grupo de Arqueologia e Arte do Centro, pp. 103–105.

Brito, B. R. (2000). O turista e o viajante: contributors para a conceptualização do turismo alternative. *IV Congresso Português de Sociologia.* Coimbra: Universidade de Coimbra.

Buckley, R. (2003). Environmental inputs and outputs in ecotourism: geotourism with a positive triple bottom line? *Journal of Ecotourism,* 2(1), 76–82.

Cabugueira, A. (2005). A Importância económica do turismo. *Revista Turismo & Desenvolvimento,* 2(2), 97–104.

Cunha, L., & Abrantes, A. (2013). *Introdução ao turismo.* 5ª ed. Lisboa: Lidel.

Farsani, N., Coelho, C., Costa, C., & Carvalho, C. (2012). *Geoparks & geotourism: New approaches to sustainability for the 21st century.* Boca Raton, Florida: BrownWalker Press.

Fennell, D. (2008). *Ecotourism.* London/New York: Routledge.

Fernandes, J. L. S. (2008). *Requalificação da periferia urbana. Expansão urbana, forma urbana e sustentabilidade urbana na requalificação da periferia de Coimbra.* Lisboa: ISCTE.

Gomes, C. (2011). Imaginários turísticos e (in)visibilidades urbanas: Geografias do turismo na cidade de Coimbra. In N. Santos & L. Cunha (Eds.) *Trunfos de uma geografia activa: desenvolvimento local, ambiente, ordenamento e tecnologia* (pp. 141–148). Imprensa da Universidade de Coimbra.

Henriques, C. (2003). *Turismo cidade e cultura – planeamento e gestão sustentável.* Lisboa: Edições Sílabo.

Hose, T. A. (1997). Geotourism – selling the earth to Europe. In K. Marinos & T. Stournaras (Eds.), *Engineering geology and the environment* (pp. 2955–2960). Rotterdam: Balkema.

Inácio, A., & Patuleia, M. (2008). Geoturismo, uma forma de Interpretação do Espaço Turístico: do Natural ao Urbano. *Revista Turismo & Desenvolvimento,* 9, 91–102.

Lockwood, A., & Medlik, S. (Eds.) (2001). *Tourism and hospitality in the 21st century.* Oxford: Butterworth-Heinemann.

Manosso, F. (2009). Geodiversidade, geoturismo e património geológico: necessidade da geoconservação. *Revista Perspectiva Geográfica*, 5(1–2), 102–112.

Martins, R. C. (2005). *Pedreiras, degradação e recuperação da paisagem. Aplicação a uma pedreira no concelho de sintra*. Lisboa: Universidade Técnica de Lisboa.

Oliveira, N. (2009). *Ecoturismo e conservação da natureza*. Avintes: Parque Biológico de Gaia.

Oliveira, S. G. B. G. (2000). *O potencial didáctico e pedagógico de objectos geológicos com valor patrimonial – o bajociano de Ançã e do Cabo Mondego*. Coimbra: Universidade de Coimbra.

Rodrigues, J. (2009). Geoturismo um abordagem emergente. *Livro das XVIII Jornadas sobre a Função Social Museu*. Idanha-a-Nova: Câmara Municipal de Idanha a Nova.

Rodrigues, J., & Carvalho, C. N. (2010). Património geológico no Geopark Naturtejo: base para uma estratégia de geoturismo. *Revista Electrónica de Ciências da Terra*, 18(11), 1–4.

Vieira, J. M. (2007). *Planeamento e ordenamento territorial do turismo – uma perspectiva estratégica*. Lisboa: Editorial Verbo.

Vieira, A., & Cunha, L. (2002). A importância dos elementos geomorfológicos na valorização da paisagem: exemplos em morfologias cársica e granítica. *IX Colóquio Ibérico de Geografia*. Huelva.

# 12 Identifying research gaps in medical tourism

*Yin Teng Chew and Alan Darmasaputra Koeshendro*

## Introduction

Medical tourism (MT) has existed since at least the nineteenth century in the form of people travelling to places such as spas and springs for healing and relaxation purposes (Hunter, 2007). According to Connell (2006), MT refers to people travelling overseas for the enhancement or restoration of their health while simultaneously spending time for vacation in the destination. While the main purpose of travel is to seek medical services, Hall (2013) stated that there is an interest among people from developed countries to undertake medical travel in combination with visiting tourist attractions. This phenomenon creates a niche market for medical and tourism industries to offer a combination of services to medical tourists (Hunter, 2007).

Resulting from globalization in healthcare, MT, as one of the fastest growing industries, has become a rising global phenomenon in the twenty-first century (Connell, 2006; Heung, Kucukusta & Song, 2011).This boom can be attributed to the number of people travelling from developed countries to developing countries for better quality care at a lower cost (Connell, 2006; Garcia-Altes, 2005; Hunter, 2007).

This study is motivated by the need to fill the knowledge gaps in the literature on MT, given that the knowledge in this field is in its infancy. There are a handful of refereed articles that tend to predominantly provide a general understanding of the development of MT around the world (Bookman & Bookman, 2007; Connell, 2006). Past exploratory studies are also mainly policy-making papers that feature the global development of MT or advice on how MT should be developed. Moreover, MT studies often provide a general view of travel motivation with a lack of focus on specific market segments that are crucial for destination promotion. Therefore, the overall objective of this chapter is to identify research gaps in MT studies. The next section is a synthesis of literature to reveal research gaps in the MT literature.

## Literature review

One of the research gaps in medical tourism is the lack of understanding of its industry from across continents to specific countries. Each medical hub possesses unique attributes and different strengths including excellence in medical speciali-zation, pricing and legal system, and tourism attractions. However, the existing MT literature emerged to predominantly describe the development of MT in general that tends to assume successful medical hubs possess similar attributes (Connell, 2006; Garcia-Altes, 2005; Goodrich & Goodrich, 1987; Lunt & Carrera, 2010).

As pioneers in health tourism research, Goodrich and Goodrich (1987) attempt to understand this phenomenon based on content analysis of 284 brochures and 206 respondents. They found that generally, cost and variety of attractions tend to be the reasons for destination choice. Garcia-Altes (2005) generally describes the driving and impeding forces of health tourism and strategies.

Using supporting statistics, Connell (2006) discusses the rise of MT as a niche market in Asia and attributes internet marketing as one of the many driving forces of MT. Lunt and Carrera (2010) provide an interesting narrative of Europe in terms of the MT market (various kind of surgeries and treatments), consumer choices (familiarity, availability, cost, quality and bioethical legislation) and the lack of comparative data of foreign institutions.

Nevertheless, there are also a handful of studies that provide knowledge of specific countries that position themselves as MT hubs (Heung *et al.*, 2011; Lee, 2010; Wingkit & McKercher, 2013; Wong & Musa, 2013). A country-level analy-sis of Singapore by Lee (2010) examines the effect of governmental efforts in establishing the country as a desired medical destination. The findings reveal that Singaporean governmental efforts would have a positive effect on international tourism only in the long run.

Researchers have also studied the factors important for the development of MT in Hong Kong (Heung *et al.*, 2011). The study by Heung *et al.* (2011) reveals that policies and regulations, government support, cost and capacity to address local community's needs are the major challenges to the development of a medical hub in Hong Kong. The authors propose that stakeholders in the MT industry should cooperate to support its industrial development.

Wong and Musa (2013) describe the development of MT in a few countries, namely, Malaysia, Thailand, Singapore and India. The common motivation for inter-national medical tourists to consider Asian countries is the low cost of treatment, cheaper than in the United States by 6–33 per cent (Healy, 2009; Heung *et al.*, 2011), and favourable exchange rates (Connell, 2006). Governmental effort to promote MT in Malaysia started in the late 1990s due to the Asian Financial Crisis. Having fewer hospitals with Joint Commission International (JCI) accreditation, the government guided private hospitals to differentiate its medical services based on their competitive edge to set up centres of excellence. Some of these centres include cardiac procedures, fertility treatment and curative medical treatments.

Wong and Musa (2013) explain that MT in Thailand was only formally pro-moted by the government in the early 1990s to cater for local elites and foreign patients, although the phenomenon started in the 1970s with cosmetic and sex-change operations (Connell, 2006). Similar to the case of Malaysia, the step to develop MT was prompted by the economic crisis in the early 1990s to help business sustainability of private hospitals. With a high number of hospitals having JCI accreditation, Thailand receives medical patients from Japan, the United States, United Kingdom and Middle East.

Unlike Malaysia and Thailand, Singapore prices its medical services relatively higher and competes on high quality and differentiated medical services (i.e. complex treatments). Its major markets are Indonesia, Malaysia, China and Japan. Its national strategy of attracting foreign patients is also to achieve economies of scale for making high technological equipment available and affordable to its small population. The government also make agreements with Middle Eastern countries to expand its market (Heung *et al.*, 2011). MT in India started in the mid-1990s and was promoted as possessing accreditations, specializations, highly trained medical personnel and a variety of services. It is also differentiated through its alternative medical services that provide traditional treatments (e.g. unani and ayurveda).

The above literature depicts the development of MT from general to specific countries. While it provides a broad overview of past research, the literature on the development aspect tends to be general and limited.

The second major research gap arises from the narrow research focus in the field of MT that neglects the motivation for leisure travel. A growing body of literature has investigated the motivations of medical tourists. Despite the fact that MT comprises both medical treatment and leisure travel, this category of research tends to focus only on the former component.

Connell (2006) and Ormond (2011) stress that it is necessary to fully understand MT by incorporating both medical and tourism perspectives in a single study. While patients with severe health conditions may not be able to undertake leisure travel, tourism services may still be engaged by accompanying family members during the patients' recuperation period. Patients with minor illness or those travelling for health examinations may engage in leisure activities more than those with critical conditions (Connell, 2006).

The literature review shows that past studies on MT tend to solely examine the medical aspects, ranging from customer preferences (Yu & Ko, 2012) and destination choice (Zhang, Seo & Lee, 2013) to motivation (Musa, Thirumoorthi & Doshi, 2012; Ye, Qiu & Yuen, 2011) and satisfaction with medical services (Musa, Doshi, Wong & Thirumoorthi, 2012). For instance, the study by Musa *et al.* (2012) on travel motivation found that the main motivation factors for medical tourists travelling to Malaysia were 'value for money', 'excellent medical services', 'supporting services', 'cultural similarity', and 'religious factors' in descending order of importance.

Yu and Ko (2012) focus on the cultural perspective and examine potential medical tourists' preferences over destination choice, comfort and preferred products across three nationalities, namely, Chinese, Japanese and Korean. They found significant perceptual differences. For instance, Japanese are most concerned with medical care and service-related convenience, accommodation, cost and insurance. Chinese tourists are more open to undertaking light surgical treatment, while Japanese tourists opt for major surgery.

In their study on satisfaction with medical services, Musa *et al.* (2012) found that medical tourists travelling to Malaysia are most satisfied with doctors, nurses, and the services, atmosphere and facilities of hospitals. Zhang *et al.* (2013) examine the impact of psychological distance on destination choice and find that, above medical competency, developed countries are preferred for major diseases, while countries with relative small psychological distance tend to be chosen for minor ones. In short, these studies reflect lop-sided attention to the medical aspect of MT.

The present study argues that motivation for leisure travel is equally important to understand why medical tourists are motivated to select certain destinations over others. If medical tourists are motivated to optimize the benefits of travel by seeking health and leisure, these motivations may influence their destination choice. Therefore, this chapter asserts that marketers of MT should understand the motivation of medical tourists in seeking *both* medical/health services and tourism abroad.

This study supports the notion that the leisure travel aspect of motivation for MT should not be ignored given that medical tourists may take the opportunity to combine medical services and vacation in exotic locations which cannot be found in the home country (Hall, 2011, 2013). By understanding the two different types of motivation, namely, motivations to travel abroad for medical services and leisure travel, marketers of MT can better combine medical and leisure services to differentiate their products and services to gain a competitive edge.

The third major gap observed among the studies on MT is the dominant reliance on a common list of motivations or intentions for medical/health services, which falls short of empirical testing (Lunt & Carrera, 2010; Ormond, 2011; Runnels & Carrera, 2012; Whittaker, 2008; Wingkit & McKercher, 2013). This is a norm for any new field of study and MT research is in its infancy. However, this simple reliance on a common list of motivations tends to ignore the uniqueness of specific consumer characteristics. This convenient approach to understanding motivation for MT seemingly assumes that motivations are the same across various consumer markets.

Each consumer segment possesses unique characteristics and needs that influence their preference for MT attributes and destination of medical hub. Understanding consumers' motives is a key prerequisite to designing and tailoring offerings to particular target markets to create favourable experience and satisfaction for those markets (Park, Reisinger & Kang, 2008). Therefore, more advanced research is required in order to provide market-specific tourist motivations for effective market positioning. Lunt and Carrera (2010) call for more empirical research on MT given that such evidence is scarce (Whittaker, 2008).

The existing literature has only a handful of studies that are market-specific, such as South Korea (Lee, Han & Lockyer, 2012), Thailand (Wingkit & McKercher, 2013), Hong Kong (Ye, Qiu & Yuen, 2011), South Korea for Korean health tourists (Kim, Boo & Kim, 2013), and Malaysia (Musa *et al.*, 2012). For instance, Lee *et al.* (2012) empirically developed salient belief items in the health treatment model and beautification model to study the motivation of Japanese medical tourists to Korea. Their study implies that easily accessible law and safety regulations are important criteria. Their advice on feedback-seeking reinforces the notion echoed in this chapter that understanding motivation of specific consumers and markets in MT is helpful for the development of marketing strategies.

One study (Wingkit & McKercher, 2013) developed four categories of medical tourists in Thailand. The largest category is the 'dedicated' type who pre-plan to seek medical help abroad which is their key purpose prior to departure or is considered as equally important as a holiday. The second category is the 'hesitant' type (15.7 per cent) who only make the decision after arrival in Thailand. The third category (18.1 per cent) is the 'holidaying' type who prioritize vacation and pre-plan to engage in medical procedure/treatment. The fourth category is the 'opportunistic' type (23.9 per cent) who prioritize vacation without a prior plan for medical services. Travel behaviours are different across these categories owing to the 'long-haul' tourists who tend to engage in multi-destination travel.

Kim *et al.* (2013) conducted a study to understand brand equity and health tourism in Jeju Island, South Korea. It was found that three dimensions of brand equity, namely, quality of nature (e.g. spa), brand recognition (e.g. health and relaxation) and brand image had positive influences on the intention of visit of 504 Koreans. Ye *et al.* (2011) conducted semi-structured interviews with obstetric patients from Mainland China who underwent the procedure in Hong Kong. They found a very unconventional motivation – Chinese medical tourists tried to avoid the 'One Child' policy in Mainland China.

The fourth and critical gap is the lack of theoretical underpinning for most of the studies and specifically on motivation in MT. Thus far, a handful of studies have made commendable effort by briefly employing pull theory (Musa *et al.*, 2012) or theory of planned behaviour (Lee *et al.*, 2012).

Musa *et al.* (2012) draw upon pull theory in guiding their study of travel motivation of medical tourists in Malaysia. They adopt the definition of the study by Uysal and Hagan (1993), which states that pull factors are specific attributes that drive people to understand their travel needs, such as natural and historical attractions, food and people.

The applicability of the theory of planned behaviour is demonstrated using structural equation modelling in Lee *et al.*'s (2012) study of motives for MT. Drawing upon this theory, Lee *et al.* (2012) empirically developed 14 salient belief items in the health treatment model and 16 salient belief items in the beautification model to understand motives of Japanese medical tourists in Korea. They suggest the use of word-of-mouth to influence customers.

The fifth research gap is the potential to study the aspect of perceived medical risks in the MT literature. This is because, similar to leisure tourism, where the nature of its product is intangible and an experience (Tasci & Gartner, 2007), MT is also exposed to risks and threats. The perception of risks may affect travel motivation which is the ultimate driving force that controls travel behaviour (Kozak, Crotts & Law, 2007; Yoon & Uysal, 2005).

The 'push and pull' theory has been referenced or briefly applied to understand motivation for MT. Although various constraints such as cost, long waiting lists, regulations and accessibility have been stated as push factors (Musa *et al.*, 2012;

Ormond, 2011; Wong & Musa, 2013), no studies appear to have paid attention to perceived risks as push factors. This study argues that perceived health/medical risk in the home environment may be a form of push factor driving medical tourists to cross borders for medical services.

Often, people may be motivated to engage in MT due to the failure of their own health system to fulfil the needs of prospective patients (Ormond, 2011). In other words, failure of the domestic health system may be perceived as a form of health or medical risk and create intrinsic needs to seek medical services abroad. Therefore, push factors in relation to medical weaknesses/challenges of the location/home country of medical tourists is a key area for future studies. To truly adopt the push and pull theory to expand the MT literature, there is a need to approach perceived health/medical risks in the home country as a push factor.

This chapter recommends the use of semi-structured interviews in future studies to identify medical risk factors of specific market segments or the home country. The qualitative findings can be then drawn upon to conduct quantitative studies to empirically test the potential effects of perceived risks on motivation to travel abroad for medical/health services and tourism.

## Conclusion

Medical tourism has existed since at least the nineteenth century in the form of people travelling to other areas for healing and relaxation purposes. It has become a fast-growing industry in the twenty-first century resulting from globalization in healthcare. However, MT in the aspect of academic research is in its infancy. This chapter has identified and discussed a number of gaps for future research in MT. In highlighting these research gaps, the importance of context-specific knowledge and theoretical underpinning as much-needed contributions to the literature on MT has been stressed.

## References

Bookman, M. Z., & Bookman, K. R. (2007). *Medical tourism in developing countries*. New York: Palgrave Macmillan.

Connell, J. (2006). Medical tourism: Sea, sun, sand and… surgery. *Tourism Management, 27*(6), 1093–1100.

Garcia-Altes, A. (2005). The development of health tourism services. *Annals of Tourism Research, 32*(1), 262–266.

Goodrich, J. N., & Goodrich, G. E. (1987). Health-care tourism – An exploratory study. *Tourism Management, 8*, 217–222.

Hall, C. M. (2011). Health and medical tourism: A kill or cure for global public health?, *Tourism Review, 66*(1/2), 4–15.

Hall, C. M. (2013). *Medical tourism: The ethics, regulation, and marketing of health mobility* (pp. 61–74). London: Routledge.

Healy, C. (2009). Surgical tourism and the globalization of healthcare. *Irish Journal of Medical Sciences, 178*, 125–127.

Heung, V. C., Kucukusta, D., & Song, H. (2011). Medical tourism development in Hong Kong: An assessment of the barriers. *Tourism Management, 32*, 995–1005.

Hunter, W. C. (2007). Medical tourism: A new global niche. *International Journal of Tourism Sciences*, 7(1), 129–140.

Kim, Y. H., Boo, C., & Kim, M. (2013). An investigation of Korean health tourists' behaviour: Benefit sought, brand equity, and intention to visit. In C. M. Hall (Ed.), *Medical Tourism: The ethics, regulation, and marketing of health mobility* (pp. 61–74). London: Routledge.

Kozak, M., Crotts, J. C., & Law, R. (2007). The impact of the perception of risk on international travellers. *International Journal of Tourism Research*, 9(4), 233–242.

Lee, C. G. (2010). Health care and tourism: Evidence from Singapore. *Tourism Management, 31*, 486–488.

Lee, M., Han, H., & Lockyer, T. (2012). Medical tourism: Attracting Japanese tourists for medical tourism experience. *Journal of Travel and Tourism Marketing, 29(1)*, 69–86.

Lunt, N., & Carrera, P. (2010). Medical tourism: Assessing the evidence on treatment abroad. *Maturitas*, 66(1), 27–32.

Musa, G., Doshi, D. R., Wong, K. M., & Thirumoorthi, T. (2012). How satisfied are inbound medical tourists in Malaysia? A study on private hospitals in Kuala Lumpur. *Journal of Travel and Tourism Marketing*, 29(7), 629–646.

Musa, G., Thirumoorthi, T., & Doshi, D. (2012). Travel behaviour among inbound medical tourists in Kuala Lumpur. *Current Issues in Tourism*, 15(6), 525–543.

Ormond, M. (2011). Shifting subjects of health-care: Placing "medical tourism" in the context of Malaysian domestic health-care reform. *Asia Pacific Viewpoint*, 52(3), 247–259.

Park, K.S., Reisinger, Y., & Kang, H.J. (2008). Visitors' motivation for attending the South Beach wine and food festival, Miami Beach, Florida. *Journal of Travel and Tourism Marketing*, 25(2), 161–181.

Runnels, V., & Carrera, P. (2012). Why do patients engage in medical tourism? *Maturitas, 73* (4), 300–304.

Tasci, A. D., & Gartner, W. C. (2007). Destination image and its functional relationships. *Journal of Travel Research*, 45(4), 413–425.

Uysal, M., & Hagan, L. R. (1993). Motivation of pleasure to travel and tourism. In M. A. Khan, M. D. Olsen, & T. Var (Eds.), *VNR'S encyclopedia of hospitality and tourism* (pp. 798–810). New York: Van Nostrand Reinhold.

Whittaker, A. (2008). Pleasure and pain: Medical travel in Asia. *Global Public Health, 3*, 271–290.

Wingkit, M., & McKercher, B. (2013). Toward a typology of medical tourists: A case study of Thailand. *Tourism Management, 38(1)*, 4–12.

Wong, K. M., & Musa, G. (2013). Medical Tourism in Asia: Thailand, Singapore, Malaysia and India. In C. M. Hall (Ed.), *Medical Tourism: The ethics, regulation, and marketing of health mobility* (pp. 61–74). London: Routledge.

Ye, B. H., Qiu, H. Z., & Yuen, P. P. (2011). Motivations and experiences of Mainland Chinese medical tourists in Hong Kong. *Tourism Management*, 32(5), 1125–1127.

Yoon, Y., & Uysal, M. (2005). An examination of the effects of motivation and satisfaction on destination loyalty: A structural model. *Tourism Management*, 26(1), 45–56.

Yu, J. Y., & Ko, T. G. (2012). A cross-cultural study of perceptions of medical tourism among Chinese, Japanese and Korean tourists in Korea. *Tourism Management*, 33(1), 80–88.

Zhang, J., Seo, S., & Lee, H. (2013). The impact of psychological distance on Chinese customers when selecting an international healthcare service country. *Tourism Management, 35(1)*, 32–40.

# 13 Destination experience for Middle East tourists

*Gürel Çetin, Batıkan Yasankul and Füsun Istanbullu Dinçer*

## Introduction

The services and products the market offers have become increasingly commoditized with little to distinguish them beyond price and availability (Pine & Gilmore, 1999). There is a general acknowledgement in the literature of a need for transformation from services to experiences within the markets. This shift requires organizations to differentiate their offerings to meet the desires of more sophisticated and demanding clients (Volo, 2009). The roles of satisfaction and quality in promoting positive customer behaviours have been replaced by experiences offered as by-products.

There are various definitions of customer experiences. For example Pine and Gilmore (1999) define them as memorable events that engage customers in a personal way. Various authors also suggest that experiences are remembered for a while and shared with others (e.g. Çetin & Dinçer, 2014; Oh, Fiore & Jeong, 2007). Thus experiences are extremely relevant in the tourism industry (Cohen, 1979; MacCannell, 1973; Smith, 1994; Uriely, 2005; Urry, 1990). Tourism destinations should be able to offer positive experiences in order to keep and increase the number of visitors they attract. Tourist experiences are able to differentiate destinations from alternative regions. They also enable destinations to create loyal clients that share their experiences, and recommend the destination to other potential travellers.

Although experiences are critical for destinations' success, offering a theoretical framework of tourist experience has been a difficult task for researchers. Creating, managing and evaluating tourist experiences have also been a challenging objective for destination planners and the travel trade. Tourists have different personal characteristics and they hold various needs and expectations, making the concept of experience a relative attribute. There is not a single experience, but several experiences for different market segments (Vega, Casielles & Martin, 2015).

Tourism is a growing international activity despite economic crises, political conflicts and natural disasters. Travelling is also becoming more global; with advancements in technology and relaxation on visa processes, the dominance of the western tourist in international tourism is declining. Far East, Middle East and CIS countries' growth rates of outbound tourism are remarkable. Although the importance of these emerging regions has been acknowledged, research on tourism has long been focused on western tourists. There is a lack of knowledge particularly on the needs, experiences and behaviours of the Middle East tourist segment.

This study adopts a qualitative method to facilitate closing the gap between importance of and research in tourist experience through exploring the experiences of tourists from Middle East countries. The chapter first briefly conceptualizes the structure of the tourist experience concept. Then Middle East tourists' experiences are discussed in the framework of factors found after analysis of qualitative data acquired from in-depth interviews.

## Literature review

Tourists are recognized as consumers as they are involved in various service exchange relationships during their travels (Gunn, 1988; Mossberg, 2007). Because of the inseparability characteristic of tourism, consumer experiences necessitate active involvement of the tourist (Brunner-Sperdin & Peters, 2009). Tourist destinations can be framed as an amalgam of services and activities (e.g. lodging, attractions) that create an overall experience of the area visited. Tourist experience is actually an output as well as a process; however, it is expected that there will be a final destination experience which is created through interacting with different elements in the destination (Hosany & Gilbert, 2010). Thus experiential value is explained based on a single experience extracted from the overall trip. Determining experiential attributes for different tourist segments would facilitate a more precise understanding of tourists and better decision-making for destinations.

One of the emerging markets for international tourism activity is travellers from Middle East countries. The Middle East region is one of the world's smallest, yet fast-growing, tourist-generating regions, with an average annual growth rate of 9.9 per cent between 2000 and 2010. The Middle East region supplied 36.2 million tourists in 2010, an increase from 8.2 million in 1990. The growth rate is the highest in the world, well above the global average of 3.4 per cent per annum for the same period, reflecting a dynamic growth trend. With a population of more than 250 million, expected to increase to over 400 million by 2050, the region promises to remain an attractive and lucrative market in travellers to tourist destinations. Outbound travel from the Middle East more than quadrupled from 8.2 million in 1990 to 36.2 million in 2010 (UNWTO, 2012).

The World Tourism Organization (UNWTO) defines the Middle East market as totalling 14 countries: Bahrain, Egypt, Iraq, Jordan, Kuwait, Lebanon, Libya, Oman, Palestine, Qatar, Saudi Arabia, Syrian Arab Republic, United Arab Emirates and Yemen. Within the Middle East, major tourist-generating markets are the Gulf countries; Saudi Arabia, United Arab Emirates, Kuwait, Bahrain and Qatar. These tourists from the Gulf constitute about 60 per cent of all outbound travel and around 75 per cent of total international tourism expenditure from the Middle East countries (UNWTO, 2012).

*Table 13.1* Arrivals from Middle East to Turkey (2008–12)

|  | 2008 | 2009 | 2010 | 2011 | 2012 |
|---|---|---|---|---|---|
| *Gulf countries* | | | | | |
| SAR | 55,636 | 66,938 | 84,934 | 116,711 | 175,467 |
| Kuwait | 22,084 | 26,801 | 27,281 | 41,617 | 65,167 |
| BAE | 19,676 | 22,051 | 30,480 | 35,579 | 48,071 |
| Bahrain | 8,081 | 9,090 | 9,375 | 9,712 | 13,342 |
| Qatar | 4,862 | 4,902 | 6,043 | 7,661 | 13,971 |
| *Other countries* | | | | | |
| Iraq | 250,130 | 285,229 | 280,328 | 369,033 | 533,149 |
| Lebanon | 53,948 | 71,771 | 134,554 | 137,110 | 144,491 |
| Syria | 406,935 | 509,679 | 899,494 | 974,054 | 730,039 |
| Jordan | 74,340 | 87,694 | 96,562 | 94,914 | 102,154 |
| Yemen | 4,971 | 6,181 | 6,344 | 8,066 | 11,826 |

Source: Istanbul Culture and Tourism Directorate (2013).

The Middle East market is also an important generating region for Turkey. This segment is critical for Istanbul as these tourists tend to visit the city during the summer months, one of the shoulder periods for Istanbul when considering international tourism demand. According to the Turkish Ministry of Culture and Tourism (2014, p. 8), more than 15 per cent of visitors to Istanbul are from the Middle East. The total number of visitors from the Middle East to Istanbul jumped from around 700,000 in 2010 to 1,700,000 in 2013. Table 13.1 shows the growth of Middle East tourists travelling to Turkey between 2008 and 2012. According to the table the total number of arrivals from Middle East countries more than doubled despite the increased political unrest in the region during recent years (Çetin & Sunar, 2012).

## Methodology

In order to explore the Middle East travellers' overall tourism experiences in Istanbul, a qualitative technique based upon semi-structured, in-depth interviews was chosen. Travellers from Middle East countries were interviewed about their experiences, as events and perceptions in Istanbul that are personal, memorable, unique and worth sharing with friends. Interviews were all electronically recorded with respondents' consent, and transcribed verbatim within the same day by one of the authors. This whole procedure filled 96 pages in total. Transcripts and field notes were then analysed multiple times and coded by each author to reach a consensus on overall dimensions, concerning experiential attributes of tourists' visits to Istanbul. Istanbul is a popular destination for international travellers and it is also attracting a large share of the Middle East tourist market mainly because of cultural and geographic proximity. The city receives more than ten million international travellers and it offers diverse products and services (e.g. heritage, cultural events, natural attractions, shopping, night life and business). Hence Istanbul can be considered as a good domain for the study of experiences.

Interviews were conducted between August and October 2013 for a period of 13 weeks. The screening criteria used for the interviewees were being above 18 years old, and to have stayed in Istanbul for more than one full day. In the case of this study, after interviewing 61 tourists, and transcribing relevant data, authors agreed on the data saturation level and that no additional interviews would provide new findings (Glaser & Strauss, 1967). Interviews took around 25–40 minutes in duration and were conducted randomly at multiple well-known cultural sights in the city centre (e.g. Topkapi Palace) and at transfer vehicles to/from excursions, as well as hotel lobbies and two international airports.

After the analysis and discussion phase was over, common themes and significant statements were extracted from the transcribed data and were coded, singled out and grouped under broader content-related categories (Cozby, 2004; Creswell, 2007). Data were than compared with previous literature for deduction and validation. At the end of this categorizing process, 43 items were merged under five themes: culture, social interaction, shopping, nature and service. The results of the research are discussed in the next section.

## Results

This study has attempted to comprehensively explore the experiences of travellers from the Middle East, and it offers valuable insights. The interview questions also included demographic information as well as questions related to experiences. Out of a total of 61 respondents, 39 were male. Their ages differed between 19 and 67; 34 of them held a university degree and the majority (88 per cent) had more than €20,000 annual income. Most were in Istanbul for leisure purposes; six were on business trips. They can also be considered as experienced travellers, travelling outside their home country approximately 3.3 times on average in 2012.

A total of five main categories describing the experiential elements for Middle East travellers in Istanbul are found. As shown on Figure 13.1, these are culture (e.g. heritage, food, modernity, arts, entertainment, night life, religion), social interactions (e.g. social local people, hospitality, safety, friendliness), nature (e.g. location, Bosphorus, islands, sea, climate, natural sights), quality of service (e.g. hotels, recreation and health facilities, convention centres, service quality) and shopping (e.g. grand bazaar, shopping malls, variety, quality, value for money, brands). These dimensions are explored further below.

*Figure 13.1* Experiential attributes for Middle East tourists.

*Culture*

Local culture was perceived as an important part of travel experience by most of the participants. The heritage, monuments, architecture and history of the city were frequently mentioned by respondents as unique characteristics of the city. Being a melting pot for different civilizations, the city also reflects a diverse background of traditions, religions, arts, food and entertainment. Particularly the variety, taste, freshness and cooking styles of the local food were perceived as positive factors by Middle East travellers. Although local gastronomy was first conceptualized as a separate theme in this study, after negotiation and discussion, authors agreed that this dimension should be a subgroup of culture dimension in line with previous literature (Çetin & Bilgihan, 2014). Local food represents an intangible cultural heritage and an important part of destination experience as well (Binkhorst & Den Dekker, 2009). Quan and Wang (2004) also discuss culture and heritage as important components of destination experience for tourists.

*Social interactions*

Interactions with locals were also expressed as one of the factors affecting respondents' experiences in Istanbul. The locals' friendliness, helpfulness, sincerity, goodwill and kindness were frequently mentioned by Middle East tourists. Turkish people were perceived as hospitable. Turkey also shares the same dominant religion (Islam) as most Middle East countries. Rather than being strangers, the tourists are perceived as guests and highly respected. Traditional hospitability, protection and special care for guests has been a typical characteristic of Turkish people that has survived for generations. Social interactions with locals during the trip are also reflected as one of the main desires of travellers by various authors (Butler, 1980; Crompton, 1979). Local hospitality in the traditional sense is assumed as an important part of the tourist experience (Mill & Morrison, 1985) and it has also been found as an important dimension of the destination's competitive advantage (Kozak & Rimmington, 1999).

*Nature*

Although Istanbul is a crowded city hosting more than 17 million inhabitants, the nature of the city is so unique that it has attracted attention of the respondents as well. Istanbul is situated between Asia and Europe with Bosphorus waterway dividing the two continents. The city is also surrounded with woods (Belgrad, Yildiz etc.) as well as islands (a total of nine, collectively known as the Prince Islands), that are among other natural attractions which make the travel experience in the city unique. MacCannell (1999) reflects tourism activity as a desire for authenticity, novelty and change. According to Urry (1990), gazing of tourists is actually a process of them turning ordinary local objects into sacred ones. Nature is also a part of the tourist experience; it represents locality and novelty (Perkins & Thorns, 2001).

Therefore, nature, places and scenery are among phenomena that are important for tourists' experience. Istanbul also offers various unique natural sights and scenery. For example, Bosphorus, the waterway that divides the city into two as Europe and Asia can be enjoyed from most of the tourist districts. The Prince Islands, spreading into the Marmara Sea and visible from the city, are also able to attract millions of visitors every year (Demiroglu, Çetin & Izgi, 2007).

### *Quality of service*

The tourism-related services (e.g. hotels, restaurants, transportation, recreation, landscaping) in Istanbul were also perceived to be high quality. Respondents frequently mentioned how satisfied they were with their hotel, the cleanliness of the streets and professionalism of the service in general. The hotels in Istanbul have been receiving various international awards (e.g. Conde Nast, Leading Hotels of the World, World Travel Awards); the prestigious facilities of international brands are also located in Istanbul (e.g. Four Seasons, Swiss, Kempinski, Ritz Carlton, Hilton) (Çetin & Walls, 2015). These member facilities in Istanbul are considered among the top facilities in the international brand portfolio of chain hotels considering service quality. Tourism-related services were seen as hygiene factors of an experience according to McCabe (2002); the overall experience might be ruined if supporting services are not up to standard. Although travellers desire authenticity and novelty in their experiences, they also seek a degree of quality, safety, comfort and predictability (Dearden & Harron, 1994). Hence both tangible and intangible service quality influence tourist experience.

### *Shopping*

Shopping is also mentioned as a part of the tourist experience in Istanbul by travellers. Istanbul offers a wide variety of alternatives to shoppers, from modern shopping malls to traditional shopping complexes such as the Grand Bazaar. As Turkey has been an important textile exporter the city is also considered to be one of the centres of world fashion. Besides the local brands, major design brands also have branches in the city. Most participants also expressed shopping as an interesting activity in Istanbul. Shopping has emerged as the second common leisure activity after visiting heritage attractions of the city. The participants mentioned that they liked the shopping experience in Istanbul even when they did not have any intention to buy; this also corroborates with Yuksel and Yuksel (2007). In particular, the traditional shopping experience in Grand Bazaar, the negotiation process, the variety of brands and products, and the fusion of different colours and noises during shopping attracted tourists' attention.

## Conclusion

Identifying experiential attributes in destinations has important implications for the tourism industry and service design. Various studies have established positive relationships between customer experiences, customer value, loyalty and recommendation (e.g. Çetin & Dinçer, 2014; Hosany & Gilbert, 2010; Walls, 2009). However, destination attributes affecting overall travel experience have not been clarified in the literature so far. In particular, the differences of the Middle East segment as a tourist-generating region have long been neglected. Different clients might desire different experiences depending on different backgrounds and motivations (Cohen, 1979). This study proposes valuable empirical findings for destination planners and industry professionals as well as scholars for implications and future research concerning the experiential needs of the Middle East tourist market.

As a result of the exploratory study conducted in Istanbul, five constructs were found to be the main determinants of Middle East tourists' experiences in Istanbul. These are social interaction, nature, quality of service, culture and shopping. It should also be stated that all respondents were very satisfied with their experiences in Istanbul; they also expressed their intention to return as well as to spread word-of-mouth recommendations to others. Hence the findings can facilitate better planning, decision-making and product design for tourism professionals and destination planners who intend to attract more visitors from the Middle East as a growing market segment.

The findings of the study might also be used by policy-makers and the travel trade in order to differentiate destinations and their products. Facilitating local contact, rather than creating isolated tourist bubbles (as in the case of Sultanahmet region of Istanbul) is one of the implications. Sultanahmet is among most visited places in in the city. It has been an old settlement for locals but as the tourism investments (e.g. hotels, restaurants, leather and rug shops) flourished, the area commercialized rapidly and many inhabitants were forced out of the area because of the increased rents. Currently there are very few locals living in Sultanahmet, and it has become a ghost neighbourhood, especially at night. During the daytime, tourists still visit in order to see the monuments located in the region to satisfy their cultural desires. However, the streets empty after 6 p.m., when the cultural sites in the region close.

Therefore interaction with locals is also a part of the tourism experience and locals' rights to their neighbourhood should be balanced with the level of tourism-based commoditization. This situation has also been confirmed by the tripographic characteristics (location of hotels where participants chose to stay) of the respondents; most of them (47 respondents) stayed in more crowded and inhabited neighbourhoods of the city (Beyoglu and Besiktas), where locals also spend their free time and socialize outdoors. Thus the travel trade, for example, can promote hotels located in regions where residents live and use restaurants that locals also patronize in their packages. Tour operators might also use public transportation where convenient. The locals' use of tourism facilities and their visits to tourist attractions would also be encouraged through utilizing resident discounts and other means in order to improve the level of host–guest interaction.

The natural attractions in the destination (Bosphorus, woods and islands in the case of Istanbul) also make up and important part of the Middle East tourist experience. This might be attributed to the fact that nature is not very generous to Middle East countries and Middle East tourists consider nature as a part of their experiences; they like being outdoors, enjoying scenery with woods and water. The quality of professional (commercial hospitality) and public services (transportation, cleanliness, security) was also mentioned as an important factor. This reflects the need for coordination between public and private authorities to cooperate in order to create the desired experiences to Middle East tourists. The service theme can also be considered as the supporting experiences that augment the overall tourist experience. Without a proper level of quality in public services (e.g. security, cleanliness) and commercial hospitality (e.g. professionalism, physical facilities, courtesy), a positive destination experience is not possible.

The culture dimension is also mentioned as a unique characteristic of Istanbul that Middle East tourists would remember and share with others. Food, heritage, arts, music, religion and traditions should be supported in destinations through incentives, festivals and other means in order to increase visibility of the culture of a destination. Although usually overlooked in the literature, shopping is mentioned as a way to experience the destination. Most tourists go shopping at a destination, whether they buy or not. The shopping expenditure makes up around one-third of tourist spending (Wong & Law, 2003). Istanbul offers a wide variety of traditional and modern shopping alternatives from designer clothing to hand-made products. Middle East tourists were especially satisfied with the shopping opportunities in Istanbul; the city was also expressed as a 'shopping paradise'. Thus shopping alternatives should be promoted (e.g. shopping festivals, discounts) and made convenient (e.g. transportation, operating hours) to Middle East tourists.

This study was conducted on travellers from the Middle East only; future studies might investigate other market segments from different tourist-generating countries. A comparison between different market segments would also offer interesting findings. This exploratory study used phenomenology to identify dimensions of Middle East tourists' destination experiences, thus the importance of different attributes was not analysed. Future studies involving a quantitative measurement of experiences might offer insight into relative importance of these themes.

A limitation of the study was considered as the locality interviews were conducted. Although Istanbul is an international destination attracting more than ten million travellers per year, experiences might differ based on the characteristics of each destination. Personal, social, cultural and geographical settings might influence tourist experiences. The findings of this study need to be validated by studies conducted in other destinations. Nevertheless, for scholars, this study is among the first concerning experiences of tourists from the Middle East region conducted in a destination with diverse offerings. Future studies investigating various destinations and travellers with different backgrounds might offer valuable insight in distinguishing different market segments.

## References

Binkhorst, E., & Den Dekker, T. (2009). Agenda for co-creation tourism experience research. *Journal of Hospitality Marketing & Management, 18*(2–3), 311–327.

Brunner-Sperdin, A., Peters, M. (2009). What influences guests, emotions? The case of high-quality hotels. *International Journal of Tourism Research, 11*(2), 171–183.

Butler, R.W. (1980). The concept of a tourist area cycle of evolution: Implications for management of resources. *The Canadian Geographer, 24*(1), 5–12.

Çetin, G., & Bilgihan, A. (2014). Components of cultural tourists' experiences in destinations. *Current Issues in Tourism* (ahead-of-print), 1–18. DOI: 10.1080/13683500.2014.994595.

Çetin, G., & Dinçer, F.I. (2014). Influence of customer experience on loyalty and word-of-mouth in hospitality operations. *Anatolia, 25*(2), 181–194.

Çetin G., & Sunar, B. (2012). Turkish political transition and incoming tourism to Turkey. In A.E. Alonso & J.E. Curiel (Eds.), *Tourism and International Relations* (pp. 151–168). Madrid: Dykinson.

Çetin, G., & Walls, A. (2015). Understanding the customer experience from the perspective of guests and hotel managers: Emprical findings from luxury hotels in Istanbul. *Journal of Hospitality Marketing & Management* (ahead of print). DOI: 10.1080/19368623.2015.1034395.

Cohen, E. (1979). A phenomenology of tourist experiences. *Sociology, 13*(2), 179–201.

Cozby, P.C. (2004). *Methods in behavioral research* (8th ed.). New York, NY: McGraw-Hill.

Creswell, J.W. (2007). *Qualitative inquiry and research design: Choosing among five approaches* (2nd ed.). Thousand Oaks, CA: Sage.

Crompton, J.L. (1979). Motivations for pleasure vacation. *Annals of Tourism Research, 6*(4), 408–424.

Dearden, P., & Harron, S. (1994). Alternative tourism and adaptive change. *Annals of Tourism Research, 21*(1), 81–102.

Demiroglu, O. C., Çetin, G., & Izgi, M. T. (2007, May). Sustainable development of tourism for islands: Case of Buyukada. *Proceedings of the 2007 International Tourism Biennial*, Canakkale Onsekiz Mart University, pp. 121–131.

Glaser, B. G., & Strauss, A. L. (1967). *The discovery of grounded theory: Strategies for qualitative research.* New York, NY: Aldine.

Gunn, C. (1988). *Tourism planning* (2nd ed.). New York, NY: Taylor and Francis.

Hosany, S., & Gilbert, D. (2010). Measuring tourists' emotional experience towards hedonic holiday destinations, *Journal of Travel Research, 49*(4), 513–526.

Istanbul Culture and Tourism Directorate (2013). *Istanbul tourism statistics – 2013.* http://www.istanbulkulturturizm.gov.tr/TR,71515/turizm-istatistikleri.html, retrieved on 13 Jan. 2013.

Kozak, M., & Rimmington, M. (1999). Measuring tourist destination competitiveness: Conceptual considerations and empirical findings. *International Journal of Hospitality Management, 18*(3), 273–283.

MacCannell, D. (1973). Staged authenticity: Arrangements of social space in tourist settings. *American Journal of Sociology, 79*(3), 589–603.

MacCannell, D. (1999). *The tourist: A new of the class.* London: University of California Press.

McCabe, S. (2002). The tourist experience and everyday life. In Dann, G.M. (Ed.), *The tourist as a metaphor of the social world* (pp. 61–75). Wallingford: CABI.

Mill, R.C., & Morrison, A.M. (1985). *The tourism system.* Englewood Cliffs, NJ: Prentice Hall.

Ministry of Culture and Tourism (2014). *Istanbul tourism statistics.* Istanbul: Istanbul Provincial Directorate of Culture and Tourism.

Mossberg, L. (2007). A marketing approach to tourist experience. *Scandinavian Journal of Hospitality and Tourism, 7*(1), 59–74.

Oh, H., Fiore, A.M., & Jeong, M. (2007). Measuring experience economy concepts: Tourism applications. *Journal of Travel Research, 46*(2), 119–132.

Perkins, H. C., & Thorns, D. C. (2001). Gazing or performing? Reflections on Urry's tourist gaze in the context of contemporary experience in the antipodes. *International Sociology, 16*(2), 185–204.

Pine, J., & Gilmore, J. (1999). *The experience economy: Work is theater and every business stage*. Cambridge, MA: Harvard Business Press.

Quan, S., & Wang, N. (2004). Towards a structural model of the tourist experience: An illustration from food experiences in tourism. *Tourism Management, 25*(3), 297–305.

Smith, S.L. (1994). The tourism product. *Annals of Tourism Research, 21*, 582–595.

UNWTO (2012). World's top destinations by international visitors. *World Tourism Barometer*, UNWTO, http://mkt.unwto.org/en/barometer, retrieved on 16 Sept. 2013.

Uriely, N. (2005). The tourist experience. *Annals of Tourism Research, 32*(1), 199–216.

Urry, J. (1990). *The tourist gaze*. London: Sage.

Vega, A.V.R., Casielles, R.V., & Martín, A.M.D. (2015). La calidad percibida del servicio en establecimientos hoteleros de turismo rural. *Papers de Turisme, 19*, 17–33.

Volo, S. (2009). Conceptualizing experience: A tourist-based approach. *Journal of Hospitality Marketing & Management, 18*(2–3), 111–126.

Walls, A. (2009). An examination of consumer experience and relative effects on consumer values (unpublished doctoral thesis). University of Central Florida, Orlando, FL.

Wong, J., & Law, R. (2003). Differences in shopping satisfaction levels: A study of tourists in Hong-Kong. *Tourism Management, 24*, 401–410.

Yuksel, A., & Yuksel, F. (2007). Shopping risk perceptions: Effects on tourists' emotions, satisfaction and expressed loyalty intentions. *Tourism Management, 28*(3), 703–713.

# Part IV

# Models of destination marketing and competitiveness

# 14 A study on the flow experience relationship model of gaming activity

*Tang-chung Kan, Joyce Hsiu-yu Chen and Chelsea Su*

## Introduction

In recent years, gaming has been presented as a flourishing industry. Most of the gaming tours are not only designed for gambling, but also for other recreational activities. Tourist casinos are a source of 'no-pain' tax; that is why governments set up tourist casinos to create more opportunities for earning money during the recession. Casinos have become major tourist attractions and are acknowledged to attract millions of tourists to travel destinations (Park, Yang, Lee, Jang & Stokowski, 2002; Wong & Rosenbaum, 2012). Gaming is an emerging travel style that is growing rapidly with flow experiences playing a critical role for participation in and desire for these activities. Worldwide, the gaming industry is expanding at a rapid pace, and as a result, the increasingly diverse global patterns of travel are also expanding.

Known as the 'Monte Carlo of the Orient' or 'Vegas of the East', Macau is famous for its gaming activity. The Macau gaming industry is entering into a new era of development, with tourist arrivals and tourism revenue rising rapidly. There are currently over 200 casinos in Macau, the so-called 'brand new gambling city worldwide'. In 2011, gaming revenue alone contributed over 40 per cent of the GDP in Macau and improved its GDP per capital to reach over USD 66,000, which ranks third in the world according to the World Bank, within just ten years of its liberalization of the gaming industry (Macau Statistics and Census Services, 2012).

This chapter focuses on the gaming activities of baccarat, roulette and blackjack in Macau gaming resorts. How to create flow experiences for participants is a worthy topic for discussion. Therefore, the objective of this chapter is to build up a Flow Experience Relationship Model to improve participants' flow experiences in gaming, by indicating the effects of 'participation motivation' and 'enduring involvement' on flow experience.

## Literature review

Tourism can be considered, in one of its many aspects, as a socio-psychological experience and motivation which is a key element that determines individual behaviour in the field of tourism (Ross & Iso-Ahola, 1991). The global approach for understanding participation motivation (PM) was originally proposed by

Beard and Ragheb (1983). They have developed the Leisure Motivation Scale which comprises four sub-scales: intellectual, social, competence-mastery and stimulus-avoidance. The intellectual dimension refers to mental motivation such as cognitive learning or the opportunity to use one's imagination. The social dimension refers to the need for interpersonal relationships. The competency-mastery dimension explains the desire for competition and challenge. The stimulus-avoidance dimension refers to escape and restoration which one seeks in leisure activities. The Leisure Motivation Scale has been utilized in a variety of settings to understand PM. Mayo and Jarvis (1981) believed that the more understanding of tourist PM, the more we could do to help developing the industry of tourism in a certain region.

### Enduring involvement (EI)

McIntyre (1989) suggests that enduring involvement (EI) is viewed as the personal meaning or affective attachment that an individual has for an activity. Havitz and Dimanche (1990, p. 184) propose that 'enduring involvement is a psychological state of motivation, arousal, or interest between an individual and recreational activities, tourist destinations, or related equipment, at one point in time'. McIntyre and Pigram (1992) have developed leisure involvement scales consisting of attraction, centrality and self-expression. Kyle & Chick (2004) proposed a modified involvement scale (MIS) which consists of five dimensions (attraction, centrality, social bonding, identity affirmation and identity expression) measured with 17 items.

### Flow experience (FE)

The notion of flow has been described as the process of optimal experience (Csikszentmihalyi & Csikszentmihalyi, 1988; Csikszentmihalyi & LeFevre, 1989) and defined as 'the holistic sensation that people feel when they act with total involvement' (Csikszentmihalyi, 1975, p. 36). Status of flow experience (FE) is the psychological balance presented by the skill of participants and challenging of activities to achieve (Jackson, 1996; Ghani, Supnick & Rooney, 1991; Csikszentmihalyi, 1990). Csikszentmihalyi (1990, 1997) summarized those factors related to flow experiences into nine dimensions: (1) clear goals; (2) immediate feedback; (3) personal skills well suited to given challenges; (4) merger of action and awareness; (5) concentration on the task at hand; (6) a sense of potential control; (7) a loss of self-consciousness; (8) an altered sense of time; and (9) experience which becomes auto-telic. Voelkl and Ellis (1998) refer to flow experiences into three dimensions: skill and challenge, affect and self-affirmation.

As mentioned above, understanding the determinants of flow experience can facilitate the participant's focus on the major factors leading to PM and EI. Many studies have examined the antecedents of flow experience. Additionally, the causal relationships between PM and EI have been established by previous studies (Csikszentmihalyi, 1990; Ghani, Supnick, & Rooney, 1991; Jackson, 1992;

Chantal, Vallerand, & Vallieres, 1995). Therefore, a conceptual relationship model of this study is proposed. This study proposes the following hypotheses:

H1   Participation motivation (PM) positive significantly affects enduring involvement (EI).
H2   Participation motivation (PM) positive significantly affects flow experience (FE).
H3   Enduring involvement (EI) positive significantly affects flow experience (FE).

## Methodology

A questionnaire survey was conducted to collect empirical data from participants of gaming activity in Macau. The questions in the questionnaire are designed based on a review of the literature and specific characteristics of gaming tourism. To ensure the content validity of the scales, the selected items are mainly adopted from prior studies. The study uses exiting scales for measuring participation motivation, enduring involvement and flow experience. Apart from respondent information measured by a categorical scale, all the other items of the first four parts are measured by a 5-point Likert-type scale from 'strongly disagree (1)' to 'strongly agree (5)'.

The questionnaire was pre-tested and revised to ensure content validity. Due to limited time and manpower, a convenience sampling method was adopted. With the object of study being the gaming activities of baccarat, roulette and blackjack, we distributed 291 useable questionnaires for gaming participants at the main hotel casino sites in Macau. A confirmatory factor analysis (CFA) was performed to specify the structure between observed indicators and latent constructs, and test the validity of measurement model as well. Subsequently, structural equations among latent constructs were examined to test the conceptual structural equation model (SEM). All of the CFA and SEM procedures were conducted by using maximum likelihood parameter estimates and appropriate correlation matrix with LISREL 8.52.

Furthermore, using the time period on weekends and weekdays to collect data during February–May 2014 also helped the researcher collect samples from both peak times and non-peak times. Finally, a total of 291 valid questionnaires were received from hotel casinos in Macau. With regard to demographic characteristics, approximately 58.8 per cent of respondents were male; 35.1 per cent ranged from 31 to 40 years old; approximately 49.5 per cent had a university degree. Business people and service workers account for 56.7 per cent of the sample, and 49.4 per cent sample had a monthly income less than NT$40,000 (US$1,250). Approximately 91.8 per cent respondents lived in Mainland China (including Hong Kong, Macau and China).

## Findings

A CFA was first used to confirm the factor loadings of the three constructs (i.e. participation motivation, enduring involvement and flow experience) and to assess the model fit. PM was reduced to four dimensions, namely 'intellectual', 'social', 'competent skilled' and 'exciting escape', in which the highest average is 'intel-lectual'; EI was reduced to four dimensions, namely 'pleasure to visit', 'lifestyle centre attractiveness' and 'self-expression', in which the maximum average is 'pleasure to visit'; FE was reduced to three dimensions, respectively, 'skills chal-lenge', 'affection' and 'testimony', where the highest average is 'skills challenge' and the cumulative amount of explained variance with the overall Cronbach's α values is stable with consistency.

As shown in Table 14.1, $t$ values for all the standardized factor loadings of items were found to be significant ($p < 0.01$). In addition, construct reliability estimates range from 0.73 to 0.96, which exceed the critical value of 0.7, indicat-ing a satisfactory estimation. These indicate that the measurement model has good convergent validity. Therefore, the hypothesized measurement model is reliable and meaningful to test the structural relationships among the constructs.

The structural model is estimated with a maximum likelihood estimation method and a correlation matrix as input data. Table 14.2 summarizes the fit indices of the structural model. The overall model indicates that the chi-square value (chi-square) = 55.10, df = 38, chi-square value ratio = 2.5, the overall pattern of fit index (goodness-of-fit index, GFI) = 0.91, adjusted goodness-of-fit index (AGFI) = 0.90, root mean square residual (RMR) = 0.035, asymptotic error rms (RMSEA) = 0.068, non-basic with moderate index (NNFI) = 0.99, more suitable index (CFI) = 0.99. Comparing with the corresponding critical values shown in Table 14.3, it suggests that the hypothesized model fits the empirical data well.

Within the overall model, the estimates of the structural coefficients provide the basis for testing the proposed hypotheses. This study examines the structural model with one exogenous construct (i.e. flow experience) and two endogenous constructs (i.e. PM and EI).

Table 14.3 reports the results of the hypothesis tests. The three hypotheses are sup-ported. PM positive significantly affects EI (standardized $\lambda = 0.88$; $t$-value = 8.86).

*Table 14.1* Convergent validity

| Constructs | Item | Standardized factor loading | t-value | Standard error | Cronbach's α |
|---|---|---|---|---|---|
| PM | PM1 | 0.73 | 8.21* | 0.09 | 0.93 |
| | PM2 | 0.91 | 11.40* | 0.08 | 0.94 |
| | PM3 | 0.90 | 11.29* | 0.08 | 0.93 |
| | PM4 | 0.84 | 10.09* | 0.08 | 0.90 |
| EI | EI1 | 0.86 | – | – | 0.94 |
| | EI2 | 0.91 | 12.57* | 0.07 | 0.92 |
| | EI3 | 0.90 | 12.18* | 0.07 | 0.95 |
| | EI4 | 0.81 | 10.21* | 0.08 | 0.94 |
| FE | FE1 | 0.74 | – | – | 0.93 |
| | FE2 | 0.85 | 10.71* | 0.08 | 0.92 |
| | FE3 | 0.96 | 8.74* | 0.11 | 0.93 |

*$p < 0.05$; **$p < 0.01$.

Source: Analysis by the researchers.

*Table 14.2* Goodness of fit

| Criteria indicators | Criteria | Indicators |
| --- | --- | --- |
| Chi-square | $p > 0.05$ | 55.10 |
| Chi-square/df | 1–3 | 1.45 |
| GFI | > 0.90 | 0.91 |
| AGFI | > 0.90 | 0.90 |
| NFI | > 0.90 | 0.98 |
| NNFI | > 0.90 | 0.99 |
| CFI | 1 | 0.99 |
| RMR | < 0.05 | 0.035 |
| RMSEA | 0.05–0.08 | 0.068 |

Source: Analysis by the researchers.

*Table 14.3* Hypotheses tests

| Path structural | Structural coefficients | t | Results |
| --- | --- | --- | --- |
| H1: PM/EI | 0.88 | 8.56* | Supported |
| H2: PM/FE | 0.41 | 2.99* | Supported |
| H3: EI/FE | 0.56 | 3.88* | Supported |

$*p < 0.05. **p < 0.01.$

Source: Analysis by the researchers.

Thus, H1 is supported. PE, as hypothesized, positive significantly affects FE (standardized $\lambda = 0.88$; $t$-value = 8.86), thus supporting H2. Finally, EI positive significantly affects FE (standardized $\lambda = 0.41$; $t$-value = 2.99), supporting H3. The flow experience relationship model of participant gaming activity built by this research was one of the major contributions. The fit of this model principally meets the standard.

## Conclusion

In this chapter, using the example of Macau, one of the key destinations in East Asia, we aimed to show that the gaming industry can be regarded as a 'flow experience (FE)' relationship model from the overall tourism experience process. Based on the findings, managerial implications are discussed, and useful suggestions are also provided for applications. With a variety of entertainment and service offerings, integrated casinos are able to attract millions of tourists (Wong & Rosenbaum, 2012); when these service providers are able to fulfil their needs and meet their expectations, participants have higher motivation and enduring involvement, and flow experience is enhanced as a result.

This study suggests that holding gaming expos and multi-project experience activities may increase awareness and the fun of gaming activities; improving service levels and casino facilities, and providing customized services for the needs of different participants, may enhance the quality of participation in the gaming experience, and promote sustainable development of the gaming industry.

Further research could also apply this managing participant relationship model or employ more variables in creating, communicating and delivering value to customers in order to contribute further to the gaming industry.

## References

Beard, J., & Ragheb, M. G. (1983). Measuring leisure motivation. *Journal of Leisure Research, 15*(3), 219–228.

Chantal, Y., Vallerand, R. J., & Vallieres, E. F. (1995). Motivation and gambling involvement. *The Journal of Social Psychology*, *135*(6), 755–763.

Csikszentmihalyi, M. (1975). *Beyond boredom and anxiety*. San Francisco, CA: Jossey-Bass.

Csikszentmihalyi, M. (1990). Literacy and intrinsic motivation. *Daedalus*, *119*(2), 115–140.

Csikszentmihalyi, M. (1997). Happiness and creativity: Going with the flow. *The Futurist, 31*(5), 27.

Csikszentmihalyi, M., & Csikszentmihalyi, I. S. (1988). Optimal experience: Psychological studies of flow in consciousness. Cambridge, UK: Cambridge University Press.

Csikszentmihalyi, M., & LeFevre, J. (1989). Optimal experience in work and leisure. *Journal of Personality and Social Psychology, 56*(5), 815–822.

Ghani, J. A., Supnick, R., & Rooney, P. (1991). The experience of flow in computer-mediated and in face-to-face groups. In *Proceedings of the twelfth international conference on Information systems*. Paper presented at University of Minnesota, New York, NY.

Havitz, M. E., & Dimanche, F. (1990). Propositions for testing the involvement construct in recreational and tourism contexts. *Leisure Sciences*, *12*(2), 179–195.

Jackson, C. (1996). Rescuing gender from the poverty trap. *World Development, 24*(3), 489–504.

Jackson, S. A. (1992). Athletes in flow: A qualitative investigation of flow states in elite figure skaters. *Journal of Applied Sport Psychology*, *4*(2), 161–180.

Kyle, G., & Chick, G. (2004). Enduring leisure involvement: The importance of personal relationships. *Leisure Studies, 23*(3), 243–266.

Macau Statistics and Census Services. (2012). *Gross domestic product*. Retrieved 29.08.12, from. http://www.dsec.gov.mo.

Mayo, E., Jr., & Jarvis, L. (1981). *The psychology of leisure travel: Effective marketing and selling of travel service*. Boston, MA: CBI.

McIntyre, N., & Pigram, J. J. (1992). Specialization reexamined: The case of vehicle based campers. *Journal of Sciences*, *14*, 3–16.

McIntyre, N. (1989). The personal meaning of participation: Enduring involvement. *Journal of Leisure Research, 21*(2), 167–179.

Park, M., Yang, X., Lee, B., Jang, H.-C., & Stokowski, P. A. (2002). Segmenting casino gamblers by involvement profiles: a Colorado example. *Tourism Management, 23*(1), 55–65.

Ross, E. L. D., & Iso-Ahola, S. E. (1991). Sightseeing tourists' motivation and satisfaction. *Annals of Tourism Research, 18*(2), 226–237.

Voelkl, J. E., & Ellis, G. D. (1998). Measuring flow experiences in daily life: An examination of the items used to measure challenge and skill. *Journal of Leisure Research, 30*(3), 380–389.

Wong, I. A., & Rosenbaum, M. S. (2012). Beyond hardcore gambling: understanding why mainland Chinese visit casinos in Macau. *Journal of Hospitality & Tourism Research, 36*(1), 32–51.

# 15  A review of life cycle models by Plog and Butler from a marketing perspective

*Grace K.S. Ho and Bob McKercher*

## Introduction

Over the past few decades, Plog's and Butler's life cycle models have been criticized extensively for being impractical, for having significant flaws, and for not working in practice; yet these models are still two of the most cited and applied models within the field of tourism studies. This chapter aims to discuss the validity of both models from a marketing perspective, and will criticize the prior mistreatment, misunderstanding and misuse of the models by others.

The two models were written as conference papers and later developed as journal articles in the early years of the conceptualization of tourism. Because of their timeliness, these models formed the groundwork for much of the critical thinking about the subsequent development of tourism. While each addresses life cycles, each also has a fundamentally different focus. The model by Plog (1974) was a psychographic portrayal of tourists to explain their motivation and behaviour, what they want from a travel experience, and how they behave in choosing and taking a holiday; whereas the S-shaped resort cycle model by Butler (1980) took a geographical point of view to explain the motivation and behaviour of the travel industry in seeking to develop and promote services in and to particular destinations. This chapter will discuss the marketing concept of product life cycle, followed by the validity of the two models in order of their appearance.

## Literature review

Plog's and Butler's models were based on a marketing concept of product life cycle (PLC). The original PLC model was first used by Levitt (1965). The model suggested that, like human beings, products have a life cycle. Human beings pass through various stages such as birth, growth, maturity, decline and death. A similar life cycle is seen in the case of products with stages of market development stage, growth stage, maturity stage and decline stage (Levitt, 1965). The model assumed that products have a limited life, product sales pass through distinct stages, and products require different marketing strategies in each stage of the life cycle. The model has significant impact upon business strategy and corporate performance.

As with most models, the PLC model has its own limitations. First, the model is not well-suited for forecasting. Products do not have a predictable life as living organisms, and the specific life cycle curves followed by different products vary substantially with unpredictable duration for each stage. Second, not all products go through every stage of the PLC. There have been many cases where products have gone straight from introduction to decline, because of bad marketing, misconceived features, lack of value to the consumer or simply a lack of need for such a product. Moreover, some products have not yet experienced a decline, but remained popular over years. These limitations, not surprisingly, also apply to Plog's and Butler's models.

## Plog's psychographic curve

Plog (1974, 2001) sought to explain how the travel characteristics of the various psychographic personality types lead to destinations' rise and fall in popularity. Basically, his model was based on his social psychology research in the United States. It assumed that a destination evolves through a life cycle and attracts first the adventurers then progressively less adventuresome tourists. The psychographic types of travellers fall on a continuum with two extremes from Allocentric or Venturer to Psychocentric or Dependable, with most people falling somewhere in between (see Figure 15.1).

Summarizing his work, Allocentrics (later renamed Venturers) tend to be self-confident, intellectually curious and have a strong desire to explore the world of ideas and places. They prefer non-touristy areas, novel and different destinations. They enjoy the sense of discovery and delight in new experiences, before others have visited the area. The Psychocentrics (later renamed Dependables and since renamed

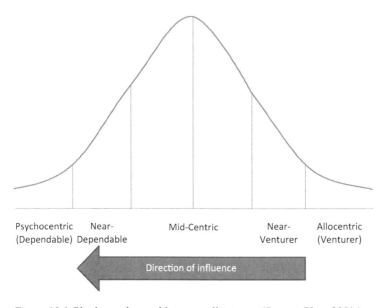

*Figure 15.1* Plog's psychographic personality types. (Source: Plog, 2001.)

as Authentics), lie at the other extreme. They are inhibited, non-adventurous and prefer a familiar atmosphere and heavily developed sites when they travel. From his study, the archetypes of the two personalities are rare, about 2.5 per cent of population can be classified as Dependables and slightly over 4 per cent as Venturers. The remainder falls into the groups in between, such as Near-Dependable, Near-Venturers, or the largest group, Mid-Centrics (since divided into Centric Dependables and Centric venturers). This mid group displays some tendencies of its more extreme end of the spectrum but to a much less extent. Some lean towards being more adventurous, while others lean toward being more cautious. But, for the most part, these traits moderate travel, rather than define it. The mid group travel for relaxation, the aesthetic pleasures of natural and historic features, need for a change, for sensual pleasure, for pleasant social interaction with friends and relatives.

Plog claimed that most destinations typically follow a relatively predictable but uncontrolled close-ended cycle from birth to maturity and finally to old age and decline, as they evolve from attraction the allocentric/venturer tourist first and then more toward a more psychocentric/dependable market. Indeed, he states:

> [W]hen the appeal of the resort passes the magic mid-point in the population curve of travellers … the destination moves towards the Psychocentric end of the continuum, in terms of its appeal in popularity, it begins to draw on a smaller number of travellers [it is approaching a declining curve, which results in] the destination moving …, however gradually or slowly, but far too often towards the potential of its own demise.
>
> (Plog, 1974, p. 58)

The destination life cycle has different stages, and at each stage the destination appeals to a different psychographic group of travellers. An ideal age exists for most destinations, which Plog called 'young adulthood', which is an early stage of development appealing to Venturer-types. In the middle of the growth-cycle stage, when Near-Venturers constitute the majority of tourist arrivals, Plog stressed it is the 'ideal psychographic positioning' for most destinations. Proper planning, protection and preservation are needed at this stage. The life cycle then reaches the peak when there are the majority of Centrics travellers.

Plog stressed that if a destination's planners understand the psychographic curve, it is possible for them to control tourism development and to maintain an ideal positioning, as there are many unplanned destinations facing a declining future because uncontrolled growth has discouraged influential Venturer-type travellers.

In the four decades since it was first published, Plog's model has received some criticism. Smith (1990) questioned the model's measurability and applicability to other cultures. Other key criticisms include the normal bell curve shape, the person specific descriptors, and the applicability of the model. McDonnell (1999) found the model had flaws when tested on Australian tourists to Bali and Fiji. McKercher (2005a) suggested that the descriptors should be trip-specific rather than person-specific as a tourist could display Psychocentric characteristics on one trip, Mid-Centric on another and be the prototypical Allocentric tourist on yet another trip. Others commented that they had tried to apply the model and found it wanting. Pearce (1993), in the comparison of motivation theories, raised questions of Plog's model on measurement, the dominance of a single trait approach, failure to distinguish between extrinsic and intrinsic motivations and lack of a dynamic perspective for individuals (compared with destinations). McKercher (2005a) also highlighted a number of questions: can destinations exist simultaneously at different places in the continuum? Can markets evolve fully through their lifecycles? Must Psychocentric destinations be in decline?

Plog's model, with its assumptions, seeks to apply a single, definitive life cycle stage descriptor to a destination, while McKercher (2005a) claimed that how a destination is classified is market-specific rather than destination-specific. He suggested that as each market has a unique perception, a destination may be Psychocentric or Dependable for some markets, Mid-Centrics for others and Allocentric or Venturer for others still. McKercher also argued that destinations can be seen to exist at multiple stages in their life cycle and serve many markets simultaneously.

### *The validity of Plog's psychographic curve*

In fact, Plog's psychographic curve is a conceptual model. It is meant to be a simplified and idealized version of the complex and dynamic reality, and one should not treat a model as simply a recipe in applying it.

Similar to the original product life cycle, Plog's psychographic curve has its own limitations. Plog's model is good for narrative and not predictive purposes. It is useful as description but not for explanation. As Leiper (1995, p. 90) mentioned, 'the theory is merely a teleology, [it is] not a useful explanation of why a process occurs.' And there are exceptional cases where the model is not applicable, where the destination has not gone through all the stages, this can be caused by poor tourism management and planning or lack of interest from tourists. Furthermore, some destinations have not yet experienced a decline.

There should be no doubt that Plog's life cycle can be applied to one single destination that appears in different markets, or targets different segments or different stages simultaneously, for the reason that the original marketing PLC model can be applied in the same way. The PLC can be applied to a specific product, and the product can appear in different stages of the PLC at the same time, and no one has claimed that the PLC model is invalid. For instance, the motorcycle used to be a popular transportation mode in the post-war period in the United States, reaching its maturity in 1980s, and the product is now at the decline stage, only left with niche market for leisure, mountain bikers, Harley Davidson die-hard fans and the scooters fan clubs. However, on the other side of the world the same product is still at its growth stage, having a huge demand, as it is still the major transportation mode in many developing cities. The product is appearing in these markets the same time, targeting different segments, with different usage and purposes of the product.

## Butler's TALC model

Similar to Plog, Butler (1980, 1990, 2009) has applied the concept of the marketing PLC model to the process of tourist development as it occurs in one particular resort over time (see Figure 15.2).

His Tourism Area Life Cycle (TALC) model stemmed from the belief that resorts are essentially products and would follow a generally similar pattern of development to that of most other products, having a product life cycle. He identified five stages of development and suggested a range of possible future trends that might occur in existing resorts that have reached the end of their product life cycle. One of the core assumptions of the model was that with an increase in the numbers of visitors, or over time, there would be a general reduction in overall quality and attractiveness after capacity levels have been reached. The development of the tourist area could be kept within predetermined capacity limits in order to maintain its competitiveness and attractiveness over a longer period of time. The implication of using his model in the planning and management of tourist resources was that tourist attractions are not infinite and timeless but should be viewed and treated as to be protected and preserved.

Butler's hypothetical cycle of area evolution defined each stage in terms of visitor numbers and changes in the tourist industry and its relationship with the local community. The *Exploration Stage* is equivalent to the introduction stage of the PLC, with a small number of Plog's Allocentrics tourists. It is characterized by difficult access, no or only limited facilities provided by local people, with limited visitor numbers. The *Involvement Stage* is characterized by increased

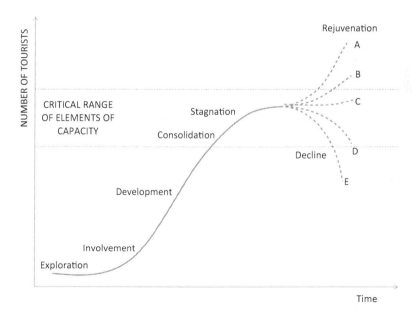

*Figure 15.2* Hypothetical evolution of a tourist area. (Source: Butler, 1980.)

numbers of tourists, with a formal tourism industry having begun and dominated by local residents. The *Development Stage*, which is equivalent to the growth stage of the PLC, is characterized by the rapid expansion of facilities, increasing investment by non-local companies to develop accommodation, natural, cultural and manmade attractions, and a large number of tourists, the type of tourist being the Mid-Centrics of Plog's classification. In the *Consolidation Stage*, which is equivalent to the maturity stage of the PLC, the growth of visitor numbers slows, but the total number of tourists continues to increase. Tourism is dominated by national or multinational organizations. Community antipathy might begin to appear as local residents feel their life styles have been compromised to serve the needs of tourism. After the stage of Consolidation, there is the *Stagnation Stage* and the *Decline Stage,* which are equivalent to the decline stage of the PLC, where the destination is no longer fashionable and sustainable, and the type of tourists would change to the Psychocentrics described by Plog.

Figure 15.2 shows that there are five possible outcomes (A–E). *Rejuvenation* might occur, which the original product life cycle does not cover, where visitor numbers pick up again as shown by curve A. The attractions change to appeal to new markets by either the addition of man-made attractions or by taking advantage of previously untapped natural resources. The new market might not be the Allocentric section of the population but rather a specific interest or activity group. Minor modification and adjustment to capacity levels, and continued protection of resources, could allow continued growth at a much reduced rate (curve B). A readjustment to meet all capacity levels would enable a more stable level of visitation to be maintained after an initial readjustment downwards (curve C). Continued overuse of resources, non-replacement of ageing plant and decreasing competitiveness with other areas would result in a marked decline (curve D). The intervention of war, disease or other catastrophic events would result in an immediate decline (curve E).

Butler's model has been empirically tested no fewer than 50 times since its first publication (Weaver & Lawton, 2006). The model has been applied by various scholars (e.g. Cooper & Jackson, 1989; Debbage, 1990; Foster & Murphy, 1991; Hovinen, 2002; Kermath & Thomas, 1992; Meyer-Arendt, 1985; Strapp, 1988). Among these tests of the model, some questioned reaching the carrying capacity threshold which could be pre-empted by human intervention to increase supply to meet demand. Some questioned the geographic scale meaning of 'destination', and thought that Butler's model could only apply to the limited scale of an individual resort concentration but not to the scale of a country. Others have debated the model's predictive value, and some criticized the model as isolationist, ignoring the external environment, as tourism might not be the only economic activity carried out in the destination.

McKercher (2005b) reflected on several features of Butler's model. First, the term used in 1980 has changed from 'tourist area evolution' to 'tourism area life cycle' over the years. McKercher suggested that evolution is defined as a continuous change from a simple to a more complex form, which implies an open-ended, ongoing and infinite process where change is part of the normal order of events.

On the other hand, life cycle is finite, and has a limited span with birth, life and death. Second, the model by Butler showed only one developmental cycle in the overall evolution of a destination rather than an entire life span of a destination. McKercher mentioned that destinations may evolve through a series of cycles, with the life of the destination portrayed by the sum of these cycles. Prideaux (2000, 2004) also disagreed with the simplicity of Butler's model which regards destinations as single entities, he recognized the complexity and suggested that destinations have multiple development cycles as they evolve from serving only local market to larger markets such as regional, national and international markets.

Moreover, McKercher (2005b) pointed out that a destination should represent an amalgam of products that are clustered geographically rather than the assumption of Butler's model that destination is a single product. McKercher suggested that it might be more appropriate to portray a destination as a product class which demands different approaches to management than single products, for the goal is to maintain the health and competitive position of the product class as a whole, rather than to ensure the continued existence of any single component.

### *The validity of Butler's TALC model*

Butler (2006) believed that the basic tenets of the model are as, or perhaps even more, applicable today than years ago. McKercher (2005b) also stressed that Butler's model remains as relevant as it was, or maybe more relevant given the dramatic changes predicted in global tourism. Butler (2006) himself strongly believes the notion of carrying capacity is still central to the process of a destination. Butler stressed that, in reality, the resort cannot exist forever and the decline is only inevitable if deliberate management and appropriate action are absent.

Butler (2006, p. 289) stressed that his model was 'a generalized simplistic model and would not fit perfectly, or even closely, all the many specific and unique cases to which it has been applied'. Johnston (2006) pointed out that the model would not capture the totality of the life cycle variation, but rather reflected one of the many possible patterns of development, whereas Weaver and Lawton (2006) found the model an 'ideal type' which showed what takes place when the distortions of real life are removed. Cooper and Jackson (1989) also claimed that the model was 'destination specific, with stages and turning points only evident with hindsight'.

Tourist destination, as defined by Butler (2009), is a place where tourists plan to spend time away from home. This geographical area could be as small as a self-contained centre such as village or town, or be as broad as a region, island or country. It encompasses all the organizations, companies, individuals and government bodies which offer products and services to people visiting the destination, as well as natural and artificial resources and attractions. Butler stressed that tourist destination is considered complex to define but it tends to refer only to the geographical unit in which products can be purchased or experienced. Thus a destination shall be not treated as a product class, but rather a 'gigantic product' or a product mix which composed of a combination of various products.

In marketing terminologies, a product class is a group or a range of products that may serve as substitutes for one another and fulfil the same need. While a product mix is generally defined as the total composite of products, consisting of both product lines and individual products. It is a range of associated products that yields larger sales revenue when marketed together than if they were marketed individually or in isolation from others.

A destination is a tourism product. Hall and Lew (2009) mentioned that a tourism product is an amalgam of tangible and intangible elements, as well as experiences, including physical resources, people, environments, infrastructure, materials, goods and services. Hall (2005) stated that most of the time a tourist is simultaneously consuming at least four embedded products, namely, service product, tourism business product, destination product, and tourist trip product. Thus a destination embedded a bunch of service products as well as tourist business products, which is the sum of all experiences at the destination including those supplied by firms and those provided through social interaction with communities, people and place.

The combination of a wide range of tourism business products are operated by different individual firms or agencies. Within this wide range of products, some can be grouped under the same product lines, such as resorts, which can be substituted for one another, whereas some are individual products which appeal to different types of tourists, such as different historical sites and theme parks. Without one or a few components of this product mix, the destination may not be as appealing to tourists as it could be. Thus individual operators shall take the initiative to manage the destination based on the stage of the cycle of a destination and take pre-emptive measures to prolong its growth stage and rejuvenate a destination before it is too late to react.

## Conclusion

The models by Plog and Butler remain relevant today; both put forward useful insights of issues a destination must pay attention to in order to ensure an ongoing sustainability. As Chen et al. (2011) concluded, Plog's model highlights the personality aspects in explaining tourist behaviour, which differ from the conventional interpretations that assume homogenous personality.

As with most models, Plog's and Butler's models have their flaws and limitations; however, they are still effective in identifying the components of any tourism system, Plog's model helps in explaining a destination rise and fall in popularity, whereas Butler's model reminds the industry players of the existence of carrying capacity of a destination, and the urgency for proper management and actions in preserving and protecting a destination to avoid a destination from reaching its decline stage.

As Levitt (1965) suggested, to extend a destination's life cycle, its related organizations should take a proactive role in long-term planning starting early from pre-introduction stage, while throughout the life cycle stages of a destination, organizations can work on four strategies (frequent usage, varied usage, new users, new uses) to prolong the duration of growth and maturity stages. A destination can attract its present tourists to visit more frequently (frequent usage), or these tourists might be attracted to the destination for different purposes such as leisure, business or special events (varied usage); a destination can also appeal to other tourists such as tourists with special interests such as skiing, hiking, golfing, heritage or culture (new users); or marketers can create new uses of a destination by providing new tourist attractions, theme parks, or facilities such as cruise terminals (new uses).

## References

Butler, R.W. (1980). The concept of a tourist area cycle of evolution: Implications for management of resources. *Canadian Geographer,* 24(1), 5–12.

Butler, R.W. (1990). The resort cycle revisited – A decade of discussion. *Association of American Geographers Conference*, Toronto, March 1990.

Butler, R.W. (2006). The future and the TALC. In R.W. Butler (ed.), *The tourism area life cycle, Vol. 2: Conceptual and theoretical issues* (pp. 281–290). Clevedon: Channel View Publications.

Butler, R.W. (2009). Tourism destination development: Cycles and forces, myths and realities. *Tourism Recreation Research*, 34 (3), 247–254.

Chen, Y., Mak, B., & McKercher, B. (2011). What drives people to travel: Integrating the tourist motivation paradigms. *Journal of China Tourism Research*, 7(2), 120–136.

Cooper, C., & Jackson, S. (1989). Destination life cycle: The Isle of Man case study. *Annals of Tourism Research*, 16(3), 377–398.

Debbage, K.G. (1990). Oligopoly and the resort cycle in the Bahamas. *Annals of Tourism Research,* 17(4), 513–527.

Foster, D.M., & Murphy, P. (1991). Resort cycle revisited: The retirement connection. *Annals of Tourism Research*, 18(4), 553–567.

Hall, C.M. (2005). *Tourism: Rethinking the social science of mobility.* Harlow: Prentice-Hall.

Hall, C.M., & Lew, A.A. (2009). *Understanding and Managing Tourism Impacts: An Integrated Approach.* Oxon: Routledge.

Hovinen, G. R. (2002). Revisiting the destination lifecycle model. *Annals of Tourism Research*, 29(1), 209–230.

Johnston, S. (2006). The ontological foundation of the TALC. In R.W. Butler (ed.), *The tourism area life cycle, Vol. 2: Conceptual and theoretical issues* (pp.7–28). Clevedon: Channel View Publications.

Kermath, B.M., & Thomas, R.N. (1992). Spatial dynamics of resorts: Sosua, Dominican Republic. *Annals of Tourism Research*, 19(2), 173–190.

Leiper, N. (1995). *Tourism management.* Abbotsford: TAFE Publications.

Levitt, T. (1965). Exploit the Product Life Cycle. *Harvard Business Review*, 43 (November–December), 81–94.

McDonnell, I. (1999). The intefrag marketing continuum: A tool for tourism marketers. *Journal of Travel & Tourism Marketing*, 13(1), 25–39.

McKercher, B. (2005a). Are psychographics predictors of destination life cycles? *Journal of Travel and Tourism Marketing*, 19(1), 49–55.

McKercher, B. (2005b). Destinations as products? a reflection on Butler's life cycle. *Tourism Recreation Research,* 30(3), 97–102.

Meyer-Arendt, K.J. (1985). The Grand Isle, Louisiana resort cycle. *Annals of Tourism Research*, 12(3), 449–465.

Pearce, P.L. (1993). Fundamentals of tourist motivation. In D.G. Pearce R.W. & Butler (eds.), *Tourism research: Critiques and challenges* (pp.113–134). London: Routledge.

Plog, S.C. (1974). Why destination areas rise and fall in popularity. *Cornell Hotel and Restaurant Administration Quarterly*, 14(4), 55–58.

Plog, S.C. (2001). Why destination areas rise and fall in popularity: An update of a Cornell Quarterly classic. *Cornell Hotel and Restaurant Administration Quarterly*, 42(3), 13–24.

Prideaux, B. (2000). The resort development spectrum – A new approach to modeling resort development. *Tourism Management,* 21, 225–240.

Prideaux, B. (2004). The resort development spectrum: The case of the Gold Coast, Australia. *Tourism Geographies* 6(1), 26–58.

Smith, S.L.J. (1990). A test of Plog's allocentric/psychocentric model: Evidence from seven nations. *Journal of Travel Research*, 28(4), 40–43.

Strapp, J.D. (1988). The resort cycle and second home. *Annals of Tourism Research*, 19(2), 504–516.

Weaver, D., & Lawton, L. (2006). *Tourism Management*. 3rd ed., Milton, Australia: John Wiley.

# 16  A new tourism map for Dubai's top source market

*Naeema Alhosani*

## Introduction

One of the most important aspects of the current economic recovery in many regions and countries around the world is a vibrant tourism sector and its related industries. Indeed, tourism has become an essential source of a country's income as witnessed in recent years in the United Arab Emirates (UAE). The UAE is located in the south-western angle of the Arabian Gulf neighbouring Saudi Arabia to the south, Oman to the east, and Qatar to the west. The UAE has an area of 77,000 km, which is mainly flat, and is 97 per cent desert. The UAE comprises seven emirates: Abu Dhabi (the capital), Dubai, Sharjah, Ajman, Ras al-Khaimah, Fujairah and Umm al-Quwain (Al Qaydi *et al.*, 2005) (see Figure 16.1). The largest and richest of the seven emirates is Abu Dhabi; the second largest is Dubai (Sharpley, 2008).

The UAE issued a long-term plan for a diverse economy, including reduced dependence on the oil sector as the primary source of economic activity, as a long-term policy. Meanwhile, the UAE will make better use of non-oil sectors which will contribute more to its Gross Domestic Product (GDP) by the year 2030. The UAE places tourism at the core of its economic development plans in order to diversify and strengthen its economies whilst decreasing its dependency on fluctuating oil prices (Sharpley, 2008). The leading emirate in diversifying its economy through tourism is Dubai. In particular, the city-state of Dubai has experienced rapid growth in tourist arrivals and is now widely acknowledged to be amongst the world's leading international tourist destinations (MacDonald, 2000; Sharpley, 2008).

Today, Dubai has evolved into a service hub with financial, shipping and commercial services, media and tourism. This is mainly due to its strategic geographic location at the 'confluence of the Middle East, Asia, Eastern Africa, and Central/Eastern Europe' (Balakrishnan, 2008, p. 64). Indeed, the highly publicized development of Dubai's tourism infrastructure has placed the city-state in a dominant position on the global tourism map (Bagaeen, 2007; Sharpley, 2008). The Department of Tourism and Commerce Marketing (DTCM) is the only authority in Dubai that is responsible for tourist planning and development in the city. It was reported in June 2014 that Dubai's top ten tourism source markets showed

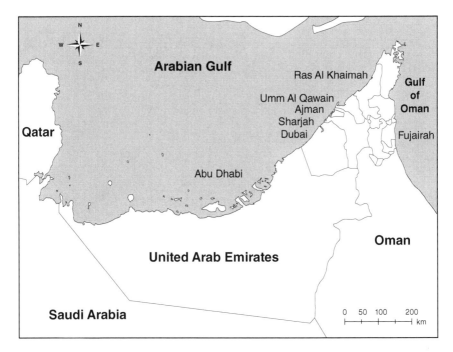

*Figure 16.1* United Arab Emirates.

some small changes in positioning and continued to show the diversity of visitors travelling to Dubai. Saudi Arabia, India, UK, USA, Russia, China, Iran, Oman, Kuwait and Germany made up the top ten in terms of tourist-generation from January to June 2014. Saudi single male tourists are the primary source of tourists in Dubai and will be the focus of this research.

Hall stated that planning is an essential element of successful tourism development (Hall, 2000). That is, effective planning is necessary to ensure that the tourism sector is developed according to broader economic and social development goals leading to its sustainability (Timothy, 1998). Furthermore, appropriate mechanisms and processes should be in place to ensure the management, promotion and monitoring of developments. Henderson (2006a) has maintained that Dubai has established a tourism environment with a sophisticated infrastructure and a high-quality chain of entertainment and tourism attractions including shopping malls, hotels, conferences, conventions, meetings and, unusually in a desert land country, a ski slope in a shopping mall.

For Dubai to live up to its ambitions in fulfilling its vision for 2020 of attracting up to twenty million visitors, it became a top priority within its planning scheme to maintain its top source market of Saudi single male tourists. However, with all the tourism accomplishments in Dubai that should be of interest to many tourism researchers, no research has so far examined tourism development planning processes in Dubai for maintaining its top source market. The main purpose of this chapter is to fill this gap; also, to call for the preparation of a new tourism map for Dubai that takes into consideration the needs of its top tourism market. The study tries to address the following key research questions: (a) what do Saudi single male tourists need to be included in the new Dubai tourism map? (b) Why do Saudi single male tourists choose specific sites to be included in the new Dubai tourism map?

## Literature review

Some research has been carried out on tourism in the Middle East (Daher, 2006; Greene & O'Loughlin, 1999; Kelly, 1998; Wahab, 2000), and there are studies that address tourism development in Dubai (Bagaeen, 2007; Balakrishnan, 2008; Govers & Go, 2005, 2009; Henderson, 2006a, 2006b; Junemo, 2004; Meethan, 2011; Saleh, *et al.*, 2013; Sharpley, 2008; Stephenson, 2014). However, there is no research on the issue of the design of a new tourism map for Dubai that takes into consideration the needs of its top tourist market. Data released by the DTCM has shown that in the first half of 2014, guest numbers across all hotel establishments (hotels and hotel apartments) reached 5.8 million, which indicates an increase in the figures for the same period in 2013.

The Director-General of the DTCM, Mr. Almarri, indicated that Dubai is the first choice for Saudi tourists as their holiday destination, since Dubai offers several tourism attractions that are not available in other Gulf Cooperation Council (GCC) countries such as luxurious hotels, imaginative shopping malls, luxurious restaurants and coffee shops, and all types of entertainment. Moreover, there are many varied events during the year which contribute to attracting larger numbers of tourists to Dubai, such as the Dubai Shopping Festival (DSF), Dubai Summer Surprises (DSS) and Eid in Dubai.

The Saudi Public Authority for Tourism and Antiquities revealed that during the summer of 2014 (June–August), Saudi tourists spent US$1.68 billion outside the kingdom, compared with US$858,666,667 for the same period in 2013, an increase of 95.65 per cent. In addition, the statistical report from the Saudi Public Authority for Tourism and Antiquities for summer 2014 stated that Dubai is the most attractive destination for Saudi tourists, visited by 51 per cent; the Middle East was visited by 6.3 per cent, South Asia by 2.9 per cent, and Europe and America by 2.1 per cent (Al Hadrami, 2014).

According to the data released by the DTCM, Saudi Arabia is the top tourism source market for Dubai. Therefore, Saudi Arabian tourists have a significant role in enhancing Dubai tourism economy. This implies that tourism planners within the DTCM should place enough emphasis on Saudi tourists visiting Dubai as they provide substantial opportunities for growth. Since no tourism scholars have designed a new tourism map for Saudi single male tourists, this chapter focuses on exploring their tourism needs in order to help in planning new developments in Dubai, and include them in its new tourism map.

## Methodology

Based on the findings of previous studies on Saudi tourists in Dubai and the statistical data on Saudi visitors to Dubai per month for the years between 2008 and 2013 (General Directorate of Residency and Foreigners) the majority of Saudi tourists were single males. Therefore in carrying out this study, the researcher utilized a qualitative method to cover more aspects of the issues involved. It was based on a series of questions which aimed to elicit more detailed insights relating to the responses in previous studies' questionnaires. The study was carried out using semi-structured (in-depth) interviews to collect data on the issue of designing a proper tourism plan for Saudi tourists. Participants were Saudi Arabian tourists who visited the sites of major tourist attractions in Dubai.

The semi-structured interviews took 10–15 minutes each. Questions were specific to experiences of Saudi tourists in Dubai: new tourist facilities they want to see in the city, what facilities they were satisfied with, and how they feel about future projects of tourism in Dubai that better accommodate their needs. The semi-structured interviews took place until redundancy was reached. For qualitative validity, the following strategies were adopted by checking their validity to enhance the accuracy of the findings: interviews were recorded and then transcribed into text; triangulating of data from different sources of information was conducted; the study data were collected from multiple sources including interviews, observations and questionnaires.

Semi-structured interviews were held with 30 Saudi single male tourists by the author in October 2014, during the Eid-Al-Adha holiday. All of the individuals interviewed were between the ages of 20 and 30, and came from different parts of Saudi Arabia. This age group represents the majority of Saudi tourists visiting Dubai and hence their answers will play an important role in achieving the study's goal. The data collection process took a week to complete.

## Findings

For the interview, six main questions were asked to Saudi Arabian single male tourists in order to help develop a proposed tourism plan for Dubai, taking into consideration the needs of its top tourist market. The main point of the interview at the very beginning was about the Saudi single males' favourite destinations in Dubai. The following represents the preferences of the majority of the Saudi tourists:

> Our favorite destination in Dubai is the luxury malls, cinema theatres, and the global village.
>
> (Saudi single male tourists, 20–30 years)

Then, participants were asked about the types of tourist facilities that they visit in Dubai which are not available in their country. The findings indicated that the majority agreed that such facilities as cinemas, luxury malls and water parks are most visited by Saudi single male tourists, particularly because such adult entertainment is banned in Saudi Arabia:

> We missed some attractions in our home country by different levels like some of them are not in the same level of luxury or quality, and some of them do not exist at all, therefore we come to Dubai to visit them and enjoy ourselves.
>
> (Saudi single male tourists, 20–30 years)

Also, to examine the perception of Saudi single male tourists about proposed facilities in the Dubai tourism map that would enhance their tourism experience in the city, the participants were asked about types of future tourism development that would meet their needs. It was found that the following were perceived as the most desired for any future tourism plans:

> Since we like very much to visit the luxury malls in Dubai, the cinemas, and the sky diving site, we want these types of places to be increased in Dubai tourism map.
>
> (Saudi single male tourists, 20–30 years)

It was also found that the participants would like to have a Disneyland in Dubai:

> Dubai has all types of activities with the exception of Disneyland park?… YES. this is what we wish Dubai government to think about building Disneyland.
>
> (Saudi single male tourists, 20–30 years)

The majority of the interviewees preferred closed places because of the weather and high temperatures in the summer:

> We can see and feel that Dubai's climate most of the year is hot and since we come Dubai most of the year we prefer to visit closed tourism places in Dubai.
>
> (Saudi single male tourists, 20–30 years)

Moreover, the following represents their preferred entertainment activities in Dubai:

> [F]or sure cinema theaters, water parks, and ski Dubai are the most activities that we LIKE to do it in our visiting to Dubai…they are Really wonderful places, as well as enjoyable places!, we feel ourselves have fun.
>
> (Saudi single male tourists, 20–30 years)

## Discussion

Tourism has become one of the fastest growing parts of Dubai's economy as it has become one of the world's fastest growing tourist destinations (Henderson, 2006a).

The purpose of this study was to analyse the patterns of Saudi tourists flow to Dubai, especially the single male tourists, and ensure that Dubai provides for them what they need and meet their expectations. The findings of this study can have a positive impact on the tourism planning schemes for Dubai vision for 2020.

The study further indicates that by comparing the tourism sites in Dubai with those of Saudi Arabia, the interviewees expressed full satisfaction with Dubai tourism facilities and especially the freedom that single male Saudis enjoy. It shows that the most places that Saudi single male tourists frequently visit in Dubai are the luxury malls, cinemas and Global Village. One key difference between Saudi cafes and restaurants and the corresponding ones in Dubai, single males are not particularly restricted in sitting in specific section for single men as the situation in Saudi Arabia. In addition, cinemas in Saudi Arabia do not go in accordance with cultural values and in some cases with religious teachings, while most of the malls in Dubai have cinemas which are the number one entertainment activity for single male Saudi tourist. Moreover, in most cases and at certain shopping peak times, single men are not allowed into Saudi Arabia malls.

In this respect, one extremely important site for Saudi single male tourists is Global Village. This tourism site provides access to the cultures of so many countries which are represented in the event. Saudi single male tourists expressed their absolute satisfaction with this tourism site.

Water parks are not available in Saudi Arabia, while Dubai has many, like 'Wild Wadi Water Park' which is considered as one of the world's most impressive water parks. This is one reason that single Saudi male tourists come to Dubai. Further, Skydive, located on the borders of the manmade islands, is considered to be the world's premier skydiving facility. They enjoyed visiting it and partaking in the many services that are provided for tourism.

In addition, single males expressed the need to establish a Disneyland park in the new Dubai tourism map. Dubai has become an international tourism destination and this attraction will increase the number of tourists from almost all over the world. It can be concluded that Saudi tourists will be the first visitors to such a park for several reasons; one of them is that Dubai occupies a geographical location or strategic location in the world map; it is a meeting channel between Asia, Africa and Europe that encourages the Saudi tourists to think of Dubai as their first, nearest and best tourism destination. Furthermore, most travellers need to get a visit visa prior to entering Dubai; however, residents of GCC countries such as Saudi Arabia can get access to Dubai without needing a tourist visa. Henderson (2006a) states that the Dubai government has simplified visa procedures to streamline passenger processing. Most Saudi tourists expressed the need for indoor tourist facilities due to the hot weather in Dubai. Also, the majority of activities that they come to Dubai for are entertainment activities, like watching movies in cinemas, and playing in Wild Wadi Water Park and in Ski Dubai; therefore, the planners have to increase these kinds of activities.

The survey results shed light on the importance of early planning for some tourist programmes and facilities that target specific groups of tourists in specific markets to achieve great results, and therefore should be the focus, according

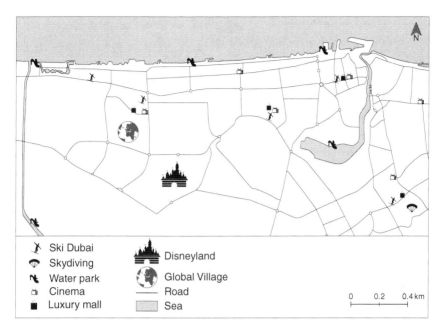

*Figure 16.2* A new proposed tourism map for single male Saudis.

to the needs of visitors and their aspirations. Dubai recognized that 'one of the key factors for the success of Dubai's tourism industry is the strategic partnership between the government and the private sector' (Sharpley, 2008). Therefore, Dubai has all the elements to attract visitors from different countries, and there is strong cooperation between the several government agencies and the private sector (tourism agencies) in order to provide facilities to increase the attractiveness of the emirate's tourism, as in the meetings between the Director-General of Dubai Municipality and the Director General of the DTCM, that seek to produce several projects that will boost tourism in Dubai and may add much charm to the city. Figure 16.2 shows a new map of Dubai's top source market, single male Saudi tourists, based on the study results.

## Conclusion

This study represents a preliminary step in understanding tourism development planning in Dubai. The survey results have indicated and offered several suggestions on how Dubai can develop tourism projects, as well as meeting the needs of its top tourism source market. These derived recommendations take into particular consideration the Saudi government social restrictions regarding the mixing of men and women. Sites of adult entertainment where men and women might socialize, such as cinemas, skydiving, coffee shops, night clubs, water parks or theme parks, are completely banned in Saudi Arabia.

In Saudi Arabia, not only may men not mix with unrelated women, they are not even allowed to smoke or wear shorts in public. These may be push factors for Saudi tourists, while Dubai as a modern and open city with all the imaginative tourism attractions it is offering are pull factors for Saudi tourists to visit Dubai more frequently.

In addition, tourism development plans should take into consideration the development of a programme of entertainment themed towards Saudi single male tourists who are coming to Dubai and thus provide them with all their favourite attractions. Dubai should consider significantly the needs of its top source market and make sure to offer what is needed and expected from their favourite tourism destination. Moreover, more opportunities should be provided for Saudi single male tourists' community participation in tourism planning and development in Dubai.

The above recommendations are to support the future development of tourism in Dubai. The study calls for a new map for tourism in Dubai with more adult activities, events and attractions. This strategy will help Dubai maintain growth rates in its tourism top markets in order to achieve its vision for 2020.

## Acknowledgements

The author would like to thank Ms. Athheba Al Ahbabi at United Arab Emirates University (UAEU) and Ms. Balqees Al Braiki for their assistance in designing the maps.

## References

Al Hadrami, M. (2014, September 9). Dubai tops the fastest growing business centers in the world. *Al-Ittihad* Newspaper. Retrieved September 15, 2014, from http://www.alittihad. ae/details.php?id=78496&y=2014

Al Qaydi, S.S. Al Ullama, H., Al Kitbi, A., & Ridha, N. (2005). *Geography of the United Arab Emirates*. Al Ain: United Arab Emirates University Publications.

Bagaeen, S. (2007). Brand Dubai: The instant city or the instantly recognizable city. *International Planning Studies, 12* (2), 173–197.

Balakrishnan, M. S. (2008). Dubai – a star in the east: A case study in strategic destination branding. *Journal of Place Management and Development, 1* (1), 62–69.

Daher, R. (Ed.). (2006). *Tourism in the Middle East*. Clevedon, UK: Channel View Publications.

Davis, M. (2006). Fear and money in Dubai, *New Left Review, 41*, 47–68.

Dubai Mall (http://www.thedubaimall.com/en/Index.aspx).

Govers, R., & Go, F. M. (2005). Projected destination image online: Website content analysis of pictures and text. *Information Technology and Tourism, 7*, 73–89.

Govers, R., & Go, F. M. (2009). *Place branding: Global, virtual and physical identities, constructed, Imagined and experienced*. Basingstoke, Hampshire, UK: Macmillan.

Greene, G., & O'Loughlin, S. (1999). Hotels in the Middle East: Trends and opportunities. *Travel & Tourism Analyst, 4*, 65–88.

Hall, C. M. (2000). *Tourism planning: Processes, relationships*. Harlow, UK: Prentice Hall.

Henderson, J. C. (2006a). Tourism in Dubai: Overcoming barriers to destination development. *International Journal of Tourism Research, 8*, 87–99.

Henderson, J. C. (2006b). Destination development: Singapore and Dubai compared. *Journal of Travel and Tourism Marketing, 20* (3/4), 33– 45.

Holly, T. (2002). Shopping spree. *Travel Agent*, 314 (12), 1.

Junemo, M. (2004). Let's build a palm island! Playfulness in complex times. In M. Sheller & J. Urry (eds.), *Tourism mobilities: Places to play, places in play* (pp. 181–191). London: Routledge.

Kelly, M. (1998). Jordan's potential tourism development. *Annals of Tourism Research*, *25*(4), 904–918.

MacDonald, D. (2000). Tourism development: The Dubai case study. In P. Dew & A. Shoult (eds.), *Doing business with the UAE* (pp. 30–35). London: Kogan Page.

Meethan, K. (2011). Dubai: An exotic destination with a cosmopolitan lifestyle. In J. Mosedale (Ed.), *Political economy of tourism: A critical perspective* (pp. 175–188). London: Routledge.

Ministry of Interior. (2013). *Statistical data of Saudis visiting Dubai per month for the years 2008–2013* Dubai. UAE: U.A.E. Ministry of Interior, General Directorate of Residency and Foreigners Affairs-Dubai.

Saleh, A., Assaf, G., Ihalanayaki, R., & Lung, S. (2013). A panel cointegration analysis of the impact of tourism on economic growth: Evidence from the Middle East Region. *International Journal of Tourism Research, 14* (4), 313–416.

Sharpley, R. (2008). Planning for tourism: The case of Dubai. *Tourism and Hospitality Planning and Development, 5* (1), 13–30.

Stephenson, M. L. (2014). Tourism, development and 'destination Dubai': cultural dilemmas and future challenges. *Current Issues in Tourism*, 17 (8), 723–738.

Timothy, D. (1998). Cooperative tourism planning in a developing destination. *Journal of Sustainable Tourism, 6* (1), 52–68.

Wahab, S. (2000). Middle East. In A. Lockwood & S. Medlik (eds.), *Tourism and hospitality in the 21st Century* (pp. 163–171). Oxford: Butterworth-Heinemann.

# 17 Innovative system indicators for Islamic tourism using C-PEST factors

*Nor'Ain Othman and Salamiah A. Jamal*

## Introduction

Malaysia is now looking for a new horizon of global tourism and plays a leading role in promoting Islamic tourism (Utusan Malaysia, 2010). The Muslim market is of great significance and the number of Muslim travellers is expected to increase as the global population increases, along with the prosperity in Muslim countries such as Brunei, Indonesia, Malaysia and Singapore (Scott & Jafari, 2010). More than 50 Muslim countries and about 1.6 billion Muslims are the potential and lucrative market. The United Nations World Tourism Organization (UNWTO) reports that international tourism continued its momentum with a 5 per cent growth, or an additional 52 million international tourists, recorded a world total of 1,087 billion arrivals in 2013. Muslim tourism contributed US$141 billion, that is, more than 10 per cent of global tourism, 78 per cent from 57 Organisation of Islamic Cooperation (OIC) Muslim-majority countries and 22 per cent from Western Muslim-minority countries. The world's Muslim population will increase from 1.6 billion in 2010 to 2.2 billion by 2020 and Muslims will make up 26.4 per cent of the world's total projected population of 8.3 billion in 2030 (Pew Research, 2014).

## Literature review

The tourism industry is volatile, complex and highly competitive. The complexity of this industry requires travel organizations to assess the external environment for outside factors that will affect the performance and existence of an organization. Besides the performance of individual businesses and attractions, the environment and community in the country will also contribute to positive travel experiences among tourists (Formika & Kothari, 2008). Economic, social and political stability is essential for the tourism industry to increase tourist arrivals, attract foreign investors and enhance profitable travel and hospitality businesses to generate income for the country. This could be seen in the negative effects on the tourism industry after 11 September 2001 and after the tsunami disaster in Phuket, Thailand, Sri Lanka and Acheh and related countries.

Malaysia is now looking for a new horizon of global tourism and plays a leading role in promoting Islamic tourism (World Islamic Tourism Conference, 2014).

As mention earlier, the Muslim market is of great significance and it is a lucrative market as the number of Muslim travellers is expected to increase in the future. Most Muslin countries realize the opportunities for tourism development in line with Islamic principles. The concept of halal or Islamic tourism is new to most tourism scholars and there are few studies carried out by researchers that integrate the teaching of Islam and tourism theories. Few tourism models fail to relate to the Islamic concepts in relations to its demand and supply of tourism. Travelling and exploring for the purpose of seeking knowledge, enriching one's experience and improving one's character has been encouraged by Islam. Islamic tourism can be defined as 'tourism activities, development of product and services, marketing strategies in accordance to Islamic values, principles and guidelines targeted to Muslim tourism for knowledgeable and holistic travel' (Othman, Taha, Ibrahim, Isa & Tarmudi, 2010). The development of Islamic tourism gives rise to various tourism business components within the tourism industry, namely tour packages, accommodation, transportation, and food and beverages which need to be studied from the Islamic perspectives. Tourism from the Islamic point of view is integrated into the global vision of civilized interdependent tourism whose principal bases are: respect for noble human values and ethics which preserve human dignity and pride; respect for the natural and societal environment; enhancement of social solidarity by ensuring local people profit from tourist activities; making an effort to give the right of travel to all people by offering services at suitable prices to all the social classes; respect for the families of various religions and various people who want to preserve their values and the education of their children; respect for people who observe Islamic values (Muhammad, 2008; Yusuf, 2009).

Even though Islamic tourism focuses on the Muslim market, non-Muslim tourists are also welcome to experience the halal activities, hotels and food and beverages that can be viewed as a knowledgeable travel and wholesome fun. 'Islamic tourism' is a new trend in the Arab region which is not simply based on the commercialization of religious pilgrimage, but aims to give a more local and regional cultural context to cultures of travel. A Euromonitor International report highlighted the potential for a boom in halal tourism, which follows Islamic rules. It forecasted 66 per cent growth in inbound tourists in the Middle East by 2011 to 55 million people due to the difficulty of getting visas from Western Europe and United States. The World Tourism Organization's 'Tourism 2020 Vision' forecasts show that international tourist arrivals are expected to reach over 1.56 billion by the year 2020. In the Middle East, the regional growth rate of tourist arrivals of 7.1 per cent will double its world market share from 2.2 per cent in 1995 to 4.4 per cent in 2020. The Arab world is at a turning point where new patterns of tourism strategies are developed to showcase novel products. Tourism Malaysia reported that there is an increase in tourist arrivals to Malaysia from countries such as the United Arab Emirates, Iran, Turkey, Egypt, Jordan and Saudi Arabia. This gives the opportunity for Malaysia to introduce Islamic tourism as a product to enhance the image of Malaysia as a halal hub.

Tourism strategies need to be formulated to meet the demand of the new Islamic market. Strategic analysis utilizes techniques for situational analysis.

This involves reporting on current and future opportunities and threats and the internal strengths and weaknesses of the situation. The opportunities and threats that summarize the external environmental factors and the key elements are C-PEST factors (which refers to the Competitive, Political, Economic, Socio-cultural and Technological), while the strengths and weaknesses analysis summarizes the state of the internal resources of the organization. The study examines other significant destinations for comparative purposes, for example some Muslim countries that are well known in promoting their Islamic heritage as their tourism products to tourists and some other countries, for example Korea and Switzerland, that are trying to provide 'halal' tourism products and services for Muslim tourists from other parts of the world. These countries are known as destinations that have become part of Islamic routes and are safely accessible for Muslim and non-Muslim tourists.

The demand for Islamic tourism, especially in relation to the needs and expectations of Muslim travellers was examined by the researcher, together with the opinions and feedback from domestic and international travellers on the importance of Islamic tourism that includes various components within the tourism industry, namely tour packages, accommodation, transportation and food and beverages, that are in accordance with the principles and rules of Islam. Islamic tourism can be targeted to both the Muslim and non-Muslim market and could be viewed as another way of seeking Islamic knowledge. Is there a demand for Islamic tourism and what are the travellers' opinions and expectations of Islamic travel?

## Methodology

The involvement and participation of the private sectors such as the tour operators, travel agencies, hotels, airlines and restaurants are essential to the success of marketing Islamic tourism in Malaysia. Feedback from the suppliers is therefore important in the formulation of the Islamic tourism strategies and the implementation of an integrated marketing communication targeted to a specific market segment:

- What are the Islamic tourism activities (including goods/products and services) that the travel and tour businesses involved and developed?
- What is the existing level of travel and tour businesses' participation in Islamic tourism activities?
- What are the benefits/contributions of Islamic tourism towards the economic, social and cultural aspects of the country?
- What are the challenges and opportunities faced by the tourism and hospitality businesses in practising Islamic tourism?

The study was carried out in three phases:

- *Phase 1. Preliminary stage.* The preliminary stage of the study identifies the related organizations that are involved in Islamic tourism such as the

Islamic Tourism Centre, Ministry of Tourism. A comprehensive literature review aims to be the foundation of the Islamic tourism concept, theory, definition, principles and other information related to Islam and tourism. Sources of information are gathered from the Holy Quran, Hadith, journals, tourism reports, books, conference proceedings and other research publications.

- *Phase 2. Data collection – tourism and tourist supplier.* The data collected are a combination of primary and secondary data. This study uses quantitative and qualitative methods. Field surveys were conducted with domestic tourists on site and potential tourists at off-site selected markets approached within the vicinity of their workplace or residency or at international airport. Personal interviews were conducted with the key informants from travel and tour operators, exhibition and convention centres, hotels and other related tourism agencies. The purpose of the interview is to identify and examine their involvement in Islamic tourism activities and promotion. This is further supported by the secondary data.
- *Phase 3. Analysis and synthesis.* The analysis of the data was carried out using frequency analysis, descriptive analysis, gap analysis, factor analysis, cross-tabulations, correlations, *t*-test, Anova and regression. There should be indicators used to construct the survey questions and analyse the outcome. The outcomes of the analysis will be extracted by SPSS and the Likert-scale technique is used in obtaining the score value. The final and complete analysis will provide the basis for synthesizing the issues.

This study is on-going and will be completed by December 2015.

## Findings

Indicators can be measured and monitored to reveal the changing conditions of a particular phenomenon. The tourism system is complex and has a number of tourism-related indicators. Factors that influence actual selection of working indicators in a particular destination or business include policy relevance, types of approach to be adopted, measurability, level of public support, politics etc. (Butler, 1999). Jovicic and Illic (2010) introduced the five groups of the comparable indicators that can be adapted to Islamic tourism, which are as follows:

- Economic indicators reflect the contribution that Islamic tourism is making to the local economy.
- Tourist satisfaction is necessarily based on tourist surveys carried out at the destination:

  perception of value for money judged by number of repeat visits;
  tourists' perception of the quality of tourist facilities, environmental quality (water, traffic, congestion, cleanliness, noise) and cultural/social conditions (general cultural interest, friendliness of residents, crime levels.

- Social indicators are related to social integrity that should be assessed in terms of the subjective well-being of the host population.
- Cultural indicators should measure cultural integrity in terms of diversity, individuality and beauty (of cultures and built heritage).
- Environmental indicators should measure environmental quality and the demands made by tourists in terms of different environmental media (water, air, biodiversity, landscape etc.).

Social indicators literature shows that visitor satisfaction can be an indicator which measures the level of visitor satisfaction which is measured using the percentage of tourists who have revisited the destinations. Ibrahim, Othman and Isa (2010) indicated that the influx, outstanding expenditure and spending power among Middle Eastern tourists have contributed to the significant impact on the economy of Malaysia. The finding indicated that Middle Eastern tourists' major activities are shopping, sightseeing and visiting beaches. Middle Eastern tourists were satisfied with the services offered by the hotel staff in terms of courtesy and performing services effectively and efficiently. They preferred Middle Eastern food and they suggested that Arabic language signage should be put up at tourist spots. Although Malaysia is the top holiday destination in Asia, it faces competition from Thailand, Singapore, India, China and Hong Kong (Insights from Tourism Malaysia Middle East Study, 2014).

According to the World Tourism Organization (2004) guidebook, socio-cultural benefits to communities can be very difficult to measure. It further indicated the components of the issues and the indicators shown in Table 17.1.

Cultural indicators express the level of protection of cultural identity of a local community from the influence of tourists who have different cultural values (Jovicic & Ilic, 2001). It involves two indicators: first, *the ratio between accommodation capacities and the number of local population* is an indicator of cultural influence, in terms of architectural appearance of the tourist region, as well as the demand for securing the necessary infrastructure, services and facilities. It can be a burden if the local community is under pressure and unfavourable. Second, *tourism intensity* shows the degree of cultural saturation of the local community. An extremely high level of cultural saturation has a negative effect on the local community, destroying its cultural identity and diminishing the quality of tourists' experience.

Social indicators show social integrity of local community from aspect of subjective prosperity of domicile population in the given tourist region. The share of tourism in the local net national product is an indicator which shows the extent to which the local community realizes the gain from Islamic tourism development. The percentage of tourists who do not travel by means of tour operators/agencies represents an indicator of usefulness of Islamic tourism for the local community.

*Table 17.1* Components of issues and indicators

| Components of the issue | Indicators |
|---|---|
| Community attitudes to tourism (including community agreement and coherence on tourism, perception and acceptance of tourism | • Existence of a community tourism plan<br>• Frequency of community meetings and attendance rates<br>• Frequency of tourism plan updates<br>• Level of awareness of local values (percentage awareness, percentage supporting)<br>• Percentage who are proud of their community and culture |
| Social benefits associated with tourism | • Number of social services available to the community (percentage which are attributable to tourism)<br>• Percentage who believe that tourism has helped bring new services and infrastructure<br>• Number (percentage) participating in community traditional crafts, skills and customs<br>• Percentage of vernacular architecture preserved |
| General impacts on community life | • Number of tourists per day, per week etc., number per square kilometre<br>• Ratio of tourists to locals (average and peak day)<br>• Percentage local participating in community events<br>• Ratio of tourists to locals at events or ceremonies<br>• Perception of impact on the community using the resident questionnaire<br>• Percentage of local community who agree that their local culture, its integrity and authenticity are being retained |
| Changes to resident lifestyles, (cultural impact, cultural change, community lifestyle, values and customs, traditional occupation) | • Percentage of residents changing from traditional occupation to tourism over previous year(s)<br>• Number or percentage of residents continuing with local dress, customs language, music, cuisine, religion of cultural practices. (e.g. change in number of local residents participating in traditional events (e.g. percentage of locals attending ceremonies)<br>• Number of tourists attending events and percentage of total<br>• Value of tourists attending events and percentage of total<br>• Value of tourist contribution to local culture (amount obtained from gate, amount of donation)<br>• Percentage of locals who find new recreational opportunities associated with tourism (local questionnaires) |
| Housing issues | • Percentage of housing affordable for residents<br>• Mode and average distance of travel to work or school<br>• Number of new housing starts and percentage of local residents<br>• Availability and access to some other services (e.g. health, water, sanitation) can also change, positively or negatively, with social effects |
| Community demographics | • Number for residents who have left the community in the past year<br>• Number of immigrants (temporary or new residents) taking tourism jobs in the past year.<br>• Net migration into/out of the community (sorted by age of immigrants and out-migrants) |

Source: World Tourism Organization.

## Development of Islamic tourism in Malaysia

Malaysia registered an estimated 5.44 million Muslim tourists in 2012 (equivalent to 21.75 per cent of Malaysia's total tourist arrivals for the same year) compared with 5.22 million in 2011. The Islamic Tourism Centre (ITC), under the Ministry of Tourism and Culture (MOTAC) was officially launched in 2009; it was established to assist MOTAC in undertaking strategic tourism research and market intelligence as well as provide training and capacity-building services in relation to Islamic tourism. The ITC serves as an advisory body, particularly in matters pertaining to Islamic tourism, and works continuously with stakeholders and industry players to make Malaysia one of the major Islamic tourist destinations in the region. The roles and responsibilities of the ITC are (1) undertaking strategic research on market intelligence for policy formulation; (2) providing capacity building in tourism human resource and professional service standards; (3) information exchange and sharing of sustainable tourism best practices; and (4) developing strategic partnerships with governmental, inter-governmental and non-governmental organizations. In terms of global recognition, Malaysia has been voted as the top destination for Muslim tourists in 2011, 2012, 2013 and 2014, Malaysia scored 8.3 out of 10, leaving behind countries like the UAE, Turkey and Indonesia, and KLIA was also voted as the most Muslim-friendly airport in the world by CrescentRating Singapore. The ITC identifies the potential Islamic tourism products in Malaysia such as history, royal heritage, Islamic education, way of life, history of independence, nature, agro tourism, comparative religion, architecture, sports and outdoor activities, arts and culture, health and fitness, and business. The composition of Islamic tourism definition introduced by ITC is as follows:

- Islamic compliance, e.g. halal food, Islamic hotel facilities, *shariah* compliant trips;
- Islamic heritage and history, e.g. Islamic museum;
- diversity among Muslim countries, e.g. countries with mainly Muslim population, cultures and lifestyle creating sense of Islamic solidarity;
- Islamic programmes and projects, e.g. *Tilawah* International Islamic seminars and conferences programme;
- learning Islamic debriefing, e.g. lesson sharing and enrichment by tourist guides from tour sessions;
- searching for value-added elements and ideas, e.g. encouraging tourists to develop new perspectives of life and find a road map for improvement.

Othman, Norhisham, Roslan and Khalil (2013) reported that more than 80 per cent of the respondents agreed that Muslim tourists prefer to stay at 'Muslim friendly' accommodation and services with halal food and no alcohol, clean and hygienic environment, direction of *qiblah* in rooms, prayer mat provided and separate or different time schedule for males and females using the swimming pool and the gymnasium. This is supported by a study conducted by Creative Minds Media which produces the Muslim Travel Index Europe 2014, resulting from research on the attitudes and behaviour of Muslim-majority populations to tourism in the future and their experiences of countries they have already visited in Europe, including questions such as 'Does the traveller follow a halal lifestyle whilst travelling abroad?'. The most important considerations of Muslim tourists are 'halal food' (67 per cent), followed by 'overall price' (53 per cent), and 'Muslim-friendly experience' (49 per cent). In another study carried by Creative Minds Media in Muslim Travel Index Europe 2014 which surveyed the attitude and behaviour of majority of Muslim tourists visiting Europe and whether the traveller followed a halal lifestyle whilst travelling abroad, the results were as follows:

- Over half from the Middle East and Far East have travelled to Europe for leisure purposes.
- England, Italy, Turkey, France and Germany are the most popular destinations of choice.
- Travellers from the Middle East and Far East choose to stay in apartments/ flats over hotels.
- Facilities that allow Islamic travellers to follow a halal lifestyle are important to everyone when considering travelling abroad.
- Providing *halal* food or appropriate praying facilities are the most important factors.
- There is room for improvement amongst the popular destination countries as around one-third rate the facilities catering to a halal lifestyle as 'average'.

Islamic tourism can contribute to social conditions that may lead to positive changes in existing multi-racial and multi-cultural countries such as Malaysia.

## Conclusion

Islam and tourism are multi-disciplinary areas and therefore a joint effort is needed to deepen the discussion on Islam and tourism. It is important to mention in this chapter that that tourism and hospitality management can incorporate the Islamic management of *Maqasid al-Shariah*. Muslim scholars hold the opinion that the ultimate objective (*Maqasid al-Shariah*) is necessary for mankind's peaceful co-existence, according to the holy Quran and Sunnah, incorporating five main areas: (1) protection of life; (2) protection of religion; (3) protection of progeny or off-spring; (4) protection of intellect or faculty of reason; (5) protection of material wealth or research (Othman, 2010). To date there is little discussion on the application of *Maqasid al-Shariah* in formulating Islamic tourism management and Islamic marketing of travel and hospitality product and services. The concept of moderation that is *wasatiyyah* should be adopted in all aspects of the management and operation of Islamic tourism. *Wasatiyyah* or the principle of moderation and balance is an important but somewhat neglected aspect of a moral virtue relevant not only to personal conduct but also to the integrity and self-image of communities and nation.

The significance of the study is the current emergence of new ideas from Islamic intellectual transformation on modern and western models with its emphasis upon the unity of Islamic tourism ideology and theories. Therefore this study will develop new expertise and approaches to establish in the study of tourism from the Islamic perspectives. The main output of the study will be the form of the development of marketing strategic plan-strategy formulation and implementation for Islamic tourism. It is to recommend a system for the development of the knowledge base for Islamic tourism and to introduce the best monitoring system for the indicators of Islamic tourism. The study will be completed in 2015 and development of the C-PEST indicator index for the Islamic tourism will assist the government agencies in measuring the values of the potential Islamic tourism market. This is in line with the Tourism National Key Economic Area (NKEA) and the Tourism Transformation Plan that aims at attracting high-yield tourist markets and contributing significantly to Malaysia's tourism roadmap in receiving 36 million foreign tourists and bringing in foreign revenue of US$54.3 billion in 2020.

## Acknowledgement

We wish to thank the Institute Research Management, Universiti Teknologi MARA (UiTM), Malaysia and the Ministry Education of Malaysia for supporting this research through the Exploratory Research Grant Scheme (ERGS) from 2012 to 2015.

## References

Butler, R.W. (1999). Sustainable tourism: A state-of-the art review. *Tourism Geographies: An International Journal of Tourism Space, Place & Environment,* 1(1), 7–25.

Euromonitor Report retrieved from http://www.euromonitor.com/ (January 2013).

Formica, S., & Kothari, T.H. (2008). Strategic destination planning: Analyzing the future of tourism. *Journal of Travel Research,* 46, 355–367.

Ibrahim, Z., Othman, N., & Isa, Z. (2010). *A study on Middle East tourists' services expectation and satisfaction gap in Malaysian accommodation providers.* Islamic Tourism Centre.

*Insights from Tourism Malaysia Middle East study* (2014). Islamic Tourism Centre.

Jovicic., D., & Ilic., T. (2010) Indicators of sustainable tourism. *Glasnik Srpskog Geografskog Drustva 2010,* 90(1), 277–305.

Muhammad, Z. (2008). Halal tourism: Knowledgeable travel and wholesome fun. *The Halal Journal,* May/June, 56–57.

Othman, N., Mohamed Norhisham, N.S., Roslan, B., & Mohd Khalil, K.N (2013). Acceptance of tourist towards the implementation of Islamic Quality Standard (IQS) at hotels in Malaysia. March-July. Unpublished dissertation for BSc (Hons) in Tourism Management. Universiti Teknologi MARA, Shah Alam, Malaysia.

Othman, N., Taha, R., Ibrahim, Z., Isa, Z., & Tarmudi, S. (2010). *'Formulation of Islamic tourism theory' Report study.* Fundamental Research Grant Scheme by Ministry of Higher Education of Malaysia & Research Management Institute (RMI), Universiti Teknologi MARA (UiTM), Malaysia.

Othman, S. (2010). Applying maqasid al-shariah to Islamic finance & economics. *Presentation at Langkawi Finance & Economics International Conference (LIFE)*.13–15 December. Langkawi, Kedah, Malaysia.

Pew Research on Religion & Public Life Project, retrieved from www.pewforum.org (12 January 2014).

Scott, N., & Jafari, J. (2010) *Bringing tourism theory and practice: Tourism in the Muslim world vol 2*. United Kingdom, Bingley: Emerald.

Utusan Malaysia (2010, April 2). Formula baharu sektor pelancongan. *Dewan Ekonomi*, 54–55.

*World Islamic Tourism Conference – Emerging trends in Islamic tourism, travel & hospitality sector*, Karthika Expo Centre, Balai Kartini, Jakarta, Indonesia, 23–26 October 2014.

World Tourism Organization (2004). *Indicators of sustainable development for tourism destinations: A guidebook*. Madrid: World Tourism Organization.

World Tourism Organization's 'Tourism 2020 Vision'. Retrieved from http://www.unwto.org/facts/eng/vision.htm (12 January 2014).

Yusuf, S. (2009) *The real sense of shariah hospitality concept*. The World Halal Forum 2009, Kuala Lumpur, Malaysia.

# 18 Competitiveness of tourist destinations and Brazilian strategy

*Rosana Mazaro and*
*Carlos Alberto Freire Medeiros*

## Introduction

In light of the current and future competitive context for tourist destinations, be it at national, regional or local level, the determinant and conditioning factors of success and special attributes required to guide strategic decisions seem to be already identified and defined. The challenge to destinations and their future is the adequate identification and study of these attributes and how each destination appropriates this knowledge and transforms it into competitive intelligence.

This perspective requires vision, and understanding that more important than having a local attraction is how you take advantage of it. This aspect emphasizes management and coordination as priorities and principles for controlling development and directing results according to what is determined within rather than outside the destination.

Based on this understanding, analysis of the Brazilian strategy to cope with international competitiveness demonstrates that the country is in tune with competitive imperatives in formulating its tourism policy and defining its strategic plan according to decentralization principles, emphasizing its own resources, 'Brazilianism' aspects, regional integration and the domestic market.

After more than a decade of efforts to enhance tourism in Brazil and a policy of empowering municipalities and micro tourist regions, called regional poles, it can be inferred from global assessment that it has improved qualitatively and quantitatively when compared with the period prior to its implementation.

The Brazilian strategy of structuring for competition in tourism, by delegating management to local and regional governments, demonstrates the correct manner of transferring technologies and power to the destinations, favouring control over the tourism development process and allowing for the strengthening of resources and attractions of each place or region. Based on these resources, the definition of priority segments is also a crucial factor for directing specific strategies and optimizing resources, given that it demarcates markets and niches for such purposes.

## Literature review

Competitiveness seems to be the most frequently used term in studies on the performance and infrastructure of tourism at national, regional and local destinations.

Understanding the foundations and conditions of competitiveness in the current context is imperative for those intending to develop tourism in accordance with international standards. The theoretical models for studies on tourism destination competitiveness are based on the work of OMT (1997) and Ritchie and Crouch (2003) who indicate conditions that favour positive performance in an environment that presents significant challenges to tourist destination management, since this requires defining clear future goals and choosing coherent strategies.

In competitiveness studies, concern with evaluating the competitive performance of destinations has dominated scientific and corporative research (Kim & Mauborgne, 2005; Gooroochurn & Sugiyarto, 2003). Academia has dedicated itself to creating tourism competitiveness evaluation models to apply at the national, regional or local level, whereas consultants have applied models to assess different destinations around the world (Genest & Legg, 2003; WEF, 2011).

It is important to note that all models dealing with defining factors that influence competitiveness of tourist destinations are based on sustainability criteria such as conditions for strategic planning and management. A review of the main models suggests that theoretical and methodological studies on destination competitiveness have already been consolidated. This differentiation is related mainly to competitiveness and what it represents for the strategic management of destinations.

If, on one hand, competitiveness is understood from a comparison of competitors, comparison of models and attributes being external to the destination and common to universal analysis, on the other, competitiveness can be interpreted from models or ideal performance standards that help in assessing the destination based on unique attributes and factors. Table 18.1 shows an inter-model comparison based on composition and application.

Since the establishment of these theoretical and descriptive conformations, there have been advanced studies of the interrelationships between variables and dimensions of local tourism from a competitive perspective and sustainable approach that have made efforts to evaluate and measure competitive standards related to global or reference parameters. Following this proposal, the model created by Dwyer and Kim (2003) goes further to define the dimensions and critical factors for local tourism and suggests a methodology for assessing destination competitiveness using multivariate statistical tools that can identify and quantify variable mobility, that is, systemically explain the logic of decision-making and action.

Along these same lines, the Comp&tenible (Mazaro, 2010) was developed to amalgamate and systematize all the factors that influence the strategic adjustment between opportunity and macro-environmental determinants into different dimensions, translated in this context by the imperatives of sustainability. These dimensions represent the anticipated influence of the main management components on results and impacts of tourism on destinations. At the international level, the study conducted by WEF is the most complete and perhaps the most important considering its methodology and scope.

The comparison between the models has revealed that the critical factors influencing the competitiveness of tourism destinations have already been

Table 18.1 Comparison of the main characteristics of competitiveness models for tourist destinations

| Model characteristics | TTCI (WEF, 2013) | Tourism-inducing destinations (FGV, 2008) | Comp&tenible model (Mazaro, 2010) | Determinants and indicators (Dwyer & Kim, 2003) | Premier-ranking (Genest & Legg, 2003) | Destination competitiveness (Ritchie & Crouch, 2003) |
|---|---|---|---|---|---|---|
| Nature<br><br>Main motivation | Methodological-applied<br><br>Institutional studies | Methodological-applied<br><br>Consultancy studies | Conceptual-methodological<br><br>Academic studies | Conceptual-methodological<br><br>Academic studies | Methodological-applied<br><br>Consultancy studies | Theoretical model<br><br>Academic studies |
| Model objectives | Apply to diagnoses and competitive ranking of destinations around the world | Apply in the self assessment of diagnoses and competitive classifications of Brazilian destinations. | Propose a conceptual model that serves as a monitoring instrument of tourist destination evolution. | Guide analysis and studies that seek to understand the inter-relationship and motricity among variables of the tourism system. | Apply in the self-assessment of diagnoses and competitive classifications of Canadian destinations | Establish conceptual competitiveness and sustainability models for tourist destinations |
| Dimensions and factors. | Subindexes; regulatory framework, business environment and infrastructure and human, cultural and natural resources | Macro-dimensions: infrastructure, tourism, public policies, economy and sustainability models | Administration: planning, management, coordination, cooperation, strategic foresight. Competitiveness: resources, attractions, positioning, profitability, tourist satisfaction. Sustainability: socio-cultural, environmental. | Local and created resources, support, administration, preservation, security, demand and market factors | Resources and essential attractions, quality and critical mass, satisfaction and value, accessibility, equipment and services, profitability, image, marketing, innovation, local sustainability | Innate resources and essential attractions, support resources, destination management, policy, planning and development, qualifiers and determinant attributes |
| Path to sustainability | | Model | Strategic, essential | Consequence, result | Model | Guindelines and premises |

Source: Authors' own elaboration.

identified, although there are some differences in the structure and organization of the variables. It is important to note that there seems to be no distinction between the target levels rated, that is, the critical factors are the same for a country, a region or a tourist location. In Brazil, the same instrument is applied to destinations and its results reflect overall results obtained for the country.

It is important to point out that all studies start from the assumption that competitiveness is inherent to the destination and not the market or competition and that their results allow comparisons among different destinations. The aim is to enhance self-diagnosis in order to outline competitive advantages and strategies in accordance with the macro-environment rather than the market or industry criteria themselves.

In the case of macroeconomic issues and particularly, the recent economic and financial downturn, Ringbeck and Pietsch (2011) analysed structural trends in the global travel and tourism industry and assessed how the economic crisis of 2008–09 accelerated these trends, which led to the sharpest decline in international tourist arrivals in history. The authors highlighted the interplay between long-term trends (such as the high growth dynamics of emerging tourism regions, increasing travel spending in the Western Hemisphere and new opportunities for domestic/regional tourism as well as short-term volatility as a consequence of disruptive events). Collectively, these represent new challenges but also opportunities in travel and tourism for national governments. The authors described countries that have suffered from the current downturn but have managed to grow despite the crisis, and present reasons and factors for their success.

The themes related to biodiversity and nature conservation are high priority. Lipman and Voerster (2011) discussed the important role played by the travel and tourism industry in the shift towards the green economy. The authors described how travel and tourism should be an integral part of this process at global, regional and local levels, compatible with a low-carbon development trajectory in addition to being a key sector in guiding the change to a green economy. In addition to compliance, market leadership, consumer satisfaction and competitiveness are also important goals. Furthermore, due to its multiplier effect, which cascades through interrelated value chains in the economy, a green revolution in the travel and tourism industry could be a catalyst for green growth and transformation in the broader economy.

Endorsing the importance of the subject, the Travel & Tourism Competitiveness Index – TTCI (WEF, 2013) underscores natural resources as another important factor underlying national travel and tourism competitiveness. The study maintains that countries that are able to offer travellers access to natural assets have a clear competitive advantage. The evaluation of TTCI 2011 included several environmental attractiveness measures, such as the number of UNESCO natural World Heritage sites, a measure of the quality of the natural environment, fauna richness, as measured by the total known species of animals, and the number of nationally protected areas.

However, the authors warned that in order to fully capitalize on its potential, the industry must abandon its inclination toward historical goals, policies and institutional frameworks that limit its decisions regarding green growth. Indeed, because of their interconnectivity and mutual dependence, the travel and tourism industry and its related industries need greater convergence and closer collaboration. Key policies should be consolidated and/or aligned to meet the twin objectives of sustainable mobility and sustainable destinations.

Convergence will enable the industry to speak with one voice on issues affecting the industry. The authors conclude by stressing the importance of transforming 'classic tourism', dominated by the considerations of growth and market share, to 'smart tourism' that is clean, green, ethical, and customer and quality oriented. This will ensure that the industry becomes a market leader in the green growth paradigm and its related green jobs, investment, trade and development.

Marton-Lefèvre and Borges (2011) indicate that the travel and tourism industry is in a unique position to integrate biodiversity-friendly practices and solutions based on nature. Biodiversity is vital for travel and tourism in many tourism products and services, due to its attractiveness to the surrounding natural environments. However, the value of natural assets used by the industry is generally not internalized, thus leading to serious impacts on biodiversity. In 2010, a new 'Grand Plan' for nature, with 20 goals for biodiversity in 2020, was approved by governments worldwide.

This 'Grand Plan' aimed to guide both public and private decision-making in the next decade. The authors pointed out that collective action to conserve biodiversity and implement this plan is a shared responsibility between the governments, the private sector and the civil society. The authors also stated that for travel and tourism to support the goals of global biodiversity, threats to nature must be minimized through the integration of biodiversity considerations in tourism management.

Moreover, there are many opportunities for industry to reap the benefits of biodiversity-friendly practices, including market differentiation, increasing competitiveness and development of products and premium services, as well as proposals for new business and emerging markets. In order to capitalize on the opportunities and minimize the risks, some focus areas are suggested for travel and tourism: adoption and integration of biodiversity-friendly operating practices in travel and tourism supply chains; destination stewardship; capacity building and marketing creation for 'biodiversity businesses'; and emerging businesses and markets based on biodiversity-friendly goods and services.

## Methodology

The present research is a case study using qualitative analysis and descriptive results. Investigative procedures adopted the methods of the content analysis of documents and specialized bibliography and observing council performance through participation in meetings and relevant activities, characterizing elements of action-research. The research uses secondary sources of data, mainly extracted from the time series competitiveness assessment produced by the WEF's TTCI between 2005 and 2013. The TTCI covers a record 139 countries, and aims to provide a comprehensive strategic tool for measuring 'the factors and policies that make it attractive to develop the travel and tourism industry in different countries' (WEF, 2011, p. xiv).

The TTCI is composed of a number of the 14 pillars of travel and tourism competitiveness. These categories are classified into three sub-indexes of the index: the travel and tourism regulatory framework sub-index; the travel and tourism business environment and infrastructure sub-index; and the travel and tourism human, cultural and natural resources sub-index. The first captures elements that are policy related and generally under the government's purview; the second captures elements of the business environment and the 'hard' infrastructure of each economy; and the third captures the 'softer' human, cultural and natural elements of each country's resource endowments.

The monitoring and systematic record of the TTCI evaluation results to the case of Brazil, produced by historical series, displays the evolution of tourism competitiveness factors of the country facing external constraints and promotes critical analysis of its institutional structure and internal political organization to the confrontation of competitiveness in tourism. Given the focus of this chapter on the instrumental and operative dimensions of tourism policies, a qualitative approach allows the specificities and nuances of the tourism policy process and outcomes to be addressed. The originality of this study lies in a monographic evaluation of a tourism programme, involving documentary analysis at different levels within the policy framework.

## Findings

It is essential to offer tourism that represents the best combination among the competitive determinants of a particular historical context and the adequate exploitation of resources and attractions available in order to be competitive. Monitoring the macro-environment to identify and seize strategic opportunities becomes the greatest challenge to tourist destinations in the current context and future. In Brazil, the subject of the competitive imperatives has been highlighted by many insightful studies that explored issues such as the impact on the tourism industry and opportunities for increasing the industry's competitiveness, since the long-term scenario is favourable.

The history of tourism in Brazil is fairly recent; during the long military dictatorship, travel was treated as a national security issue with focus on controlling the movement of people. With the transition to democracy, accompanied by open markets and socioeconomic restructuring, travel and leisure became public policy, thereby giving individuals opportunity to use their free time as they saw fit.

Since the turn of this century, Brazil has adopted a new economic development model that includes mechanisms to improve income distribution and job opportunities by favouring the inclusion of millions of Brazilians in the so-called consumer society. Therefore, Brazil possesses a positive set of economic and social indicators, which are conducive to accelerating growth. Brazil has reduced its dependence on external financing, and today, the country is less vulnerable to international crises than ever before. In recent years, the country has substantially increased its participation in international commerce.

This favourable performance allowed the accumulation of unprecedented levels of international reserves, thus transforming the country from a debtor to a creditor nation. Considering that growth in tourism is closely related to economic growth, and taking into account the current stability and perspective for expanded economic activity, it can be inferred that this is a strategic moment for Brazil filled with new tourism opportunities.

The first National Tourism Plan, NTP 2003–2007, represents a mark of political modernity in the field of tourism. The plan arose from a maturing process (in terms of the central government's approach to the industry), was initiated at the end of the last century and consists of the first formal document that establishes guidelines for its development and a definitive strategy for tourism-related issues.

The NTP is being implemented in different regions of the country, supported by a decentralized coordination structure and action management, taking into account Brazil's large land mass and in accordance with the perspective that decisions must be made by the destinations where tourist activities actually take place. The structure and organization of domestic tourism encourage cooperation and participation between different government sectors and private sectors as well as a host of institutions representing civil society, thus making the National Tourism Council responsible for planning.

The Brazilian strategy for structuring competition in tourism by means of management training, and for regional and local governance demonstrates the correct form of transfer of technology and power to destinations and control of the process of tourism development, thereby enhancing the resources and attractions of each place or region. The current organizational flowchart of tourism in Brazil is illustrated in Figure 18.1.

The second National Tourism Plan, NTP 2007–2010, continues programmes initiated in 2003 and expresses its priority direction in its title (*A Voyage of Inclusion*). It reinforces and widens its application as a planning and management instrument that characterizes tourism as an engine for development and a generator of employment and income in the country. This inclusion can be achieved in two ways: production through the creation of jobs and income and consumption by attracting new tourists to the internal market.

The NTP is structured into macro-programmes directed to large tourism intervention areas. Each is subdivided into programmes dedicated to specific topics within each policy dimension. For the purpose of this analysis, it is necessary to focus on the regionalization macro-programme, which considers strategies with a direct impact on the competitiveness of Destination Brazil, especially in the case of structuring of hundreds of destinations in all the regions of the country.

Its main objectives are to promote the development and decentralization of tourist activities, support planning and structuring of tourist regions, consider cultural plurality and natural diversity, encourage tourism-related production, add value to tourist products and strengthen their competitiveness. Tourism regionalization implemented by the tourism regionalization programme, Brazilian Itineraries, proposes:

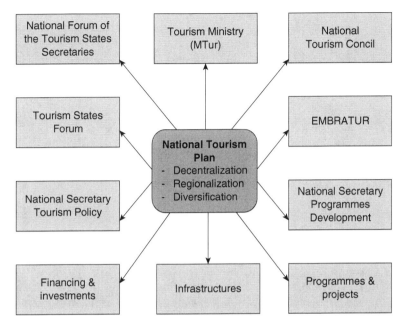

*Figure 18.1* Brazilian structure of tourism management. (Source: authors' elaboration.)

The structuring, organization and diversification of tourist products are based on the National Tourism Plan. The plan consists of a decentralized, coordinated and integrated public policy management model based on the principles of flexibility, implementation, mobilization, intersectional and inter-institutional cooperation with joint decision-making as the guiding strategy of other NTP macro programs and actions.

(Ministério do Turismo, 2007, p. 36)

When incorporated into this NTP version as a tourist program for macro region-alization, the proposal is distinguished by segmentation as a strategy to organize tourism for planning and management purposes, with the aim of conceiving prod-ucts, itineraries and destinations that reflect the peculiarities and specificities of each region, thus emphasizing Brazilian characteristics.

The tourism regionalization programme mapped 200 tourist regions in the 27 Brazilian states through a project carried out in conjunction with the State Tourism Organs and Forums. The policy of municipalizing tourism management was adopted before the implementation of the NTP in its current form, and indi-cated the path that subsequent proposals would follow: the focus on destinations.

This can be considered one of the main challenges for tourism policy in Brazil due to its dimension, diversity and large number of municipalities with more than 5,000 inhabitants. More than 3,000 of these inhabitants identified themselves as tourist destinations in a survey taken in 1998. The first significant challenge was to find the criteria to establish priorities in a universe of important questions and how to select priority destinations to implement policy.

In order to emphasize the importance of this strategy, the primary goal of NTP 2003–2007 was the structuring of the 65 tourist destinations with international quality standards, the so-called Inducer Destinations. This action must be based on the principle of environmental, socio-cultural and economic sustainability working in a participative, decentralized and systemic way to stimulate the integration and consequent organization and expansion of tourist products. The 27 capital cities and other prominent places in each state were called to induce destinations.

The strategic focus of the project consists of instituting a management system in the action plans of the 65 tourism-inducing destinations, qualifying local stakeholders to strengthen local management and expanding the knowledge of strategic planning (BRASIL, 2006). This will create a working network that maintains a constant and efficient exchange of information aimed at accelerating planning, execution and monitoring processes. The work will also determine the numbers of local managers who will receive technical support from a group of national administrators to structure and execute plans that guide competitiveness actions.

The social aspect of the plan indicates that Brazilians should be the main beneficiaries of tourist development in the country. To that end, domestic tourism has increased to generate economies of scale and widen the participation of Brazilian families in tourism. It can be observed that NTP 2007–2010 expands and strengthens the internal market, with special emphasis on the social function of tourism. This is a central aspect of tourism policy in Brazil, since it is based on and justified by its mega geographic and demographic dimensions and focuses on the potential for both supply and demand.

However, the social character stated in the guidelines is not sufficient to generate actions actually committed to Brazilians or to promote the distribution of benefits through economies of scale. Brazil does not have defined incentive mechanisms or control over activities at destinations, which ensure compliance of social proposals and more inclusive tourism. The social aspect seems to have been wrongly interpreted, thereby stimulating flow in the internal market mainly through funding programmes for specific segments, such as seniors and students, among others.

In fact, in recent years, the number of Brazilians from economic classes C and D travelling by plane for the first time has grown exponentially. This indicates that these changes drive the economy in many small towns. However, it is thought that, in addition to demands, this would require inclusion as the foundation of tourism plans for these localities and social inclusion programmes through the provision of tourist destinations. This distortion has increased the flow of travellers and allows the establishment of monopoly operators and exposes the serious problems of general infrastructure in tourist locations.

The results of TTCI 2013 and their interpretation for the Brazilian situation provide interesting inferences about its conditions of competitiveness on a global level. Moreover, comparison with internal studies reveals important elements of Brazil's tourism destinations. The overall ranking results of TTCI 2013 showed no change among countries that occupy the top rankings compared with 2011 but further strengthen European leadership in the industry. Europe holds the top five positions and seven European countries occupy the 10 most competitive positions in the world. Figure 18.2 shows the results for Brazil from 2009 to 2013.

The first inconsistency is between stated objectives and the time horizon, since four years is not enough to change the tourism scenario in a country like Brazil. This was demonstrated when it did not reach the goal of expanding participation in international tourism in NTP 2003–2007, a deficiency that was exacerbated in NTP 2007–2010.

Another important gap is between the proposed sustainable development of biodiversity and the effective measures that guarantee preservation, subsequently taking advantage of this distinctive heritage as a differentiated tourist attraction. The evaluation of TTCI 2011 clearly demonstrates loss of tourism competitiveness in the country due to poor urban infrastructure in terms of mobility, sanitation, waste treatment and disposal, security, town planning, leisure and appropriate conditions for the exercise of citizenship.

This means that the problems and gaps in competitive tourism are reflections of the appalling conditions found in tourist destinations, such as those found in the northeast region of the country, considered an important potential for tourism, attracting much of the Brazil's national and international flow. The problems relating to basic infrastructure at destinations are related to municipal management, a responsibility not adequately assumed by municipalities.

These competitive deficiencies, even though the NTP still bases its founding principles on the regionalization programme, whose priority is to empower destinations

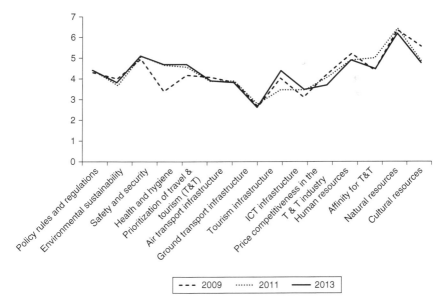

*Figure 18.2* Brazil Travel & Tourism Competitiveness Index evolution. (Source: authors' elaboration.)

for tourism management, have produced poor results in the preparation and transfer of management technologies to destinations. The TTCI has always ranked Brazil first in natural biodiversity of the *top three performing economies per pillar*. This pillar also represents the country's best score, reaching over 6 points on a scale of 0–7. The sub-index that measures human, natural and cultural groups ranks the country twelfth worldwide.

Another valuable intangible resource in Brazil is the receptivity of its people and their propensity to be happy. The importance of this factor was recognized in TTCI 2011 , which includes *affinity for travel & tourism* as a key indicator that measures the extent to which a country and society are open to tourism and foreign visitors. It is important to recognize that the general openness of the population to travel and foreign visitors has an important impact on travel and tourism competitiveness.

In particular, it provides a measure of the population's attitude toward foreign travellers; a measure of the extent to which business leaders are willing to recommend leisure travel in their countries for important business contacts; and a measure of tourism openness (tourism expenditures and receipts as a percentage of GDP), which provides a sense of the importance of tourism relative to the country's overall size. Tourism in Brazil accounts for a mere 0.9 per cent of international travellers (Ministério do Turismo, 2007).

These data demonstrate the huge unexplored potential for growth in the industry, especially when based on the attributes of sustainability and within a strategic perspective and vision for the future (Dwyer & Kim, 2003; Mazaro, 2010). Determinants that have shaped the competitive context underscore that strategic opportunities are limitless in terms of tourism for destinations that transformed macro-environmental imperatives into strategic guidelines.

Therefore, in the case of Destination Brazil, the competitive advantages can and must be sustained. This means market insertion and positioning in different segments depend on natural diversity for their development and find fertile terrain for growth in the current competitive context.

## Conclusion

At first glance, Brazil's results were not positive. The country lost seven positions in the overall ranking between 2009 and 2011, but recovered two positions in 2013. It is ranked 51st overall with an index score of 4.4 points. However, a closer look at the partial data for the sub-index reveals a more promising scenario for Brazil.

However, the most important and significant gap in the implementation of the programme is between the diagnosis of destination conditions and poor implementation of strategic objectives'committed to high levels of competitiveness on the part of local management. The fragility and lack of management, in some cases, displays the chronic situation at Brazilian tourism destinations. The country exhibits a number of cases where the concept of efficiency and effectiveness predominates in the municipal management of regular population flows rather than in the management of tourism flows. Tourism management is often referred to as the administration of cities and towns, tangible places where tourism actually materializes.

If we analyse the NTP under the criteria and principles of strategic planning and tourism sustainability, it is apparent that this is essentially a political document and that, although it has the undeniable merit of being in printed format, representing a more formal and professional management approach to tourism in the country, it also displays a number of inadequacies and inconsistencies that can compromise its effectiveness.

Another important indicator is the detailed analysis of pillars displaying the competitive advantages of the highest placed countries in the overall ranking. Noteworthy is the predominance of leadership in dimensions related to general infrastructure and tourism, health and public health, safety and other factors directly related to planning and management of localities and mainly conditioned by decisions under the control of managers. The pillars in which Brazil fared worst, causing a drop in ranking, were attributes related to management skills that can be assimilated and factors that can be controlled.

This interpretation is based on studies indicating an important driving force of variables, management decisions and strategic choices regarding competitive destinations, including factors that have an impact on more general issues, such as local sustainability.

However, the application of tools for evaluating consolidated competitiveness emphasizes the format and management criteria adopted by the destinations in successful tourism strategies. This finding is crucial for the analysis of long-term strategies for tourism in Brazil, considering the factors and indicators of the study showing Brazil's weak competitiveness in international tourism is subject to change by the acting managers of the destinations.

## References

BRASIL (2006). *Segmentação do Turismo: Marcos Conceituais*, Brasília, Ministério do Turismo, available at www.turismo.gov.br (accessed 4 June 2007).

Dwyer, L., & Kim, C. (2003). Destination competitiveness: Determinants and indicators, *Current Issues in Tourism,* 6(5), 369–414.

FGV (2008). *Indice de Competitividade dos 65 Destinos Indutores do Desenvolvimento Turístico Regional: Relatório Brasil*, Brasília: Ministério do Turismo. Retrieved from http://www.turismo.gov.br/export/sites/default/turismo/o_ministerio/publicacoes/downloads_publicacoes/xndice_de_Competitividade_do_Turismo_Nacional_-_Relatxrio_Brasil_2011.pdf (accessed 8 May 2009).

Genest, J., & Legg, D. (2003). *Premier-ranked tourist destinations: Development of a framework for analysis and its self-guided workbook,* Ontario. Retrieved from http://www.tourism.gov.on.ca/english/research/pdf/self-guided-workbook.pdf (accessed 20 April 2004).

Gooroochurn, N. & Sugiyarto, G. (2003). *Competitiveness indicators in the travel and tourism industry.* Tourism and Travel Research Institute, Nottingham University Business School, G8 1BB, UK.

Kim, W., & Mauborgne, R. (2005). *A estratégia do oceano azul,* Rio de Janeiro: Elsevier.

Lipman, G., & Vorster, S. (2011). Green growth, travelism, and the pursuit of happiness. In *The Travel & Tourism Competitiveness Report 2011: Beyond the downturn*, Retrieved from http://www.weforum.org/reports/travel-tourism-competitiveness-report-2011 (accessed 4 March 2012).

Marton-Lefèvre, J., & Borges, M.A. (2011). A new big plan for nature: Opportunities for travel & tourism. In *The Travel & Tourism Competitiveness Report 2011: Beyond the downturn*, Retrieved from http://www.weforum.org/reports/travel-tourism-competitiveness-report-2011 (accessed 7 June 2012).

Mazaro, R.M. (2010). Atualização da Sustentabilidade Estratégica como Instrumento de Gestão de Destinos Turísticos. *Revista Turismo & Desenvolvimento*, 2(13), 771–781.

Ministério do Turismo (2007). *Plano Nacional de Turismo 2007–2010*, Uma Viagem de Inclusão, Brasília. Retrieved from http://www.turismo.gov.br/export/sites/default/turismo/o_ministerio/publicacoes/downloads_publicacoes/plano_nacional_turismo_2007_2010.pdf (accessed 2 August 2007).

OMT. (1997). *Guía práctica para el desarrollo y uso de indicadores de turismo sostenible.* Madrid, OMT.

Ringbeck, J., & Pietsch, T. (2011). Crisis aftermath: Pathways to a more resilient travel & tourism sector. In *The Travel & Tourism Competitiveness Report 2011: Beyond the downturn.* Retrieved from http://www.weforum.org/reports/travel-tourism-competitiveness-report-2011 (accessed 7 June 2012).

Ritchie, J., & Crouch, G.I. (2003). *The competitive destination: A sustainability perspective.* Wallingford: CABI.

WEF (2011). *The Travel & Tourism Competitiveness Report 2011: Beyond the downturn.* Retrieved from http://www.weforum.org/reports/travel-tourism-competitiveness-report-2011 (accessed 4 March 2012).

WEF (2013). *The Travel & Tourism Competitiveness Report 2013: Reducing barriers to economic growth and job creation.* Retrieved from http://www3.weforum.org/docs/WEF_TT_Competitiveness_Report_2013.pdf (accessed 10 March 2014).

WTO (2006). *Tourism 2020 vision: Global forecasts*, Madrid.

# Index

188    *Index*